*From* The Women's Press Ltd
124 Shoreditch High Street, London E1

*Joanna Ryan and Sue Cartledge*　　　　Photo: Jo Valentine & Jessica James

*Sue Cartledge* lived with friends in London, where she died at the age of thirty-four. She contributed articles on sexual politics to magazines and to two anthologies. She worked for most of her life in the housing service of local government and was involved in her local Women's Aid Group, as well as other feminist groups, for several years.

*Joanna Ryan* has worked in the field of psychology and mental health, at different times as research worker, teacher, advice worker, campaigner, psychotherapist and writer. She has co-authored (with Frank Thomas) *The Politics of Mental Handicap* (1980), as well as contributing to many other publications. A feminist ever since she can remember, she has one son and lives in London with friends.

# Sex & Love

## New thoughts on old contradictions

*Edited by*

Sue Cartledge & Joanna Ryan

The Women's Press

First published by The Women's Press Limited 1983
A member of the Namara Group
124 Shoreditch High Street, London E1 6JE
Reprinted 1984

British Library Cataloguing in Publication Data

Sex & Love
    1. Women—sexual behaviour
    2. Interpersonal relationships
    I. Cartledge, Sue      II. Ryan, Joanna
    306.7'088042      HQ29

    ISBN 0-7043-3913-7

Typeset by MC Typeset, Chatham, Kent
Printed by Nene Litho, Wellingborough, Northants
Bound by Woolnough Bookbinding, Wellingborough, Northants

## Sue Cartledge

Sue died on 22 February 1983 after a long and bravely borne illness. I would like to record the love, clarity and vigour with which she worked on this book despite the gravity of her illness, until the manuscript was finished shortly before her death. I would also like to express my appreciation of her as co-editor and friend, and the pleasure it has been for me to have worked so closely with her. Sue will be sorely missed by many people and I hope that this anthology will remain a testimony to the imagination and thoughtfulness with which she pursued her life and expressed her deep commitment to women.

Joanna Ryan
March 1983

# Contents

# Acknowledgements

We would like to thank Stephanie Dowrick for the original suggestion of this anthology, and for her helpful advice and encouragement; The Women's Press for their enthusiasm and hard work; Lucy Goodison and Lynne Segal for some last-minute very practical help. We are indebted to Sue's friends for nursing her through many months of illness, and to Jo's friends for constant and loving help with child-care: all their unstinting support has made this book possible.

S.C.
J.R.

# 1
# Introduction

Sue Cartledge and Joanna Ryan

Sexuality has always been of major importance to feminists. Our preoccupation with it expresses a fundamental tenet of feminism: that not only is the whole area of 'personal' relationships a highly political one, steeped with the power relations of the wider world, but also that we cannot countenance a politics that promotes a deep split between the two. Our preoccupation also reflects the overriding social definitions of women in terms of their availability as sexual objects for men. And above all it reveals our persistent desire for a better life now, in one of the most pervasive aspects of our being.

'Sexuality' encompasses a vast range of issues, from the most private to the most public, the most violent to the most tender. In the last fifteen years feminism has thrown up enormous challenges in the whole field of sexuality. We have challenged the 'rights' of men to women's bodies; the compulsory nature of heterosexuality; the stigma and invisibility of lesbianism; the primacy of the nuclear family; rigid gender roles; patriarchal definitions of what is 'natural'; the violence of rape; the exploitation of pornography; sexist imagery and symbolism. Even the importance and priority given to sexual relationships have been questioned. The autonomy and diversity of women's sexual desires have been affirmed.

This book is about sexual love relationships: what we bring to them; the strengths, the problems, the dilemmas we experience within them; our hopes of how to change them. We are not thereby prioritising this area of our sexuality over other, possibly more public, areas as targets of our political energy. Nor are we supposing that the various areas are ultimately independent of each other. Indeed one main theme of this book, approached from many different angles, is the social construction of our sexuality: the intricate and multiple ways in which our emotions, desires and relationships are shaped by the society we live in.

This project – the examination and exploration of sexual relationships – has been with us from the very beginning of the present women's movement. It has expressed itself in many ways: in the revelatory discussions of consciousness-raising groups; in 'alternative' life-styles and domestic structures; in the endless personal testimony of stories, films, poems and works of art; in theoretical writings; in various forms of therapy. These have all reflected the multiplicity of our concerns, the creativity of our continuing efforts towards a fuller understanding. Debate about sexual relationships has surfaced with more or less intensity, more or less visibility, in the various phases of our recent history. Following the initial explosive years, there was an apparent waning of interest and a turn to other issues. Many of the questions we asked led not to answers but to new questions. It has not been easy to chart new territory, to construct new relationships or even to agree what these would feel like. We have had continually to face the many barriers to change, internal and external; to re-assess our goals and means of action. We have had to grapple not only with the overwhelming social definitions of our sexuality, but also with the debates and conflicts between ourselves as feminists about what is politically desirable, about what and how to change, indeed about the whole notion of prescriptive ideas in this area.

This anthology reflects a resurgence of interest in sex and love. Our original intention was to collect together some of the writings we thought existed in the scattered publications of the women's movement. To our surprise we found relatively little, and certainly not enough to reflect the wealth of ideas and activities we were aware of through conversation and more formal discussion. So instead we invited original contributions on a range of topics which would illuminate how some feminists were now thinking about sexual relationships.

Resting as it does on the diverse activities of the present and recent past, this book could not have been written ten years ago. This is especially clear in the recognition of the power of the unconscious and in the sophistication with which ideas of psychology and therapy are used: different versions of which inform many, although by no means all, of the chapters of this book. It is also evident in the complexity with which 'social construction' is understood: the diversity of influences, material and ideological, acting on us; the mediation of these through the family and other institutions; the internalisation of social forces in our feelings and personality structures. While clearly rejecting any kind of 'naturalism' about sexuality, there is a recurrent tension throughout the book, as within feminism, about how to describe our own identities. How do we reconcile our deepening sense of what 'social construction' means with the experience that many women have of discovering, often through feminism, something real or authentic about themselves, something relatively untouched albeit suppressed by patriarchal society? The theme of personal autonomy as a precondition of intimacy in relationships has also come to the fore, as women are struggling to have control in all areas of their lives, and realising the reverberations of this in their close connection with others. This is explored from several different angles, as is the vulnerability and passion of being 'in love'. We have come a long way towards finding the language, concepts and forms in which to think about and live our sexuality. Many of the chapters in this anthology are direct evidence of this, whilst others reflect on this process as part of our collective history.

There is inevitably a large element of selection involved. Although we think that this anthology will speak widely to the experience of many women, it does not represent anyone other than the contributors themselves, their thoughts and allegiances. In particular it does not bear witness to the specific experiences of black women, of women with disabilities, nor of young women. Class is present, not as the focus of analysis but as an implicit factor in the different personal histories. Several chapters could be broadly, although inadequately, described as emerging from a socialist–feminist tradition; some as taking a more radical feminist position; others it would be misleading to label at all. We have chosen to include both lesbian and heterosexual relationships within one book, not from any false idea that 'really we are all the same', but because this reflects the reality of our own personal experience and that of many other women.

For both of us, the editors, the women's liberation movement has been decisive in creating a shift to lesbian relationships after a substantial personal history of heterosexuality. We are thus aware of both forms of relationship, or aspects of both. We are also aware of the significance, personal and political, that such a shift in sexual orientation carries; and of the questions it raises about the formation of our sexual feelings and the construction of our sexual 'identities'. There has also been an increasing recognition of the diversity of women's experience – both within the categorisations 'lesbian' and 'heterosexual', and across the whole continuum – and the plurality of options this necessitates. Encompassing some of this diversity within one book can illuminate the variety of interconnected processes that shape our sexuality and that make the expression of our sexual and emotional desires so problematic. In doing this we are not denying the specificity and overriding nature of lesbian oppression, nor the particular strengths and joys of lesbian relationships.

The anthology as a whole is a particularly feminist fusion of emotion and intellect, theory and practice. As Adrienne Rich has commented, discussing the western polarisation of thought and feeling: 'The fear of change . . . intersects with a fear that lucidity and love cannot coexist, that political awareness and personal intensity are contradictions, that consciousness must dissolve tenderness, intimacy and loyalty.'[1]

It is in the belief that lucidity and love not only can but must coexist that we have included different forms of understanding and styles of writing. The chapters range from the mainly historical and theoretical, through others which combine in many creative ways personal accounts with theoretical and political understandings, to the specifically autobiographical.

Lucy Bland's historical chapter provides the context for what follows, by describing the changing conceptions of women's sexuality throughout the century, and the different definitions of 'natural' and 'desirable'. She emphasises the lack of language, other than that of the prevailing culture, in which feminists of all periods could articulate their demands, and traces the continuities between past and present feminist debates. She situates the present women's movement as developing out of and in reaction to the pro-marriage ideologies of the 1950s and the 'permissiveness' of the 1960s, using and criticising the ideas of behaviourist psychology and sexual liberation. This theme is developed further by Lynne Segal (Chapter 3) who locates her own experience of fantasy and masochism within a critique of the ideologies of feminist sex manuals. She argues for a wider recognition of the complex and often disturbing nature of the emotions we experience around sex, and the diverse ways in which these can reflect social and personal reality, both past and present. The power, rational and irrational, of 'falling in love', and its connection to sexuality is explored by Lucy Goodison in Chapter 4, which emphasises the contradictory and transcendent nature of this experience. Drawing on a diversity of personal accounts and theoretical frameworks, she considers how we can value and use the power involved rather than losing ourselves and our sense of personal autonomy in it.

Chapter 5, written separately by Jo Chambers and Jill Brown, describes two women's views of their relationship with each other. Both recount their loving but painful search for clarity, and their use of co-counselling methods to explore and shift deeply ingrained

4

patterns. Jo Chambers describes her intention to start the relationship free from some of the traps of previous relationships, and the ways in which she coped with the terror of rejection and with Jill's pregnancy. Jill Brown shows vividly how lesbian oppression is internalised and the deep and damaging effects of this for individual lesbians. She explores the connections for her between sex and feelings of loss and wanting to be cared for, as they relate to both past and present. She also describes the confusing vacuum surrounding lesbian motherhood.

Heterosexual motherhood and sexuality are analysed in Chapter 6 by Lesley Saunders. She looks at the contradictory expectations and demands that face women around and immediately after childbirth, the enormous changes in our bodies and sense of ourselves that we have to cope with, and the inappropriate nature of most available understanding.

The following chapters present different views of male power in heterosexual relationships, with different suggestions for change. Angela Hamblin, drawing on women's replies to a questionnaire, describes the many processes whereby male-defined heterosexuality is imposed on women, and stresses the importance of women discovering their own authentic sexuality in order to create the terms on which they are prepared to engage sexually with men. Wendy Hollway, using both psychoanalytic ideas and interview material, looks at women's and men's power in relation to sex. She describes the dynamics of projection, resistance and defence with which men hide their vulnerability to women and which lead them to maintain a façade of invulnerability or indifference: a façade that is easily experienced as 'power' by women because of their particular social roles and the expectations projected onto them by men. Without ignoring all the other sources of men's power, she argues that unpacking these dynamics can help change the way power is experienced and used in sexual relationships.

In Chapter 9 Debby Gregory explores bisexuality and the potential this creates for increased personal autonomy. Using her own and other women's experiences she presents bisexuality not just as a question of the gender of our sexual partners but as a positive expression of many different aspects of ourselves. She argues for the importance of many more feminists' acknowledging and exploring their bisexuality.

Shifting the ground away from the various experiences of being 'in' a relationship, Tricia Bickerton (Chapter 10) looks at the particular dilemmas of women without a primary sexual relationship. She

5

describes the contradictions of this situation: the social and other pressures on women which may make them internalise the absence of a sexual relationship as their 'failure'; and the various reasons why such relationships may seem impossible or undesirable. Without denying the pain involved in being 'alone', she considers ways in which women can recognise their own strengths outside of relationships.

Sue Cartledge (Chapter 11) looks at the question of what we consider 'right' or 'wrong' in sexual relationships and by what principles we decide this. Drawing on many examples from her own life, she discusses the conflicts that often arise between our own and others' needs and looks at how feminists might try to approach the resolution of such conflicts.

The final three chapters extend many themes raised earlier in the book. Elizabeth Wilson surveys the changing conceptions and forms of representation of lesbianism. She points to the difficulties we have with the notion of lesbian identity, arguing against the desexualisation of lesbianism that she feels has occurred within feminism, and also against any form of politics that denies the specificity of lesbianism. She advocates the greater recognition of unconscious forces in sexuality, a theme which forms the focus of the next chapter on psychoanalysis. In this Joanna Ryan considers some feminist uses of psychoanalytic theory in relation to the questions of attraction, sexual orientation and identity. She looks at the notion that infantile feelings are evoked by sexual involvement, and that our sexual orientation 'comes from' our relationship with our parents. Finally Sonja Ruehl considers the functions and value of theory, feminist and otherwise, in relation to the questions posed by feminism. She discusses different feminist views of how our sexuality is socially constructed, and then considers in more detail Lillian Faderman's approach to lesbianism and Michel Foucault's theorising of sexuality as a whole, arguing for the advantages of the latter.

The process of working together on this anthology, and with all the contributors, has been exciting and sustaining. The enthusiasm and creativity of the authors has continually inspired us, as has the realisation that so much more than we have been able to include is going on. We hope this book will encourage more women, particularly those whose experience is not encompassed here, to value their own thoughts and discussions about sexual relationships, and to share their ideas and activities more widely. Breaking down isolation, of whatever kind, and sharing experiences will always be an essential aspect of feminism: this book is a contribution to that process and to

the various debates within feminism as we continually travel in new
and uncharted directions.

J.R.<br>
S.C.<br>
January 1983

# 2

# Purity, Motherhood, Pleasure or Threat? Definitions of Female Sexuality 1900–1970s

Lucy Bland

> Surely the ideal should be that sex relationships and sex organs should be held absolutely sacred to the production of children, and never be degraded to minister to a lustful pleasure.
>
> Mrs P. Sherwen, correspondent to the feminist journal
> *The Freewoman* 25 January 1912

> Nature seems to have designed definite roles for the two actors in the sex drama . . . the husband, understanding his wife's nature, has the joy of rousing her gradually, of creating in her an ardour equal to his own. A woman's body can be regarded as a musical instrument awaiting the hand of an artist.
>
> Dr Helena Wright, *The Sex Factor in Marriage*, 1930

> The establishment of clitoral orgasm as fact would threaten the heterosexual institution.
>
> Anne Koedt, *The Myth of the Vaginal Orgasm*, 1970

The feminists quoted here were writing at different times, in very different ways, of ideal sex for women as they saw it. We may feel that we've come a long way from such statements: that obviously we no longer see sex for women as sacred, or tied to reproduction, or needing the 'magic touch' of a man, nor believe that the clitoral orgasm alone is much of a threat to heterosexuality. However, before we arrogantly claim that at least we are clear as to what we *reject*, it is salutory to reflect on whether we are also clear as to what we *want* from sex, mean by sex, define as our sexuality. I think it is only too apparent that many of us feel unclear about the whole issue. Certain questions are of central concern to feminists today: what we mean by a right to determine our own sexuality; what a self-defined sexuality means; what the role of sex is in relationships with men or women;

8

what role we feel it should have; how we can challenge power in sexual relationships and encounters? Some similar questions, some very different questions, were asked by earlier feminists.

We face a past and a present in which there has never been a *language* allowing us to think about and define women's sexuality. Previous feminists have also been aware of this difficulty. Stella Browne, for instance, noted that 'the realities of women's sexual life have been greatly obscured by the lack of any sexual vocabulary.'[1] We have as our heritage a dominant definition of sex that is based on a male hydraulic model of sex: sex as a 'natural' energy or force 'needing' release or control, a force basically seen as male (penetrative) and heterosexual, its release involving a linear progression from arousal to penetration to orgasmic release. Women, in effect, provide the 'outlet' for male sexual force – figuratively as repositories of male desire, literally as receptors into which semen is released (in nineteenth-century language the act of 'spending'; in the twentieth-century of 'coming'). Since the 1960s, in particular, women have been informed by sexologists and sexual 'radicals' that female sexuality is the *same* as men's. Nevertheless, to commonsense ideas, men engage in 'sex acts', they are active and genital, women have 'sexual relationships', they are more passive, emotive. Their sexuality is seen essentially as a response to male sexuality. In a sense, male sexuality is also thought to involve response – reaction to female *precipitation*. But male sexuality is crucially construed as having an existence independent of women, an existence central to male culture. Women's sexuality, though, is not seen as autonomous; it exists by virtue of male presence, male desire. For women, sex is still thought of as preferably tied not merely to a relationship, but to romance and love. Romance still stands as the acceptable face of desire for women in our culture.

To understand the power and deep-seatedness of these definitions of sex and sexuality, and the forms of their control, we need to locate their roots within earlier historical periods. The ways we feel about our sexuality have been formed in relation to these definitions and images. However, as a women's movement we have another heritage which needs uncovering: past feminists' attempts to explore questions of sex and sexuality and to take on and challenge the power-relations involved in sex. It is important to look at this tradition for a number of reasons: to learn from earlier insights; to recognise how, like us today, their ideas and struggles were, on the one hand, up against the lack of a language to define female sexuality, on the other, working within as well as against the dominant defining

9

ideas and practices; to recognise that while we have made certain gains in the arena of sexual politics, in other respects some of these supposed gains may, in a different light, be revealed as Pyrrhic victories. Finally, in achieving some understanding of past struggles *within* feminism over a politics of sexuality, as well as between feminism and society at large, we can perhaps learn important lessons for today.

Of course in the small space of this article, I cannot hope to offer anything but an extremely schematic and selective account of such issues. What I attempt to do is present on the one hand, what I take to be part of the legacy of dominant definitions of female sexuality, and on the other, indicate some of the feminist responses to such definitions.

## Victorian sexualities: asexual lady/degenerate whore

The 'liberated', 'sexualised', twentieth-century woman has frequently been favourably compared to the image of the asexual Victorian lady. In the late nineteenth century, although such a representation of womanhood was both widespread *and* an ideal to which women were expected to aspire, it coexisted with other conflicting representations of women (including that of the *sexual* working-class woman). Late nineteenth-century evolutionary theory held that in the highest level of human development (Victorian society with its patriarchal monogamous family), evolutionary 'needs' allocated woman to the private sphere in her role as reproducer and moraliser, man to the public sphere as competitor (latterday hunter). This stage of human development was believed to involve a heightening of gender difference, and one aspect of that difference was thought to relate to the 'sex instinct': man's insatiable urge, woman's virtual lack. *Her* instinct lay with motherhood. The work of Darwin[2] explained and justified female asexuality in terms of woman's evolutionary importance in harnessing and controlling male sexual energy. Darwin (and following him Freud) saw sex as an instinct rooted in our ancient animal heritage, the 'beast in man', forever lurking and threatening the higher and 'human' developments of Reason and Civilisation. Woman's 'civilising' 'moralising' powers were believed necessary to curb man's animality and lust, to aid the development of his Will in conquering such urges. But although a mark of bestiality, man's sexual urge was also viewed as biologically 'natural', and it was this that gave the rationale for the double standard: that unchastity was excusable and understandable in man, but both unforgiveable and

10

unnatural in woman. Man's sexual urge, 'naturally' unfulfilled in the marriage bed by the virtuous asexual wife, 'needed' fulfilment through the institution of prostitution, the prostitute standing in contrast to the bourgeois wife as Magdalen to the Madonna. For if middle-class women were dominantly defined as asexual, prostitutes (and often working-class women generally) were seen as sexual and thereby aberrant, sometimes conceived of as atavists – biological throwbacks to an earlier evolutionary stage (akin to the 'promiscuity' of 'primitives').[3] The prostitute was 'needed' to keep the middle-class home and its female homemaker unsullied and pure.

Further, although man was more 'animal' in relation to the proximity of his sexual desires, woman was deemed inferior, more primitive, less evolved in every other respect, and ultimately more fundamentally defined by her biology, for woman was believed to be unable to escape the total domination of her reproductive system. While man was thought able to curb his sexual desire through the training of Will, for woman there was no escape – her behaviour, 'normal' or 'pathological', lay in the action of her reproductive organs. As Havelock Ellis put it 'Women's brains are in a sense . . . in their wombs.' To the medical profession (and the nineteenth century saw the medicalising of all things sexual) manifestations of sexual desire, and of most other pathologies, were to be dealt with through the treatment, and possibly removal, of those offending 'causative' organs – hence oviotomy, hysterectomy and clitoridectomy.

In the early twentieth century, along with concern over the falling birth rate, high infant mortality and fear of national 'degeneracy', emphasis on the woman's maternal role heightened dramatically.[4] On the one hand, women were beginning to be seen as having a normal, rather than pathological sexual instinct, on the other this instinct, for women, was seen primarily *in terms of* a maternal instinct. In other words, women's sexual instinct and maternal instinct tended to be conflated. As August Forel, an influential sexologist, expressed it: 'the most profound and most natural irradiation of the sexual appetite in women is *maternal love*' (his emphasis).[5] To the popular medical writer, Elizabeth Sloan Chesser,

> The longing of every normal woman to find happiness in sex union and to exercise her functions physically and psychically in marriage and motherhood is an ineradicable instinct.[6]

Further, sex for women (and ideally for men too) was thought to be 'normally' and 'naturally' tied to love:

In normal women, ecpecially young girls, the sexual appetite is
subordinated to love. In the young girl love is a mixture of exalted
admiration for masculine courage and grandeur, and an ardent
desire for affection and maternity.[7]

## Feminist responses: Purity or free love?

One prevalent image of the Victorian period is of a time of silence and
repression and prudery on the question of sex, broken by the 'speaking out' of sex-reforming sexologists such as Havelock Ellis. This
image needs challenging. Those same social purity feminists, who
were labelled prudes and puritans by contemporary sex reformers,
also 'spoke out'. In the early twentieth century feminism was itself
divided over the problem of sex: how to define it, how it was experienced by women, and what to demand sexually from the state and
from men. One strand of feminism, with its roots in the radical liberal
and social purity campaign work of Josephine Butler,[8] drew largely
on the language of Christianity, with its notions of purity and
impurity, virtue and vice, but also on aspects of the contemporary
theories of evolution. Religious language, especially that of
Evangelicism, had allowed many women a voice in the public sphere
from the early part of the nineteenth century – not as individual
women in their own right but as the instruments of religious
inspiration. Religious rhetoric increasingly framed nineteenth-
century feminism, including the feminist campaign against the
Contagious Diseases Acts in which feminists publicly broached the
question of 'immoral sex' itself, the most 'unspeakable' of subjects.

The strand of feminism opposed to social purity also utilised certain
evolutionary ideas. However, it drew not on the language of religion
but on a politics of radical individualism, libertarianism and the
ethical socialism of figures such as Edward Carpenter[9] (with notions
of communal living and 'free love' unions). It also and increasingly
drew on the emergent ideas of sexologists – the new so-called 'science'
of sex. This grouping termed themselves the 'new moralists'. I want to
look here at the feminist debate over sex in the years before and
during the first world war, largely between social purity feminists and
the 'new moralists' (although there were differences between women
within each grouping, and also women involved in the debate who
didn't fit easily into either camp). It would be wrong to divide these
women into those who were anti-sex, those who were pro it. Both
groupings were debating and struggling over what role sex should
ideally play in human life generally, and in women's lives in particu-

lar. This inevitably involved consideration of the definition of sex and female sexuality. Both agreed that, ideally, sex was not an uncontrollable physical force or urge, indiscriminate in its object; both were opposed to promiscuity. Both grounded their convictions in notions of the place of sex within the evolution of humankind. Both held to the principle of a woman's right to control her own body. However, the ways in which this was thought about differed markedly between the two groupings.

To social purity feminists, the right to control one's own body referred to the right to say 'No' to all undesired male sexual advances – *including* advances from one's husband.[10] It also implied a right to control conception – a right to 'voluntary motherhood'. 'Motherhood can be sacred only when voluntary, when a child is desired by a woman who feels herself fit to bear and rear it'.[11] In this respect social purity feminists were in favour of a form of birth control – the practice of what was termed continence or abstinence within marriage. However they were not in favour of artificial contraception (the sheath, cap, sponge or syringe), known in this period as Malthusian appliances/practices, or of artificial sterilisation. Contraception was thought to be a means by which men could indulge their lust while escaping the consequences of their actions: 'artificial sterilisation [makes] easier the indulgence of uncontrolled passions unfortunately *outside* marriage as well as inside.'[12] Since contraception was believed to be widely used by prostitutes, many 'respectable' women felt that use of such appliances reduced them to the status of a prostitute. 'Common Malthusian practices are . . . a gross outrage on the aesthetic sensibilities of women and the final mark of their sexual degradation.'[13] Further, artificial contraception was also deemed unnatural and declared by the medical profession to be detrimental to health.

Informing social purity feminists' view of sex was their conviction that sex should ideally be reserved for the act of reproduction. Control of reproduction made restriction of sex desirable. I quoted Mrs Sherwen at the beginning of this paper. Christabel Pankhurst held a similar position: 'sex powers are given . . . as a trust to be used, not for . . . immorality and debauchery, but . . . reverently and in a union based on love, for the purpose of carrying on the race.'[14]

For unmarried women, social purists advocated chastity. At the turn of the twentieth century many feminists claimed the identity of 'spinster' or 'single woman' and argued for a positive celebration of celibacy. Through the nineteenth century and into the twentieth, the proportion of women to men gradually rose. The excess of women was referred to negatively as the 'surplus' or 'superfluous' woman problem, and the spinster was subjected to much ridicule. But certain feminists presented positive arguments for women's celibacy: it gave women more time;[15] it enabled women to channel their energy into the public world;[16] rather than impairing health (as medics and sexologists claimed), it allowed women to *avoid* the ill-health encumbent on marriage and motherhood; and it indicated women's freedom from slavery to 'our lower appetites'.[17]

Social purity feminists distinguished love from lust. 'Sexual indulgence' – sex sought for itself – was thought by some social purity feminists to reduce humankind to the level of lower animals. 'We women are miles above and beyond men . . . [who] still have a long way to go before they are really emancipated from the lower orders.'[18] Certain other social purity feminists, drawing on ideas from evolutionary theory, argued that while evolutionary development had led to a lessening of the sex drive, 'man' was the only animal within the animal kingdom to indulge in sex.[19] One social purity feminist asked rhetorically: 'What male creature below humanity ever infects or abuses his mate?'[20] She was referring here to venereal diseases – the notorious 'social diseases', the 'hidden scourge'. A number of feminists in the early part of the twentieth century orchestrated a campaign against venereal diseases in which they relocated blame away from the prostitute and onto her male client. Male lust lay at the base of prostitution and thus of VDs, they claimed. VDs were the punishment for the 'unnaturalness' of male sexual immorality: 'vices like curses come back to roost.'[21]

> Immoral intercourse with prostitutes men are pleased to term 'the exercise of their natural functions' . . . and those who wage campaigns [against prostitution] are accused of defying nature. Nature, indeed! As though Nature had not decreed a punishment for sexual immorality such as she imposes in respect of no other sin.[22]

It wasn't a new point – feminists, such as Josephine Butler, had made the same argument forty years earlier. However, it was the *degree* of feminist 'speaking out' about the issue of VDs and male sexuality which was new. A number of recent reprints have given us access to several feminist texts which deal with the VD question.[23] The period's best known text, Christabel Pankhurst's *The Great Scourge and how to end it* (1913), a composite of a series of articles which first appeared in the *Suffragette*, argued that so-called 'women's diseases' were not intrinsic to the female constitution (as many medics

14

claimed), but the effects of VDs surreptitiously imposed by phil-
andering husbands on their unsuspecting wives. Drawing on medical
sources, she argued that 75–80 percent of men had had gonorrhea,
and a large minority had had syphilis. To another contributor to the
debate such a husband represented to his wife 'the death-distributor
at her own hearth'.[24] To Christabel Pankhurst, the solution lay with
'Votes for Women, Chastity for Men'.

The feminist arguments concerning VD represented a stringent
critique both of the double standard and of male sexuality. Even
Rebecca West, a feminist deeply opposed to the social purity position
and, at the time, hostile to Christabel's *Suffragette* articles on VD,
later admitted the power of their impact: 'The articles . . . were
ill-informed and badly written, but they scattered like wind an age-
old conspiracy of prudishness, and enabled society to own the
existence of these diseases and set about exterminating them as never
before.'[25] The social purity feminists also attacked the basic male
predatory view of women: 'Men have sought in women only a body.
They have made it the refuse-heap of sexual pathology.'[26]

The feminist 'new moralists' were far fewer in number than the
social purity feminists. They stood for 'limited monogamy' and 'free
unions': monogamous relations that could be freely entered and
freely left.[27] They opposed the hypocrisy of indissoluble marriage
(the 'old morality'), with the married woman maintaining her 'purity'
at the expense of the prostitute. Feminist 'new moralists', like social
purists, argued for the right to freedom from unlimited pregnancy,
but they differed as to the means of arriving at this freedom. Rather
than sexual abstinence, they argued for the separation of sex from
reproduction through the use of contraception, including 'artificial',
mechanical methods. High on their agenda was the demand for
women's sexual pleasure and the destruction of the myth of women's
asexuality, 'the belief that the majority of women . . . feel neither
curiosity, nor desire . . . while they are maidens. And that when their
sexual life has begun, its physical side is quite subordinate, and
merely a *response* to their husbands'.'[28] They held that not only
should women be allowed to be sexual, but that sex was a natural
function, needing frequent exercise like all natural functions,[29] which
over centuries had evolved a distinctly human and spiritual aspect –
the capacity to love. As a corollary, it was dangerous to deny or
repress one's sexuality. Rebecca West authoritatively declared:

Many of the evils of our social system spring from perversions that
arose when all education and much of the land was in the hands of

monks and nuns who were professedly leading unnatural lives of repression. And in the same way the lady – who is simply the well-repressed woman – may be a source of danger to the State.[30]

Looking back from the feminism of the 1980s we are likely to find problems with *both* these strands of feminism. The social purity feminists believed that sex should be preserved for procreation, and many held women to be far less sexual than men. The woman 'is so little sexual that non-sexual matters can exclusively engross her. Sex instincts of both sexes cannot be compared . . . in the majority of women, the desire for children is inherent, but the necessary process abhorred.'[31] 'Woman has been the scapegoat [of male lust] . . . though she has far less strenuous sexual proclivities than those which curse men.'[32] Women were passive sexual victims and those who advocated 'the new "morality" . . . would permit for women the same degrading laxity in sex matters which is indulged in by most of the lower animals, including men.'[33] In other words, women who were sexually active were degraded women.

One of the problems with the new moralists, on the other hand, was the centrality to their view of sex of 'the sex act' (penetration): 'the highest form of sex giving and of self-expression'.[34] Other forms of sexual expression were either of no value and bordered on the pathological, or were merely useful in aiding the attainment of the ultimate expression of love: mutual orgasm through penetration. This was a theme taken up and developed in the interwar years by the writers of marital sex manuals (see below).

Both social purity and new morality feminists dictated standards for other women. The concern to protect women from male sexuality could be double-edged, sometimes taking the form of active supervision and control of women's sexuality. In the first world war, certain feminist groupings were responsible for setting up women patrols and women police. The women patrols, initiated by the social purist feminist organisation 'The National Union for Women Workers (with women and children)', saw their role as moral watchdogs, concerned to

> influence and, if need be, restrain the behaviour of women and girls who congregate in the neighbourhood of the camps and to safeguard our girls from the result of unnatural excitement produced by the abnormal conditions now prevailing,[35]

and to warn those girls who'd been 'speaking to men on duty or behaving unsuitably'.[36]

The move for the setting up of uniformed women police came from two separate quarters, Nina Boyle of the Women's Freedom League (WFL) and a grouping around another suffragette, Margaret Damar Dawson, but when the latter permitted women police to be used to enforce a curfew on women in certain districts, the WFL severed all connections. However, it was Damar Dawson's lot that won the day and gained recognition from the Home Office and the Metropolitan Police. The stress lay on protection: 'the protection of women by women was the root principle underlying the whole project',[37] but the degree of surveillance open to the women police in the war makes for disturbing reading. For example, Damar Dawson's Second-in-Command records how a regulation in the area where the curfew on women applied. It

> gave us power to go into the women's houses to see if the girls were in bed, and to see who was in the houses. We found that the women were getting large quantities of drink into the house instead of being . . . in public houses, or in the streets where people could see them. We turned out hundreds of soldiers and girls, and reported it to the military authority and to the Chief Constable.[38]

The new moralists also dictated standards for other women. It was above all in relation to the spinster that condemning pronouncements were made. It appears that in order to claim their right to sexuality the new moralists felt the need to lampoon those women socially labelled 'asexual'. Anti-spinster imagery was widely prevalent in society at large,[39] but it is galling to find it so repetitively on the pages of the feminist journal the *Freewoman*. For example, the spinster was referred to as 'the withered tree, the acidulous vestal under whose pale shadow we chill and whiten. . . . She is our social Nemesis. . . . She rules the earth. . . . A restive but impotent world writhes under her subtle priestly domination.'[40] To Stella Browne, spinsters 'spend lives of sterility and a slow atrophy of bodily and mental power.'[41] In her protest against the preaching of abstinence for all women, single or married ('do not let them make their temperamental coldness into a rigid standard for others'[42]) Stella Browne effectively dictated her *own* standards for other women.

*'Tender wooing' and marital 'bliss': Sex literature of the interwar years*

In the years after the first world war and the winning of the vote, the

17

biting feminist attack on male sexuality went into abeyance; its only manifestation was anger at male inconsideration of female sexual needs and pleasures. With the 'sexualising' of women and women's recruitment into active participation in heterosexuality,[43] the demand for the right of married women to say 'No' to sex with their husbands effectively disappeared. But this is not to imply that feminists were inactive on the question of sexuality. In the interwar years feminists took up the issue of sex primarily in relation to sex education, artificial contraception and the right of women to sexual pleasure. Marie Stopes was a key figure on all counts.

In relation to women's right to sexual pleasure, her various writings, especially *Married Love*, were of great importance. *Married Love*, with an objective 'to increase the joys of marriage and to show how much sorrow may be avoided', was published in 1918, sold over 2000 copies in a fortnight and by the end of the year was already in its sixth edition. As Stopes wrote later:

> Its explosively contagious theme – that woman like man has the same physiological reaction, a reciprocal need for enjoyment and benefit from union in marriage distinct from the exercise of maternal functions – made Victorian husbands gasp.[44]

While drawing on some of the work of sexologists (although she appears to have been largely untouched by Freudianism), her language retained much of the religious and sentimental inflection of an earlier period and in this she was not unique. Most of the pamphlets and books on marital sex produced in the interwar years, and right up into the early 1960s, displayed a similar rhetoric – a language sitting uneasily within the same text alongside the more medical 'scientific' discourse of sexologists and psychiatrists. Stopes was in fact explicit as to their coexistence: 'I herald a new epoch, in which Science and Religion will be one. I wish that I could blazon to the world in burning words their essential unity.'[45]

Part of the importance of *Married Love* lay in her denial that women were irrational, capricious and sexually cold, and with her claim that if women were disinterested in sex, it was due to man's lack of consideration and knowledge of the nature of woman's sexual desire. Thus, unlike the new moralists' blaming of desexed women, she put the blame mainly on men. Other sex reformers followed suit in this respect; as Bea Campbell has expressed it: 'his failure was her frigidity'.[46]

However, the sexual norm for women was still represented as

monogamous marital heterosexuality ('conjugal bliss'), with penetration as the ultimate experience and woman the passive partner. A 'successful' sexual union (that which culminated in simultaneous orgasm) was the 'work' of the man:

> The Supreme law for husbands is: Remember that each act of union must be tenderly wooed for and won, and that no union should ever take place unless the woman also desires it and is made physically ready for it.

Women were only likely to desire 'it' when at the peak of their cycle of desire (termed by Stopes the 'Law of periodicity of desire in women'), generally fortnightly (mid-month and just before menstruation). Recognition that women's sexual desire varied through the month was indeed radical. Unfortunately, however, she did not encourage the wife to express her desire, it was 'against the true ideals for a woman to advertise to her husband that he is wanting',[47] but the husband must 'carefully study his wife, observe how far she has a normal rhythm, and in what she has little personal traits. He will then endeavour to adapt his demands on her so that they are in harmony with her nature.'[48]

After the publication of Stopes' *Married Love* other popular books on marital sex appeared in increasing number. *The Sex Factor in Marriage* (1930), the bestseller of the feminist Dr Helena Wright, had many parallels with Stopes' work. The woman was viewed as passive, needing to be 'sexually awakened' by the 'right man', (her husband). In contrast, the man did not need arousal but 'knowledge' in the 'art of love-making'. Men were thought of as permanently 'on the brink': 'she needs arousing; he needs relief.'[49] Wright urged every husband to remember Balzac's aphorism that 'woman is a harp who only yields her secrets of melody to the master who knows how to handle her',[50] while Havelock Ellis approvingly quoted Balzac's view of woman as 'a delicious instrument of pleasure'; 'man had to learn to play its quivering strings . . . timid keyboard . . . changing and capricious fingering.'[51]

Rev. A. Herbert Cray's introduction to *The Sex Factor* conveyed grave disapproval and threat to any woman who wasn't willing to co-operate in the whole exercise:

> If you do not consent to be awakened your husband will be deeply disappointed. . . . He will not call it purity, he will call it prudery; and he will be right. . . . He will know that you have not fully *given*

yourself in marriage; and married joys are for those who *give* with royal generosity (his emphasis).[52]

The prevalent language of Christianity, with its emphasis on the *union* of body, mind and soul of husband and wife, the merging of two into one through mutual orgasm, acted to reinforce the emphasis on the sex act as the ultimate sacrament – the 'sexual communion'.

As with the new moralists, all this stress on the 'sex act' rendered other sexual behaviour aberrant or mere foreplay to the 'real' event – in spite of recognising the erotic importance of the clitoris. The pleasures of the clitoris were but the gateway to the higher (but harder to achieve) mature pleasure of the vagina.[53] Stopes' theory of the enormous benefits of the sex act contributed to this belittling of other forms of sexual activity. Her ideas on this score took what today seem a rather strange direction in her emphasis on the value of 'secretions'. In *Enduring Passions* she developed this point at some length. After the mutual orgasm, the man should remain with his penis inside the woman so that

> the seminal fluid is enclosed in the vagina in which the penis lies so that *both* are in a position to absorb and benefit from all ejaculated secretions.[54]

Not receiving the secretions was, to Stopes, the main argument against lesbianism:

> The bedrock objection to lesbianism is surely that women can only *play* with each other and *cannot* . . . have natural union or supply each other with the seminal and prostatic secretions which they ought to have, and crave for unconsciously. Lesbian love . . . can never supply the actual physiological nourishment, the chemical molecules produced by the accessory glandular systems of the male (her emphasis).[55]

Perhaps significantly Stopes wrote this in 1928, the year of the trial and subsequent banning of Radclyffe Hall's lesbian novel *The Well of Loneliness*. Prior to the trial, lesbianism, in the sense of *sexual* relationships between women, appears not to have been widely known about, let alone spoken of. The attempt to criminalise lesbianism through a clause in the 1921 Criminal Law Amendment Bill (to place it on par with the 1885 criminalisation of male homosexuality) foundered on the conviction that drawing attention to the existence of a practice unknown to most women might itself incite the practice.

However, within sexology lesbianism had been an object of study for some years. Havelock Ellis distinguished 'true' congenital 'inversion' from a temporary acquired perversion. 'Inversion' represented biological deviation from the norm of heterosexual procreative sex and thus, in relation to women, evoked barrenness in a manner similar to the depiction of the spinster. In an excellent article on the trial and reception of the *Well of Loneliness*,[56] Sonja Ruehl demonstrates how Hall, working within Ellis's category of inversion, highlighted the 'sterility' of lesbian relationships. Further, Hall's thinly disguised autobiographical novel stood as a plea from a self-confessed lesbian for toleration, rather than condemnation of a state of sexual being over which the invert had no choice. The idea of 'congenital inversion' freed lesbians from moral blame. Hall thereby opened up space for other lesbians to claim an identity and speak for themselves, (a theme which is discussed further by Elizabeth Wilson in Chapter 12). The prosecution of the novel, and the concomitant media coverage of the trial, led precisely to that process so feared by Parliament: the entry of lesbianism as a practice and identity into common parlance. The novel was to represent a central definer of lesbian identity for many years, and had at least sown the possibilities of a separate identity, even if by moving the category of 'lesbian' away from sin and sickness it defined it as innate sexual nature. However, it didn't affect how female sexuality within heterosexual relations was perceived.

What of the attitudes towards the spinster in the interwar years? Stopes was keen for them to fill themselves with 'pluriglandular compounds' – all those 'secretions' they were missing out on in their celibate lives. However, although Stopes was apparently impervious to the influence of Freud, many others, *including* a number of social purity feminists, were not. By the 1920s, with the impact of 'new psychology' (the biologistic form of psychoanalysis influential in this country), many people's view of the spinster had decidedly shifted. The dangers of repression that 'psychology has taught us' led Maude Royden, a social purity feminist, to view the enforced celibacy of the spinster as pitiful and potentially stultifying.[57] However, hope lay in the re-channelling of the sex instinct into creative vocations other than motherhood and marriage. Until the 1960s, the 'solution' of 'sublimation' was to become the main advice for all unmarried women.

The ideological equation of sex and reproduction might have been loosened in the interwar years ('the false idea that intercourse undertaken for a reproductive purpose is more meritorious than intercourse performed purely as an expression of love, is dying'[58]). But as Beatrix Campbell points out,[59] if sex meant penetration, women were always put at the risk of pregnancy. This was *despite* contraception becoming increasingly available and respectable. Apart from the fact that for many women birth control was not an option (lack of information, lack of co-operation, even prohibition from the husband, unavailability in the area, difficulties with using the different kinds of contraceptives, etc.), no birth control method was 100 percent reliable. Nevertheless, the huge growth of birth control information and clinics in the 1920s and 1930s must be recognised as a crucial gain for women sexually. The grounds on which birth control was largely argued for and won – the basis on which the birth control movement gained respectability – are not so encouraging. A small minority of feminists, including Stella Browne and Dora Russell, did make an explicit case for birth control as a woman's right to self-determination, but the main body of the movement fought for contraception on the grounds of eugenics and health. Marie Stopes is far more famous today for her birth control work than her pronouncements on marital love. A committed eugenicist (the name of her organisation, the Society for Constructive Birth Control and Racial Progress, hinted at such an association), her arguments for contraception took the form of a plea for fit breeding and healthy mothers rather than for women's pleasure. To Stopes, birth control enabled on the one hand, the 'fit' married woman to space her children for reasons of health, rather than to choose a life of childlessness, and on the other, the 'unfit' woman to do her eugenic duty and refrain from breeding entirely. Other women's organisations were also, on occasion, influenced by eugenics. For example, the National Society for Equal Citizenship and the Woman's Co-operative Guild both supported the campaign to legalise sterilisation in the 1930s for certain groups of 'unfit' persons. That birth control was not generally argued for in terms of women's sexual pleasure in this period is hardly surprising – eugenics and a concern with health were central issues of the day, and by all accounts sexual pleasure was lacking in many women's lives anyway.[60] However, the virtual absence of this way of seeing birth control has meant that the dual potential of birth control – as a *woman's* right to control of her reproduction or as *population* control – has not always worked for the benefit of women. Today, the imposed use of the dangerous contraceptive Depo-provera on certain working-class and black women in this country, often without their prior knowledge of the dangers and sometimes without their consent,[61] indicates the continued presence of a eugenic influence. Until recently, a woman's use of contraceptives was acceptable only as a means for the married woman to space her family responsibly: birth control as family *planning*, rational regulation of family size rather than a woman's control of her own fertility. Since the late 1960s, of course, unmarried women have had far easier access to birth control, although for an unmarried woman to be on the pill, especially an 'unattached' unmarried woman, still has a stigma attached in certain contexts, for instance its 'relevance' in rape trials as means of discrediting a woman who has been raped.

## Post-war 'love without fear'

The way that women's sexuality was written about in the post-war marriage and sex education manuals showed marked continuities with the interwar years, despite the intervening upheavals. Sexual intercourse was still seen as legitimate only within marriage, and with the perpetuation of Christian concepts ('union', 'one flesh', sex as sacrament), the 'sex act' with mutual orgasm remained *the* definer of sex-as-love. The need for the husband to learn the 'techniques' of 'love-making' remained a continuing theme, as did the ideas of the essential passivity of the wife awaiting the 'awakening', and requiring a longer duration than the man to reach the 'summit of the mountain of desire'.[62] 'Unlike a boy, a girl has no biological urge at all unless stimulated, thus her sex drive makes no troublesome demands.'[63] Thus the woman was thought *naturally* to respond differently from a man; she was also thought to crave 'gentle' sexual domination: 'the normal woman likes to feel herself *conquered* . . . she demands in her lover a combination of masterfulness and kindliness, of confidence and consideration'[64] (my emphasis). The ideal of 'purity' for the unmarried woman clung on tenaciously:

> If a woman is a virgin when she is married, she need have little fear that her husband will ever leave her, providing of course, she is a wife to him in every possible sense. He feels that she really does belong to him, and him alone.[65]

In the post-war years, masturbation was generally no longer dangerous (and had long ceased to be sinful), it was simply selfish, solitary, self-indulgent and probably just a 'phase' to be passed through on the path to maturity. 'Maturity' for a woman still lay with the move from the clitoris to the vagina as her 'true' seat of pleasure. Freudianism was now much in evidence in substantiating both this view of masturbation's 'adolescence', and the definition of the lesbian as the woman 'stuck' in an immature stage, with libidinal attachment to the mother, a definition of lesbianism that quite obviously competed with the 'congenital' definition. However lesbianism tended not to be mentioned widely in the 1940s and 1950s, almost as if, like Parliament's sentiment in the 1920s, the manuals believed that lesbianism 'unspoken' held back its 'doing'.

Freudianism, or rather the biologistic variant influential in this country, also emphasised the completion of women's sexuality in motherhood. As is well-known today, the 1950s was a period of great emphasis on mothering, in which the writings of Melanie Klein and others (Bowlby, Winnicott, Isaacs) were highly influential. It became almost impossible to imagine women not wanting to be wives and mothers since this was the area in which they could really 'find' and fulfil themselves. The stress on women-as-mothers may at first sight appear to be contradicted by another long-term tendency that had been in evidence since at least the turn of the century: the move to smaller families. By the 1940s and 1950s, it was generally recognised that the small family was here to stay, and that most married couples used some form of birth control some time or other. Indeed birth control was on occasion argued for as a means of avoiding sexual 'perversions': 'Many perversions are practised for no other reason than that the couple concerned are afraid of pregnancy. . . . Why not, instead, apply modern methods to "space" children?'[66]

If motherhood centred on the mother–child couplet (for Klein, as opposed to Freud, it was this relationship, rather than the Oedipal triangle, that was all-significant), the post-war notion of marriage stressed a different factor for the relationship of husband and wife. It is here that the question of women's non-reproductive sexuality came to the fore. 'Marriage' was a central organising concept in the 1940s and 1950s for everyone across the political spectrum. Part of the social democratic ideology of the period was the view of women as equal marital partners – though it was an equality in terms of 'equal but different'. This concept was enscribed in the Beveridge Report in 1942, the blueprint of the welfare state, and mobilised throughout the debates on marriage and the position of women that took place in the period. Concern with the maintenance of marriage became a major issue after the war. The factors contributing to this ranged from the increased entry of married women into waged work, to the enormous post-war leap in the divorce rate and the compression of women's child-rearing years.

With married couples facing the possibility of years ahead together *without* the preoccupation of children for more than a few of those years, and with widespread acceptance of birth control as a legitimate part of family life, pleasurable, non-reproductive sex stepped in as the 'cement' of the marital relationship. It was, of course, a view of sex that Stopes and others had long been arguing for. It also laid the ground for the positive sanctioning of women's non-reproductive (hetero)sexuality outside marriage, although, as we well know, this didn't come into effect until the late 1960s/early 1970s, and then in a very ambiguous way. (See below, and Lynne Segal's chapter.)

One new development of the post-war years was the appearance of books and pamphlets addressed to the adolescent, and not simply to the married or 'about to be married', as was always the case before the war. (This needs to be seen in the context of the period's wider concern with 'youth', 'youth culture' and the new phenomenon of the 'teenage consumer'.)[67] Jeffrey Weeks[68] rightly points out that stress on petting in sex literature underlined the ambivalence of the period: recognition of the need for sexual outlet (for men and boys at least), but fear too of promiscuity. For example, as one sexologist put it:

> It is unwise to allow the lovemaking [of engaged couples] ever to lead to more than mutual masturbation. It is very poor feminine tactics to permit the pleasures of marriage without any of its responsibilities, quite apart from the probable tragedy of unwanted pregnancy.[69]

Here we see an increased tendency to demand sexually *responsible* behaviour from women – men act, but women use 'tactics', and they must use them wisely.

Missing from all this discussion of marital sex was any *feminist* voice. The feminists of the 1940 and 1950s tended not to address questions of sexuality. Adhering to the 'equal but different' ideology, they were primarily concerned with single-issue campaigns relating to improving the law in relation to marriage, divorce and waged work (especially the demand for equal pay), or were involved in the international peace movement. Marriage and motherhood as women's true vocation were generally unquestioned.[70] However, as Beatrix Campbell points out,[71] one lone(?) feminist did address the question of women's sexuality, namely Dr Helena Wright, in her 1947 autocritique of *The Sex Factor in Marriage*. Written in response to

25

years of patients' complaining of their inability to achieve vaginal orgasm, she blamed male domination for the 'penis–vagina fixation', which in turn obscured the crucial role of the clitoris.[72] That her insights and challenge went largely unnoticed indicates only too clearly the period's widespread consensus on the correct role of sex for women: as not simply marital, monogamous and heterosexual, but, above all, directed to the sex act of penetration. However, the 1953 Kinsey Report on women's sexuality[73] did have a large initial impact in that it was sensationally presented by the media (labelled the 'K' bomb), and quoted widely. Yet the Report's findings, in particular that masturbation and homosexual practices were more sexually satisfying for women than heterosexual intercourse, were not incorporated into current sex manuals. As with Helena Wright, Kinsey's challenge to the vaginal orgasm was unpalatable. So too was the 'amorality' of his anti-Freudian behaviourism and the divorcing of sex from love, romance, motherhood and marriage. Kinsey was seen as having reduced sex to statistics, with a wide variety of different sexual acts put on a par. As one commentator expressed it: 'Nocturnal emissions, rape, Romeo spending the night with Juliet are made equivalent outlets.'[74]

The 1950s thus continued the equation of love, sex and marital bliss, but it arguably upped the pressures on women to fit in with the 'divine' plan. Women – or rather married women – were caught in contradictory demands: on the one hand they were required to maintain their passivity and let men always take the lead; on the other, they were required to learn the requisite response, to display a 'knowing innocence'. For, it was argued, 'a sexually illiterate woman is as unfit for wifehood as a mental defective is for motherhood.'[75] As for what sexual *literacy* might entail, however, it was not entirely clear; whatever it was, it certainly wasn't premarital sex.

## Chastity outmoded: the permissive 1960s

By the late 1950s/early 1960s, with the publication of books and pamphlets such as Chesser's 'Is Chastity Outmoded?', the possible legitimacy of premarital sex was, for the first time, widely contemplated. Initially the answer was usually a resounding 'No': but not for long. The 1960s are now remembered largely as the era of 'permissiveness'. For many feminists today it was also the period of our adolescence in which sexual expectations and explorations were likely to have been a major preoccupation. A variety of rather different factors contributed to the 1960s' reputation as permissive, few of

26

which were, in truth, any clear-cut sexual liberation for women.

However, the advent of the contraceptive pill in the early 1960s was a landmark: for the first time sex appeared *potentially* separable from reproduction for the majority of women. In 1964 the opening of the first Brook Advisory Centre, catering exclusively for the young unmarried, presented the possibility of premarital sexual intercourse without the fear of pregnancy. Subsequent clinics were not always established without fierce resistance. In Birmingham, for example, the proposed Brook Clinic was hotly opposed by doctors, clergy and councillors.[76] Nevertheless, it could be said that the 'Brook' laid an important basis for legitimate 'sex for the single girl'. In a retrospective article in 1969, one journalist cited the two separate but simultaneous developments he believed responsible for 'the fastest revolution in sexual habits and attitudes that this country has ever seen' as the decline of religion and the arrival of the pill.[77] This would be to simplify the causes of change. For a start, it was not just a matter of decline in religion; the Anglican Church had itself shifted. The debate around John Robinson's *Honest to God* in 1963 represented a move to greater permissiveness – the placing of *love* and individual choice at the heart of morality, which thereby made possible the contemplation of sex within a long-term loving relationship that was not necessarily one of marriage. Further, developments within fashion were central to the sense of greater 'sexual liberation'. The new blatantly and publicly sexual fashion, aimed particularly at young women and epitomised above all in the mini-skirt, at one and the same time freed us from constricting clothing while establishing us ever more firmly as objects of the male sexual gaze. It also infantilised women – the obsession with youth, with hindsight, looks almost paedophilic.

Fashion, along with the multiplication through consumerism of areas of women's bodies defined as sexual, and the sexualisation of situations previously tabooed (work and the street) all contributed to the claim of women's 'sexual liberation'.[78] But at what price? As Beatrix Campbell expressed it:

> the permissive area had some pay-off for women in so far as it opened up political–sexual–space. It permitted sex for women too. What it did not do was defend women against the differential effects of permissiveness on men and women . . . and it was primarily a revolt of young *men*. . . . The very affirmation of sexuality was a celebration of *masculine* sexuality.[79]

The work of the sexologists Masters and Johnson and the take-up of Reich and Marcuse were all part and parcel of the idea of 'sexual liberation'. Since Masters and Johnson's work is discussed further elsewhere in this book (see Chapter 3), I only want to make a couple of points. Masters and Johnson saw women's sexuality as *equivalent* to men's – give or take a few little differences. Their work was extremely important, not least their claim that women's sexual drive was as great as men's, their sexual capacity even greater (their capacity for multiple orgasm) and that 'the primary focus for sexual response in the human female's pelvis is the clitoral body.'[80] Women were being recognised as sexual subjects not merely objects – a huge advance indeed. However, rather than decentring penetration as *the* Sex Act, they re-established it by claiming that clitoral stimulation could be synchronised with vaginal penetration. The linking of their work with the ideas of the so-called 'sexual revolution' had certain oppressive implications for women. The break with chastity as 'old-fashioned' meant the removal of unmarried women's right to say 'No'. Further, the insistence that sex was not only 'good' for you, but essential for one's liberation, together with the availability of the pill, and thus the removal of an 'escape clause' for saying 'No' to undesired sex, reinforced the pressure on women to fuck.

### The language and demands of the women's liberation movement

With the rise of the women's movement in the late 1960s, and in the context of consciousness-raising groups, the oppressiveness of 'permissiveness', and of the centrality of penetration and hetero-sexual genitality, began to be subjected to close scrutiny. Rather than detail the various ways in which feminists have thought about sex (many of which are addressed in other chapters in this book), I want briefly to take stock of where we stand in relation to our gains and losses since the early years of this century.

At the turn of the century, social purity feminists had demanded the right of women, including married women, to say 'No' to sex with men. As we have seen, with the married women's 'sexualisation' in the interwar years, this demand was effectively lost. With the 1960s' sexual revolution and the final denigration of chastity, the right of unmarried women to reject male sexual advances was also lost. Today, feminists have renewed the earlier social purity feminists' demand, claiming the right of *all* women to reject unsolicited male advances as central to our sexual politics. The demand for rape to be recognised within marriage ensures the inclusion of married women's right. However, unlike the social purity feminists, we claim the right to *be sexual*; in contrast to the new moralists we demand this right *on our own terms*. We are having to develop our own language with which to describe and define our sexuality. We have rejected the confining definitions of religion which yoke sex to monogamous heterosexual union. We reject much of the language of sexology – particularly its past definition of lesbianism as sickness or perversion, and its current behaviourist view of sexual behaviour as separate from human relationships (see Chapter 3). Evolutionary language, favoured by certain past feminists, is today utilised by sociobiologists to convey an inevitable and biologistic sexist world of predatory male, passive, domesticated female.[81] We also reject the ideology and practice of 'permissiveness' and its perpetuation of the double standard: the idea that 'anything goes' (yet heterosexual fucking is still the ideal), that casual sex is desirable and 'natural' (but a 'promiscuous' *woman* is a slag).

Our heritage is not a linear story of progress, nor the 'glorious unfolding' which Marie Stopes believed would occur.[82] Along the way, certain demands were lost, certain developments became oppressive and coercive. As we have seen, past feminists were sometimes complicit in dictating sexual standards for other women. We need to learn today from the past, taking care not to apply new coercive standards to women who at present live by different sexual codes from ourselves. As feminists, we are for the first time decentring heterosexuality from the dominant definition of sex, arguing for lesbianism as a *political* and not simply a personal choice, and for celibacy as an option that doesn't necessarily spell no-sex, but sexual *self*-pleasure. Further, in recognising that our sexuality is socially and psychically *constructed*, we recognise that it is open to change through collective self-determination. Building a new language to describe our actual and potential sexual experience is part of the task of effecting such a change.

*Acknowledgements*

Many thanks to Janice Winship, Jo Ryan and Sue Cartledge, Mary Ballard, and Richard Johnson for their help and encouragement.

# 3

# Sensual Uncertainty, or
# Why the Clitoris is not enough

## Lynne Segal

'In this society the nearest any of us reach freedom, honesty and spontaneity with others is in bed with a lover or in the street hurling beer cans at the police.'[1] Some may question the anarchic 'freedom' we express through a riot in the streets, but most of us share the illusion that we are expressing something *natural, private and uniquely ourselves* in our sexual behaviour. And yet we are also, and women in particular, deluged from all sides with earnest and enthusiastic advice on how to enjoy this supposedly natural sexuality. Although some of the advice has been coming from within feminist writing, just how we follow its dictate towards adopting a positive and progressive attitude towards sexual pleasure remains both confusing and mysterious. I shall argue that much of the advice is misleading and inadequate, failing to identify the most significant problems.

Emerging as feminists from the end of the 1960s, many of us had experienced the increasing contradictions of 'sexual liberation'. Women, we had been told, were 'free now as never before', yet the underground press was alive with sexist porn imagery of women as 'chicks', all cunts and boobs, 'happily' screwed every which way by the steely cock of the urban guerrilla. The ubiquitous symbolism of male conquest and female submission, built into almost every image of heterosexuality, depicted a strange 'liberation' for women. And by the end of the 1960s many women were to recognise the male domination anchored in such a 'sexual liberation', as well as to express a deep dissatisfaction with the sexual experiences it had provided for them. When sexual expression and political liberation were believed to go firmly hand in hand – as ironically Mary Whitehouse and her opponents both agreed – women were largely excluded from that fraternal handshake.

30

But more available contraception, abortion law reform, and the general permissiveness of the 1960s had indeed raised women's expectations of sexual pleasure, or some sort of pleasure, even if we were disappointed more often than not. A desire for sexual freedom, to be active sexually outside of marriage, and a desire for more satisfactory heterosexual relationships were important reasons many women came to the women's liberation movement in the early 1970s. Sex and relationships with men were the focus of intense discussion. Most often it was full of resentment and frustration, yet at the same time there was optimism, and we were almost never without hope for some possible, much sought-after change. The early writings on sexuality were optimistic, whether describing possibilities for heterosexual or lesbian pleasure.

In the second half of the 1970s, however, much less was written about sexuality, and most of us rarely even discussed it within the women's movement. There were many reasons for this. First of all theoretical developments, even within socialist feminism, stressed that it was not just capitalism but a separate power-relation between men and women that maintained women's oppression. Connected to this, there was a growing tension between separatist and non-separatist feminist politics. More feminists came to support a strategy and tactics which eschewed any contact with men, as types of radical feminism grew which focused primarily on male behaviour, alongside a cultural feminism which celebrated the ways of women. And finally, the voluntarism and cheery optimism of much of our early writing on sexuality were shaken by a growing awareness of men's hostility and violence towards women. These factors all tended to silence discussion on heterosexuality. Heterosexual women were also attacked by separatist feminists not only as masochistic perpetuators of their own oppression (and unhappy in love many of us were), but as sharing in heterosexual privilege (which we did), and even as encouraging rapists and male violence. (Of course, we could as plausibly argue that heterosexual feminists might be expected to be rather actively discouraging rape and male violence towards women. But tactical and moralistic rhetoric is at issue here, not empirical assertion.) Soon it was not only feminist debate on heterosexuality – outside of the prescription to reject it – but any more complex theoretical work on sexuality which became rare as attention focused on the dangers of male sexuality and the seeming inevitability of rape. Today that debate and theoretical work is hesitantly re-emerging, or at least some examination of the reasons for our silence. It's not easy to begin again.

31

Re-assessing our early writing on sexuality can perhaps suggest new directions. For I do think that the inadequacy of our early theorising on sexuality fed into a growing uncertainty over the relationship between women's sexual experience and oppression. For example, most feminists had begun, as Pat Whiting was to argue in her 1972 article, by seeing women's sexual problems as stemming from their having 'accepted the male definition of their own sexuality, or at least pretended to'.[2] These definitions, she wrote, were now 'obsolete' as they did not correspond to reality. Women were therefore confused about their own sexual responses, and could not communicate their needs, so they remained sexually frustrated, which in turn led, she warned, to physical and mental disorders. Whiting attacked Freudian psychology, with its emphasis on the vaginal orgasm, as a 'disaster' for modern women, and a large part of women's sexual problems. The empiricist research of Masters and Johnson, by contrast, she saw as dedicated to liberating women's sexuality, suggesting that women had greater sexual potential than men. So Whiting was to conclude that: 'The research of Masters and Johnson indicates that widespread acceptance of female masturbation and learning to masturbate to orgasm in the post-puberty period would eliminate most of the female's sexual problems.'[3] Knowledge of women's 'sexual response' will show women 'where their male-inspired hang-ups end and their real sexual feelings begin.'[4]

That same year Angela Hamblin wrote of how women had been cut off 'from the inner core of their own sexuality'.[5] Because women's sexuality had been, as of course it had, defined in male terms, feminists argued for some 'natural' or 'authentic' *female* sexuality, which we need to 'rediscover'. Quoting Susan Lydon in the USA, Hamblin saw Masters and Johnson as 'truly revolutionary and liberatory', moreover she claimed that 'when we reclaim our sexuality, we will have reclaimed our belief in ourselves as women.'[6] Though the American actress Viva was to compare the rejection of the vaginal orgasm to news of the birth of Christ, and Eva Figes to see modern women's discovery of the orgasm as another nail in the coffin of patriarchy, such proclamations were perhaps premature.

Masters and Johnson had become the authority on female sexuality, as feminists not surprisingly welcomed their critique of centuries of 'phallic fallacies'. Yet though feminists have been and still are greatly influenced by the theoretical perspectives of Masters and Johnson, these are, I believe, fundamentally flawed and misleading. It is easy, none the less, to understand the appeal of the empirical studies of sexologists over the last thirty years. They have begun to explode some aspects of the myths and moralisms surrounding human sexual behaviour, and in particular contributed to the long haul towards a positive assertion of female sexuality in contemporary western thought. They have not, however, represented as decisive a break with earlier conceptions of sexuality as most people have assumed.

The late nineteenth-century approach to sexuality, with its newly emerging 'science' of sexology – developed most systematically in the work of Krafft-Ebbing – was to give sexuality a central position in human motivation. Indeed the very concept of sexuality, as some internal bodily desire, rather than as sex acts, only emerged at this time.[7] Sexuality became a new but pressing 'problem', a dangerous, overpowering, biological urge, fortunately for civilisation confined mainly to the male sex. From childhood masturbation – which was seen as linked to subsequent 'perversion', sex murder and madness – sexual behaviour was seen then as essentially destructive and anti- →animal social. Freud's vast and elaborate theorisation of sexuality from the turn of the century did introduce new and radical understandings of human sexual behaviour. No longer was sexuality to be located first of all in the norm of adult genital heterosexuality, from which all other manifestations deviated. It was to be seen instead in the variously located, continuously unfolding possibilities for physical sensuous gratification through auto-erotic and social encounters, from birth onwards. But the Freudian model also saw sexual desire as both central to human motivation and potentially dangerous, for both the individual and society. Mature female sexuality, because of women's lack of 'the phallus', was seen as attenuated – ideally passive, receptive and essentially responsive to male sexuality, as the girl abandoned her active clitoral sexuality to accept the phallus and vaginal orgasm.

So the 'revolutionary' appeal of the massive statistical surveys of sex behaviour by Alfred Kinsey and his co-workers in the 1950s, and of the elaborate anatomical and physiological recordings of sexual response by Masters and Johnson in the 1960s, was its reflection of a change in certain assumptions about sexual behaviour. The centrality of the sex drive in human behaviour remained, as well as its conceptualisation as some sort of biological demand which needed to be satisfied, somewhat analogous to the drive for food or water. What was different from Krafft-Ebbing or Freud was that both Kinsey and Masters and Johnson saw this pivotal sex drive as both healthy and good for society. They saw *mutual* enjoyment of sex as the basis for ⊲ marital harmony, and sex as essentially harmless, if not beneficial,

33

even in its 'deviant' expressions – outside of marriage and in homo-sexual encounters. Both Kinsey and Masters and Johnson emphasised the similarity of male and female orgasmic potential, and stressed the necessary role of the clitoris in female orgasm; while Masters and Johnson stressed that women had a higher potential for orgasm and a more infinite variety of sexual response patterns than men.

Feminists and non-feminists alike have agreed that Masters and Johnson's work on female sexuality is both radical and progressive. Yet this is a strange state of affairs, when not only is their sexual therapy *always* geared to maintaining traditional marriage and the family, but it falls strictly within a behaviourist psychology which in other contexts most feminists and radicals have rejected as superficial, manipulative and misleading. This is because it looks at and attempts to modify individual behaviour in isolation from social relations. Human behaviour, on this view, has no cultural meaning, historical significance or even subjective importance, but is understood simply as physical response to physical stimulation. In this individualistic psychology sexual liberation is not about social relations or subjective experience, but about individual sensation. And sexual desire is understood not in terms of a person's relation to the object desired, but as some bodily state.

Indeed masturbation and auto-eroticism become the explicit paradigm of satisfactory sexual behaviour for Masters and Johnson, and always provide the model 'for any successful sexual experience'. Sexual behaviour is no longer seen, as in Freudian psychology, as a complex mixture of psychic longing, desire, anxiety, fear, hostility and repression built up over a lifetime of personal erotic encounters with others. Instead, it narrows down to become 'the effective stimulation for orgasm' – a straightforward physical event. And even this physical event is more or less the same for everybody on every occasion, never more or less significant, except that the orgasms in masturbation tend to be stronger and more multiple in women than those resulting from encounters with others.

When they venture at all from anatomical detail into acknow-ledging a psychological side to sexual arousal, Masters and Johnson provide only voluntaristic platitudes. Sexual arousal may be blocked by general negative attitudes either towards all sexuality or particular sexual acts (nothing interpersonal!) and the goal of sexual therapy is to replace these negative attitudes with positive ones. A person needs only anatomical information and the instruction to think positively, to 'correct' any lack of sexual pleasure. Sexual behaviour is seen as always malleable, and negative feelings of shame, disgust or hostility

34

can always be replaced by favourable ones if the person really tries hard enough.

> When the partners in the sexually inadequate relationship see themselves as they have permitted the co-therapist to see them, when they can have their rationales for sexual failure and their prejudices, misconceptions and misunderstandings of natural sexual functioning explored with non-judgemental objectivity and explained in understandable terms with subjective comfort, a firm basis for mutual security in sexual pleasure is established.[8]

(We can only assume, I suppose, that Masters and Johnson must use slightly less pompous and stilted language when instructing subjects how to orgasm, than when describing this passage to victory!)

Most of the more recent popular feminist writing on sexuality, though now sparse, still remains heavily influenced by this crass and simplistic psychology of Masters and Johnson. In 1976 a series of articles appeared in *Spare Rib* by Eleanor Stephens presenting 'a feminist approach to female orgasm'. Based solidly on Masters and Johnson, masturbation is the route to sexual pleasure; orgasm the route to women's greater confidence and power in the world; and ignorance and superstition the obstacles in our way. Stephens sees everything in physical terms, 'every woman with a clitoris can become orgasmic given the right kind and amount of stimulation', though mysteriously, the physical becomes spiritual when we are told that for women to have orgasms is 'literally [for them] to learn to love themselves'.[9] (Really? Even if my orgasm is dependent on my imagining myself tied up, beaten, degraded and fucked up the bum by a diseased rhinoceros? Presumably, since Stephens can recommend reading pornography to obtain a suitable 'mental attitude' for orgasm.)

Stephens draws upon the work of Lonnie Barbach in the USA, *For Yourself: The Fulfilment of Female Sexuality*. Contrasting the good-natured, independent and strong orgasmic woman with the bitter, immature and sulky non-orgasmic woman, Barbach stresses, over and over again, the *unique* nature of each woman's 'very own' orgasm, 'each as unique as the woman herself'.[10] That responses, again seen in purely physical terms, are quite so unique is surely surprising – the knee-jerk like none other! Whatever uniqueness attaches to sexual behaviour one might have expected to arise from the complex histories that have created our particular objects of desire, not the particular rub that ignites the clitoral nub.

No respecter of the power of unconscious mental processes,

Barbach tells us that negative ideas of sexual repulsion or disgust 'may have been perceived unconsciously'. But looking at our genitals in the mirror will eliminate this.[11] Once we have studied our unique sexual response all sexual problems are solved. 'If you can have orgasms with one partner, you can probably have them with another. . . . No one "gives" you orgasms. You are in control.'[12] No one turns you on, you do it yourself? This goal of individual autonomy, applied to sexual encounters, seems to me remarkably odd, not to mention unerotic. How is it that in what is seen as our most intense and intimate connection, the other person slips into irrelevance? And Barbach's conclusion that 'After you find out what really turns you on, you can change your sexual practices to fit your responses'[13] suggests we reign supreme in some solipsistic sexual universe where other people simply don't matter, or can be chosen at will.

Barbach does ask how sexual arousal occurs in the first place, and we quickly learn that once again we do it all for ourselves. (She admits it's exhausting, and a lot of 'hard work' – whoever said it would be fun?) We do it by focusing on sexual, particularly genital, sensations, by removing all sources of distraction (closing the kids' door), and by providing 'erotic stimuli', like candlelight, a roaring fire, roses or pictures of naked bodies; women can 'recondition themselves to respond positively to erotic stimuli'.[14] If such banal advice does not work for you, Barbach recommends pornography. And don't worry about the masochistic fantasies it feeds, because you 'probably' would not enjoy being raped. (No, you probably would not, particularly if you were murdered or mutilated as well – probably not!) What women might find reassuring about their own masochistic fantasies is surely not such unconcerned irrelevance as this, but some insight into the possible appeal and obsessive nature of masochistic fantasy.

At the very least Barbach could acknowledge that it does not feel like personal liberation to be able to orgasm to intensely masochistic fantasies. Instead Barbach nonchalantly advises us to 'stop psycho-analyzing our fantasies' and try enjoying them 'fully and freely', since anyway they 'change over time'.[15] But change over time is exactly what masochistic sexual fantasies usually do not do. They usually survive, often despite the pursuit of autonomy and strength in our everyday lives, to create a puzzling and frightening contrast which can make sex a difficult and disturbing area of life. Nor is it helpful to be told, if we don't like imagining ourselves as helpless and humiliated objects in sexual activity, simply to forget it because, anyway, 'your sex life is private' so nobody need know about it.[16]

Barbach will admit no real impediments in the pursuit of sexual pleasure, so we should just stop imagining them! 'There is probably no reason why you can't enjoy sex fully and be orgasmic,'[17] Barbach assures us. Well, thinking of my own sexuality and that of other women, I would say that there is probably every reason why we can't enjoy sex fully, *whether or not we are orgasmic*. And these reasons often have little to do with anatomical misinformation. Barbach tells us that the sex manuals written by men did not match women's experience, making them feel inadequate and abnormal. Her own book, by contrast, based on women's sexual experience, will she asserts promote 'liberation in the most basic sense' for women, since sexual liberation leads on to personal liberation.[18] I can assure her that her sex manual, self-consciously 'feminist' as it is, made me feel inadequate and abnormal when I first read it, having been given it by a feminist therapist. This was not because I had trouble having orgasms, I never have, but because I nevertheless did find my sexual experiences unsatisfactory and problematic. The enormous importance and value placed on satisfactory sexual experience, as expressing what is most *distinctive* and *unique* about ourselves – though now a part of the ideology of sex – seems more likely to produce anxiety and doubt than the biological bliss Barbach prescribes, where in the words of one newly orgasmic client 'I always think "this is the best *ever*".'[19]

The most ambitious study of female sexuality by a woman is the American *Hite Report* of 1976. Feminists welcomed it widely. The opening is promising, telling us that previous research has asked the wrong questions for the wrong reasons, and that what we need is a new theory of sexuality. I completely agree. But what we get, as Hite continues, is over 500 pages devoted to the same questions, asked for the same reasons, as Masters and Johnson – how do women reach orgasm? Her final section, offering a new theory of sexuality, is less than fifty pages and offers nothing new. She maintains the incorrigible optimism of contemporary sexology, which finds nothing problematic about sexuality, least of all our understanding of the meaning of the term. True to empiricist traditions, she makes no links between sexual experience and culture, not even between sex and gender – though she easily could, if only on the evidence she has collected.

Again, she does not acknowledge that there are any *unconscious* mental processes, and sees people as infinitely malleable: 'it is *we* who know what we want at any given time, and we who create sex in whatever image we want.'[20] And once we have learned to orgasm, as we should by now expect, we are becoming 'free'. 'Controlling your own stimulation symbolizes owning your own body, and is a very important step towards freedom.'[21]

Nowhere does Hite consider as a problem that women might *desire* sex where they can be passive, feel overpowered and *not* in control, though many women tell her this. Nor does she dwell on the problem that she is told that men still feel hostile to women, that there are still sexual double standards. Such observations are apparently trivial compared to what Hite sees as *the problem* – that girls are still kept in the dark about the clitoris. Yet some of us I suspect do manage to find our clitoris – even in the dark (especially in the dark). But more seriously, while knowledge of our genital organs can be important both for self-gratification and for seeking what we may want from sexual partners, Hite's attention to bodily reaction rather than social relations ignores what I see as critical in social relations – their connection to other relations of power, dependence, desire, hostility and fear. The message she has for us, and delivers as she tells us in her preface 'with great joy', is that 'You are free to explore and discover your own sexuality, to learn or unlearn anything you want, and to make physical relations with other people, of either sex, anything you like.'[22] Amen.

And finally, with masochistic delight, I have tormented myself with the most recent feminist 'present' on sex, Anja Meulenbelt's *For Ourselves*, published in Britain in 1981. I may not like it, I certainly did not, but I 'deserve it', she assures me, like a bunch of flowers or a box of chocolates – or a hole in the head! The theme again: we must get in touch with our own needs (through masturbation) and then give ourselves what we want. Strangely, though within recent sexological fantasy not so strange at all, what we want, still seen entirely in terms of those bodily sensations we enjoy, turns out to correspond to 'feminist' aspirations. Our 'real needs', as Meulenbelt illustrates them, are all positive and progressive. They are about wanting equality in relationships, wanting to feel independent and in control. The good sensations are mostly unconnected to genital penetration, and above all they always create the basis for that happy 'love affair' we can have with ourselves.

Oddly enough, Meulenbelt adopts the idea (which, as we've seen, feminists have frequently expressed) of there being some sort of fundamental 'natural' female sexuality, which is uniquely '*our* sexuality', even while also denying that there is such a thing as natural sexuality. 'Sexuality isn't "natural" but learned behaviour,' she says, and 'There is no natural way for people to have sex.'[23] And yet she feels it important for us 'to distinguish our own needs from those imposed on us by society', and tells us 'our sexuality belongs to us, it isn't something we get from someone else.'[24] If sexuality is learned behaviour, and there is no 'natural' way to have sex, what is it that we are to distinguish from all that is social? The way to clap with one hand, that is to ignore the logically impossible, is at least in tune with what some feminists think ought to be our '*real*' sexual needs.

So, for example, admitting that many women *do* like penetrative sex with men (a deviant '30 percent of them' even orgasm that way!), Meulenbelt tells us that here 'the excitement seems to be emotional rather than something to do with getting an orgasm'[25] (!) For, if we are to have sex without problems, orgasm must be something quite separate from emotions when: 'the most important thing is not to wait for someone else to make us happy, but to choose what we want for ourselves'.[26] I don't think Meulenbelt intends this as a licence to rape. (Is it beyond the contemplation of any but de Sade that a woman might have aggressive sexual desires?) So I assume she intends only to assure us that we can 'make' orgasms for ourselves – we can masturbate to orgasm and that even if we think we desire a *particular*, other person, we don't really need them for orgasm; nor do we need them for cuddles, which we can get quite easily from our feminist friends.

I am aware that books like the *Hite Report* and *For Ourselves* have been enjoyable and relevant for many women. Most importantly, they have encouraged us to be more assertive sexually, and to object to the male arrogance and insensitivity which sees sex in terms of penile performance. But though women have been strengthened by a stress on *women's* sexual pleasure, and knowledge of the dismal failure of many men to provide it, these books leave aside what is most complex and problematic about sexuality.

Sexual *desire*, for example, is rarely mentioned in *For Ourselves*. A very brief mention of sexual fantasy tells us that it can be fun, and that 'the images which surface in our fantasies will certainly change as our sexual relationships change.'[27] That is not my experience. And this new feminist sexuality, about loving ourselves and cuddling our friends, can become a new morality which does not in any way connect up with our erotic fantasies. However well-intentioned the gift, these books are no longer what I want. I think we deserve a more sophisticated analysis than they can provide.

What I do want to read and to hear is feminist reflection on sex which is less naïve, less prescriptively optimistic, and less individualistic. (You too *can* change your sexual life and fulfil all your own sexual wishes.) I think, on the contrary, it would be more helpful for us to understand why it is so very, very *hard* for us to change our erotic life, even when we do consciously desire to. We can consciously restrain or try to forget about our sexual desires – that may seem a sensible choice. But we cannot consciously change them at will. Since some of us do want to make the most of whatever sexual pleasure we can find, thoughtless Polyanna promises – 'The moon within your reach'[28] – can deepen our frustration.

Sex is a problem. But this is neither because men are *by nature* sexually aggressive and coercive, nor because women have lost touch with their own natural sexuality which, rediscovered, would be wonderful. It is ironic that having exposed the myth of the 'liberated sexuality' of Lawrence, Miller and Mailer in the 1960s as little more than a homage to masculinity, some feminists seem in danger of coming up with a new version of the same myth. Transforming the myth into a naturally joyful, self-nourishing female sexuality may inspire some of us some of the time, but it also obscures much of the reality of much of our sex lives most of the time.

Sex is still a problem because whatever the current sexological steps to orgasmic happiness, at a more fundamental level many of the ideologies surrounding 'sex' have remained *unchanged* over the last hundred years. What we call sexual behaviour is still concealed from children, confined to a very special area of life, cut off from other activities, and acceptable only in certain types of relationship. It is still surrounded by taboos, shame, disgust and fear. Above all, sex remains the endorsement of gender. Language creates sex as the symbol of the male and the female. And whatever the questioning which is going on, and whatever the tolerance for 'deviance', sexuality is still seen in terms of its reproductive functioning, symbolised by a genital heterosexuality which men initiate and control. The culture of masculinity, rooted in male sexual assertion and domination, constructs heterosexuality as a symbol of male power over women. It fosters the use of male sexuality as a means of coercion of women. So the context for sexual development for everyone remains both repressive and deplorable, but for women in particular, subordinating and dangerous. That cannot be shrugged off, or rather overcome, with just an extra flick of the wrist – on the clitoris.

What might help us grapple with some of these problems is theoretical exploration by feminists of the links between sex and power, and sex and gender. And we need also to examine, rather than reinforce, the anxieties produced by the high valuation given to sex in our society, as that which most clearly expresses our true selves and identity, the place where we are most 'free' from social constraint. We need to understand why sexual behaviour is still largely secret and

40

forbidden, despite its celebration in certain contexts. This would all entail looking at sexuality as it develops *through* social relations, and a genuine rejection of any notion of sex as an innate or biological force, either male or female. Anthropological and cultural studies indicate that human potential for physical pleasure – or anything else – is always mediated by society. Sexual behaviour is culturally and historically specific, including the ideas we hold about what is and is not 'sexual' or 'erotic'. While there is all sorts of evidence that people need physical comfort and physical contact (though no evidence for any overriding *exclusive* need for genital contact) there are an infinite variety of ways in which we may (hopefully) receive that contact.

Beginning here, as indeed some people do today, feminists might have more to say on the dynamics of women's sexual desire and how we strive for sexual pleasure even within deplorable constraints. Perhaps then we could touch upon, rather than ignore, women's actual sexual longings. We could explore how power is entangled with desire and pleasure in ways which may foster, disconnect from, or seek to redress more general relations of dominance and submission between men and women, one person and another.

In an illuminating study of mass-market romance, which feminists have rarely studied, Anne Snitow looks at the deep psychological structures to which they appeal. She sees them as 'accurate descriptions of certain selected elements of female consciousness'.[29] These books, written by and for women, vibrate with 'phallic worship' of men – men as cruel, arrogant and threatening objects of enormous power and strength. The point of the romance, however, is for all this male power and strength to be ultimately, and despite all appearances to the contrary, laid at the feet of the swooning heroine.

Snitow sees the novels as women's pornography (or erotica, if you can maintain that fractured line), with all the contradictions of women's sexual desires in a sexist world. The titillation has little to do with any physical event. It is a 'social drama', and exists in the anticipation, anxiety, suspense and fear of waiting for the manifestation of – the impossible. The impossible longing is to be both helpless and in control, ravished and adored, powerless and yet supremely powerful. It's easy for feminists to see that the sexist imagery of the male sexual aggressor and passive heroine creates a sexual climate which condones rape and male coercion of women. Yet it also connects up with real romantic desire in a way which we cannot simply dismiss as a male plot.

Nowadays I never read these romances – just as I never look at porn – but I know they correspond to the impossible drama of my own

41

sexual feelings. And these being the product of a social and shared, as well as a personal history, I suspect they are *far from* unique. As far back as I can remember, I have always spent substantial amounts of time in erotic daydreams. Once upon a time the object of desire in the daydreams was always a powerful woman (teacher or prefect) who was moved to comfort, stroke or cuddle me in response to my undeserved and humiliating suffering. Later the object of my desire, but also the one with whom I came to identify in the fantasy, was always a man. And I would have to invent circumstances for the most bizarre and impossible distortions of power-relations between the man and the woman (myself), but with me now more the object than the subject in the fantasy. The man whose feelings and behaviour I played out in the fantasy would be apparently totally powerful and the woman would be apparently totally powerless. But the impossible circumstances would mean that the man was really totally vulnerable and dependent on the woman, who was therefore *really* totally powerful. Yet it would be always important that in every way, to the woman and others, he would still *appear* all-powerful. In every fantasy, this powerful/powerless man always ended up in a situation of having to make devoted reparation to the woman for some accidental abuse of his ambiguous power, for having caused her (me) some pain or injury.

I think these daydreams, despite their appearance, are in fact barely masochistic at all. But they do express a rather unhealthy admiration for the appearance of strength and power which I wish, by some means, to gain for myself. I think they do connect up with ambivalent feelings of desire for and hostility towards people I see as powerful. And this indeed can create sexual relationships which are ambivalently hostile and dependent, and therefore painful and unstable, as rejection becomes the proof of a person's superiority and hence desirability.

The fantasies which I have always needed to come to orgasm, by any methods, are for me far more tedious and obnoxious. In them I am always passive, objectified, humiliated and whatever abuse I can imagine to be happening at the time also contains the threat of even worse to follow. Since I avoid masochistic pornography, because it distresses and pains me, at the same time as titillating sexual desire, it is hard work to imagine this ever more hideous threat. I resent the content of the fantasies. And I resent the effort I have to make to produce them, and the disconnection which occurs with lovers who, at least recently, are most caring, gentle and as extensively physically stimulating as I could wish. Orgasm, as I said before, is simply not the problem. Part of the problem is that the magical impossibility of the daydream, of being all-powerful and powerless, cannot manifest itself in any actual sex life. Obviously!

What all this suggests to me, apart from the irrelevance of sexology to sexual desire, is that we must seek to understand how sexual desire comes to express such a variety of other social needs: needs which are irrational, unconscious and not easily understood and changed. Certainly until we attempt to understand what feeds our desire, prescriptions for change can seem repressive or irrelevant. I suspect that some of the emotional horror feminists and other women feel towards sexist pornography (which I share) is not simply that they think it encourages men to rape and objectify women (there is no evidence that they need pornography for that), but that it is obnoxious because it both degrades and titillates us. And that is *not* a connection which we like. It feels as though the connection is thrust upon us from outside, by pornography itself, which if removed would sever the connection. But it is not so unusual for feelings we dislike to seem to come from somewhere else, when in fact they are buried inside us as well as reflected in the social world which shaped them to begin with.

So when we talk as feminists about our efforts to understand and satisfy our sexual needs, and of the changes we are trying to make in our lives, it seems to me that these two goals may not flow together in the straightforward way feminists might hope and have suggested. The changes we might want to make may relate quite ambivalently to the needs our sexuality expresses. We may have to begin from accepting and attempting to understand what appears as a split between the social relations of equality and autonomy which we seek (and some times find) in our domestic and working lives, and the sources of our sexual desire. The satisfactions of the latter, however, do *not* determine the success of the former. Whatever the sexologists, feminist or otherwise, may claim, the relation between sexual desire and the achievement of power or autonomy in the world is very complex. For example, a recent study of the sexual activity of men in power has found that 'By far the most common service politicians demand from call-girls is to be beaten.'[30] This masochistic eroticism *accompanies* the achievement of and attachment to enormous power in the world – not its forfeiture.

It is because we cannot easily understand the nature of sexual desire that some feminists, and in different ways, have used psycho-analytic concepts which at least address the problem. They would suggest that it is not some straightforward need for physical grati-

43

fication which motivates sexual behaviour and erotic desire, but rather, sexual desire is knotted through with all sorts of other emotional needs – to obtain approval and love, express hostility, dependence and domination, relieve anxiety, and repair deep-lying psychic wounds of rejection, humiliation and despair. Each of us has a particular history of psychic joys and misery, but we do share two crucial experiences – the dependency and relative powerlessness of childhood, and the overriding cultural significance attached to our biological sex from which we form a gender identity. The ambivalence of female sexuality and the prevalence of masochistic fantasy are hardly surprising in a cultural context where femininity defines weakness, and masculinity strength. Obtaining mythical strength and power through erotic fantasy (if not practice), even if it is as the weak gain power through the seduction of the strong, connects up with both what has been pleasurable in our experience of femininity as well as the pleasures of childhood recalled. As babies we have been the passive and powerless, but also powerfully demanding, recipients of enormous parental attention and, hopefully, physical gratification and love. One woman, writing in *Spare Rib* of her sexual relations with a man, confessed: 'I discovered that I didn't get any satisfaction from exciting him and what I wanted was to have things done to me.'[31]

So, passivity and masochism in sex can, paradoxically, be demanding, self-centring and pleasurable. In her book, Maria Marcus describes how she always wants to see herself as 'the object' in sexual encounters, then she knows where she is. 'If a man looked at me I seemed to exist more clearly.'[32] Marcus uncovers some of the contradictions of masochistic fantasies, where the 'masochist' is actually the consumer, the one receiving all the attention, to whom things are done. 'I am really the main character. I am the one who receives the right service to enable me to think I am nothing.'[33]

The problem with masochistic fantasy, I find, is *not at all* that it encourages real submissiveness, and most certainly *not* any desire for real pain, hurt or humiliation, but rather that, like any reliance on fantasy, it can make your sexual partner irrelevant, reducing sex to masturbation. I think it interferes with the feeling of personal connection, of being one with another, and therefore makes sex more rigid and less satisfactory (and orgasms less significant and cathartic!). I could feel, of course, that my masochistic fantasies provide me with an 'autonomous sexuality' – it is always me who is in control. But the problem is *I don't want to be*. I would like not to have to do all this work 'for myself'.

44

My masochistic fantasies seem to be unconnected to any attempt to rationalise actually existing personal power relations of hetero-sexuality – quite the contrary, in fact – though this is a common feminist interpretation of masochism: 'Perhaps fewer people would dream of being dominated if it weren't assumed that we ought to be underneath.'[34] They pre-dated by over a decade any conscious experience of sex with men, and were first of all a part of sex play with girls and to accompany later sexual experience with women. Sexism and repressive attitudes to sex have certainly fed these fantasies. But on a more personal level I think they began as consolations for particular circumstances of a quite unusually extreme experience of loneliness in infancy and childhood, with the magical belief that somehow reparation should and would be made for suffering. I see them as, among other things, a way of making myself the centre of attention, when in fact I knew for certain that there was actually nobody there for me at all in reality. They express hostility and despair, mixed up with desire for attention and physical contact.

In describing her erotic passion for Sita, Kate Millett described similar sources of desire feeding her sexual excitement. 'How she knows me, rules me, masters me, plays me, pleasures me . . .'. 'How I envy her everything.' 'How enormous my sense of inferiority.'[35] Sita is 'all-powerful'. Kate Millett's desire is triggered by envy, resent-ment, submission, and yes, hostility, she 'envies' and 'hates' Sita. And in this context, she can have truly thunderous orgasms! Sexual excitement is generated by, and in the service of, a multitude of needs, not all of them 'nice'. Whereas some feminists have claimed that the sex act for men serves as a kind of rape to express power, domination and hostility, we have usually written as though female sexuality is totally bland, devoid of any such emotions. I think it is wrong to see such emotions as present only in male sexuality and absent in female sexuality, or present in female sexuality only because of 'male definitions' of sexuality. I think it is also wrong not to see that men's sexuality as well expresses complex desires – for dependency, submission and forgiveness; of envy and fear of women; as well as the desire to dominate and control. Though of course it is hideously true that men's greater power in the world and the particular construction of masculinity both allow and *encourage* men to express domination and power through sex.

Anne Snitow, in another article, looks at sex in recent women's novels. She shows them describing mainly women's disappointments, deprivations and difficulties in sexual relations (whether heterosexual or lesbian) through which women nevertheless search for whatever pleasure they can find.[36] Whatever our sexual preference, it would seem, our desires are imbued with both sexism, and all the socially structured anxieties, disturbances and humiliations that are generated endlessly throughout our lives under capitalism. Snitow writes 'Women have had to enjoy sex in ways that were destructive to them. Instead of calling this masochism, one might say that it has been life affirming for women to embrace sex even on painful terms, to find ways to enjoy sex in spite of sexism, *including their own*.'[37]

I agree. And would argue that it is not necessarily orgasms that we are deprived of, but more likely any possible sexual scenarios for exploring and enjoying the contradictory tensions of erotic desire – dependence and strength, control and passivity, love and hate – in any playful, yet intense and pleasurable way. A possible scenario is hard to find when heterosexual relations are so fraught and bitter because of women's struggle against male oppression, while lesbian relations as well exist in reaction to, and against, our heterosexist, male-dominated erotic world. Anna Coote and Beatrix Campbell argue that what remains to be done in relation to sexuality 'is to explore the experience that lesbians and heterosexuals share and to build on this common ground a political understanding of sexuality.'[38] Again, I agree. But what they do *not* indicate is that what we 'share' is likely to involve all sorts of things we would rather avoid: masochism, self-objectification, domination, guilt, hostility and envy. We must accept and explore these censored emotions, and see how they might conflict with a now fashionably radical but somehow tritely optimistic vision of 'female eroticism, as something powerful and autonomous, which is shared by heterosexuals, lesbians and bisexuals',[39] and transcends all those categories.

Feminists who are not separatists do engage with men. We engage with men politically, in fighting the oppression of class, race and other hierarchies, because we also to a certain extent share a common fate with particular men. We engage with men because of our personal histories – with fathers, brothers, sons, friends and yes, some of us engage with men sexually, because we desire them. The prescription that women should repress heterosexual desire to further the cause of feminism is one I believe to be strategically and morally wrong. Although our sexual pleasures are formed and deformed within the power relations of sexism and capitalism (as are all our pleasures), I do not conclude that we should give them up. But I would like to understand this formation in a way which increases my security, rather than exacerbates my doubts that I can accept and enjoy the tensions of erotic desire, even though I may as yet only very partially transform them from the sad and sorry state of their emergence into something closer to what our feminist hearts might consciously desire. At the same time, I agree with those who would like to see sex given a less privileged place in determining our 'unique identity'. What is wrong with our lives is perhaps not so much the lack of orgasms as our perpetual craving for that orgasm which can obliterate the isolation and emptiness we feel in the rest of our lives.

# 4

# Really Being in Love means Wanting to Live in a Different World

Lucy Goodison

So reads a situationist leaflet lying on my bedroom floor.[1] Since 1968 the Left and the women's movement have given 'falling in love' a very bad press. Women have pointed to the way it tends to make us feel helpless, passive, uncomprehending, dependent, immobilised: the very feelings we are struggling to leave behind. From a socialist and feminist viewpoint we have been reminded how 'falling in love' is individualistic, objectifying, linked to escapist notions of romantic love, exploited by advertisements to encourage consumerism, and tied firmly at the far end to the great institution of marriage which helps to keep the cogs of society ticking over. All in all we can see that it is clearly 'incorrect', and one reaction has been to ignore it.[2]

And yet falling in love does not go away. We all do it. It is gripping, exciting. We long for it. It makes other more politically 'correct' areas of our life pale by comparison. It keeps cropping up. Its power is unquestionable.

Perhaps somewhere between the traditional view of accepting it as an inevitable part of human nature, and the tendency to dismiss it as a capitalist con, there is a third path: one which involves looking at the experience in detail and grappling with its process. In this way we might gain more access to using its power rather than becoming its victim. This has not been done. As a subject it has largely remained untouchable. Perhaps we secretly like having an area of our lives that we cannot explain and are not expected to.

As with a religious experience, no one can contradict our feelings.[3] We are sent reeling into talk about 'wonderful feelings' which 'just happen'. We seem to fear that if we look too hard its magic will vanish. We can however try to chart unknown seas, not in order to plunder them, or cut them down to size, but the better to explore and

48

travel them. We are not trying to reduce the excitement in our lives, but to increase our ability to choose and direct that excitement.

So what is falling in love like? How does it happen? What are the steps, the progressions? It is not one unitary or primary experience, but rather a number of experiences bound up together, different feelings present in different people in different proportions. It may vary as widely as one orgasm from another. However, there are certain common experiences, and before investigating the 'whys' and 'wherefores' I shall briefly sketch what these seem to be. From women's accounts, some common threads seem to recur whether the object of our passion is a man or a woman, so I shall describe both together as different aspects of the same process. I shall use women's novels, poems and personal accounts, as well as some of the media clichés which have influenced us so strongly and which remain the backdrop of our efforts to create a new language for our experience.

Over the years I have done extensive field work on this subject. I am not describing a place where I have not been, though I have never written about it before. My account feels very tentative, like early maps of uncharted territories, and much of it is written in blood.

Step one, you find someone to love. It often happens through 'love at first sight', the impact of a first encounter:

> Who is this stick of corn? or is she a lion?
> she's doing yoga on the lawn
> brown body bending like a snake
> her face is miles wide; she is open
> eyes welcome. . . have I really known her
> somewhere before? was I born with her?[4]

A bell rings, something beckons far beyond words. Yet often the reason for the attraction is not obvious. The objects of our passion often lack traditional 'qualities' like money or looks. They may also be too old, too young. They may be different from us, unsuitable or unavailable. But the line is cast, the bait is taken, and we are hooked.

What happens next? One friend compared falling in love to LSD in the way it changes reality. Another woman writes that it is as if the world has been stopped and started again.[5] We often hear about a general sensation of disorientation, a feeling that the cosmos has moved in its tracks, the concrete and the clay beneath our feet have crumbled. And this shifting world is permeated by a terrible wanting. Marge Piercy, in her novel *Small Changes*, describes how Miriam experiences the power and relentlessness of this yearning:

49

Where so much had been, plans and projects and curiosities and relationships and speculations and histories, was now everything and nothing in one: this painful hollow wanting, this fierce turbulence, this centring about him white hot and icy, cold and dark and bright.[6]

Miriam lies on her bed in embryo position curled round her obsession and feels as if her self and identity are dissolving. Her ability to operate in the world is seriously impaired. 'I can't do my homework and I can't think straight,' sang Connie Francis in my teens. Miriam has a more grown-up version of the same problem:

> When she did her work at all, she did it perfunctorily . . . she would resent the trivial chatter about programming languages that made her for a moment unable to loose her whole energies on her obsession. . . . She seemed to have nothing left for anyone else, anything else. She was stupefied in general and in that one touch point intensely burning like a laser.[7]

Though the overwhelming feeling is of emotion or intensity, it is very localised and there can be a narrowing of vision, a deadening of other areas of life. Stored aggression erupts as violence; stored love, too, seems able to break out with an edge as cutting as a knife.

It is this laser-like cutting quality which can give being in love an active, rebellious, even political flavour. Sometimes there can be anger contained in that ferocious energy: a schoolteacher angry at the reactionary staff falls in love with a sixth-former; a teenager falls in love with someone who will shock her parents. It can be a way of cocking a snook at authority, of striking a blow at society. Traditionally falling in love is a great defier of convention, breaking barriers imposed by class, race and prejudice: the lady of the manor who falls in love with the gypsy, the Capulet who falls for the Montague. It can act as the beam of light which cuts through the crap, which reveals the mediocrity, hypocrisy and banality of so much in our society. As the libertarian magazine *Ink* pointed out in their 'In Love' issue:

> The experience . . . gives us a glimpse of the exuberance and energy which might be set free when our relations with one another are liberated from the system that perverts them. . . . Being in love shatters . . . constraints. We give presents instead of

50

buying and selling, we touch instead of avoiding one another's eyes.[8]

Amidst alienation it makes us feel inexorably connected; amidst deceit its sheer impact makes us feel that something is real; in muddy waters of pain and compromise it can feel like a lifeline. Though it can obliterate the rest of the world, sometimes it can also make the whole world come alive. Sometimes its light, rather than turning inwards, can turn outwards to infuse the whole range of vision. Something in it tells us it could be a revolutionary force: 'They never wanted us to feel like this. Killers beware! With love like this we can move mountains and break your prisons down. It is no dope to help us to forget, oh no. This love is dangerous.'[9]

Another contradiction with falling in love is that although we may feel vanished and drained into the loved one, we may also at some level feel ourselves more intensely. We are super-conscious of something important happening to us. We step into the limelight in our own lives. There can even be an unwonted narcissism or relish in our experience. The strength of our feelings imparts a new self-confidence and meaning to life.[10] Though we are not in control of it, we are undoubtedly the carriers of some huge power:

> I have a feeling, a strange feeling:
> she seems to potentiate me. I am expanding: will I burst
> like a star on the world?[11]

Or as Marge Piercy describes it: 'Much of the time she felt lucky, chosen, exalted. Her life seemed infused with intensity, a plenum, shining and holy. She was never bored. Her previous life seemed vacuous by comparison.'[12]

How does this whole experience connect with romantic love? Romantic fantasies (about moonlit nights, wedding bells, true love to the death against all opposition, and so on) may be an important element, but from all accounts they are rarely central. They may be the preformed moulds which society offers us to pour our love into: but they are not its source. These fantasies are pretty, while the central drive of falling in love seems to be more of a blood-and-guts affair. It is not just glamorous and appealing. More than wanting to cosset the beloved, we may feel we want to eat them alive. We may idealise the loved one, but that may slip away like a mask to reveal ferocious hatred and rage if things go wrong. Romantic feelings and fantasies may be the blossoms produced by being in love, but its roots lie deeper in the earth. The power it feeds on is not essentially romantic, but one that tears at the innards.

So what is this strange and physically overwhelming power? Is it primarily sexual? Here comes another irony. In some of the most passionate accounts of 'being in love', the sexual experience itself is not totally satisfactory. Erica Jong writes in an autobiographical novel about a woman who leaves a very compatible sexual relationship with her husband for a love-affair in which at first she finds it very hard to reach orgasm:

> He fucked as if he wanted to get back inside the womb. My heart was beating so hard I couldn't come. . . . Josh felt like kin to me, my long-lost brother. . . . I went right to the edge of orgasm and wasn't able to come. This had happened the night before. . . . And the oddest part of it was: I didn't care. . . .
>
> We locked together like two pieces of a puzzle. . . . What other point was there in bringing a man and woman together *except* to stretch the soul and expand the imagination, except to tear things apart and put them back together in new ways? . . . . The mere rubbing that sooner or later results in orgasm was not all one looked for. A vibrator could do that.[13]

Here is another woman's experience:

> The sex was wonderful, overwhelming, not because it worked particularly well in itself, but because it was with him. One of my most most precious memories is of a night when I simply lay sleepless and blissed-out in his arms. What was most powerful was not the sex but the *intimacy* I felt with him.[14]

We hear accounts of passionate love where sex 'works' perfectly, or relationships which centre on the strong bonding of sex, but there are also accounts of sexual difficulties and incompatibilities which are dwarfed by the power of being in love. Some intense bonding seems to occur which may channel through sexuality, but is not subsumed in it. Pure lust is generally recognised as a different experience. It is possible to feel a magnificent lust for a person, to connect with her or him intensely and magically through sex, without ever feeling 'in love'. Sexual feelings may be an important factor in falling in love, but it is as if those feelings are informed from another source, from some other connection between the two people.

Finally, I need to mention how falling in love can end. Sometimes it endures, developing into a long-term relationship. What is then retained or lost of the original impetus is part of a wider discussion about long-term sexual relationships. Does the intensity of the passion fade, endure, transmute? Is it compatible with daily life, living together, children? What is the difference between 'falling in love', 'being in love', and 'loving' someone in a steadier and more whole way? These issues fall outside the scope of this piece. But perhaps more common than the happy-ever-after ending is for a relationship to die young. Apart from cases where circumstances tear lovers apart, this generally happens through one person 'falling out of love'.

Like falling in love, falling out of love can happen suddenly. You may wake up one morning and feel different. It can be as if a dream has passed to be replaced by reality. The person suddenly looks very ordinary. What did I see in her/him? Sometimes there is a sensation of relief at the return to 'normality'. Sometimes there is a vague sense of loss at the inexplicable passing of passion:

> Where are the sons of summer now?
> The winter has come
> And you don't know how to turn your dreams into coal. . .
> And I can't help but get a little bit blue
> Thinking about the precious nothing we once knew.
>
> (Carly Simon)

A few nostalgic grains of stardust are left in the hand, and life goes on as normal.

Alternatively, it happens the other way round. Some loves are unrequited from the start, or the other person may start to give you a hard time or fall out of love with you. Then comes more than a vague sense of loss. That is when the heartaches really begin. In *Small Changes* Miriam feels her strength and identity slip away:

> She waited. She waited two hours, while anger and resentment wound her tighter and tighter. She tried to fight her tension. . . . Why must she sit like – like a woman was supposed to, stewing? Her anxiety stripped away her sense of herself as a strong person moving through things in her own style. She became dependent woman. She became scared woman. This waiting had teeth. [15]

Very recognisable is the process whereby Miriam becomes more and more desperate to regain the love that is slipping away from her. Our efforts to recover, to rebuild our power in ourselves, are continually dogged by referral to that other person who remains the magical standard by which everything is measured, the philosopher's stone without which nothing can be gold.

What is so excruciating about this state is its closeness to the worst stereotypes of how women are meant to be: dependent, empty, passive, waiting, pleading. However hard we fight it consciously, we can feel drawn to wallow in the 'rich stew of masochism'.[16] It hurts so *good*. We feel 'right', we feel in character, as if the pain is part of our birthright as women, so intimate and close that it almost becomes precious to us, as Marge Piercy writes of Janis Joplin:

> You embodied the pain hugged to the breasts like a baby.
> You embodied the beautiful blowsy gum of passivity. . .
> That willingness to hang on the meathook and call it love,
> That need for loving like a screaming hollow in the soul.[17]

When the beloved is completely and irrevocably lost, the immensity of love's joy can turn its flipside to reveal an immensity of pain. The craziness of happiness can come perilously near real craziness and self-hatred, as one woman writes:

> The same waves that crested in the elation of BE HERE NOW and ALL IS ONE sucked me back under and I was CRAZY as never before. I lost control. I suffered disbelief and an excruciating desire not to BE ME that allowed me to touch bottom in some amorphous way . . . and declare 'I am bankrupt.'[18]

This love that can be like a meathook, this love that can drive us crazy, where does its power come from? I have described the terrain, the superficial process, but what are the force fields at work under the earth? Like many major experiences, falling in love is perhaps overdetermined and can be explained on a number of different levels. I shall mention some of these, and describe some of the factors which may conspire to send us hurtling over the abyss. I shall also mention various theoretical frameworks which may throw light on the process, drawing mainly but not exclusively on psychological models placed within the social context of capitalism. Knowing whether the same factors would be present or relevant in another culture or another period of history would illuminate our political understanding of falling in love, and our sense of how that experience could be transformed; but this question would need a separate article to do it justice, and here I can only bear it in mind.

One precipitating factor seems to be immediate life-circumstances, which often include some kind of 'rebound' situation, or a reaction to suppression. People often seem to fall in love as a reaction from another relationship. The original relationship may be deteriorating, or there may be unexpressed resentment in it, perhaps due to infidelity, neglect, or subtle domination by one partner. A certain level of need or tension has accumulated. Strong feelings are present but they are blocked or stuck. Then suddenly an outburst of passion shoots, not into hurt or anger in that relationship, but into overwhelming love for a different person. The new relationship allows a release of feeling and expression which had been blocked in the first relationship. The connection of the new passion to the original person is rarely felt; often s/he appears to be completely wiped off the map. Thus Erica Jong's heroine reacts with total blankness to the husband she has just left: 'Couldn't he hear in my voice that I didn't miss him at all, that he had never even existed, that he was a ghost, a shadow? I suppose not.'[19] This view of falling in love presents it as a substitution, its fierce energy partly fuelled by the need to escape from an existing situation.

Sometimes that situation does not involve another person. Sometimes it is simply a long period in an emotional desert, a long period without joy or sexual satisfaction or physical affection or expression or intensity in any relationship or activity, which builds up until there is a 'charge' of need which will eventually spark across to make contact with another person. Is this level of repression, in relationships and outside them, a feature specific to capitalism? *Ink* suggested that even in a Utopia we might need 'release in concentrated bursts of energy. Would communal, ecstatic, religious, spiritual, sexual experiences be a feasible alternative?'[20] However the charge builds up, that charge and the readiness to fall in love lie in the subject. She may even make a false start and have a short-lived infatuation with one person before falling deeply in love with another: a kind of practice run. Her antennae are out. Falling in love is what she needs. The timing is hers.

But how do we choose the object of so much unstinting affection? What qualifies them for the job? One theory proposed by various schools of psychology is that they fill gaps in ourselves, resonating with qualities which are absent or not fully realised in our own personality. This means we love not the whole, but only that part of the person which we need to complete us. As Fritz Perls of the Gestalt school of therapy put it:

We don't usually love a *person*. That's very, very rare. We love a certain *property* in that person, which is either identical with our behaviour or supplementing our behaviour, usually something that is a supplement to us. We think we are in love with the total person, and actually we are disgusted with other aspects of this person.[21]

So what kind of properties do we love in the beloved? Often it is something which is forbidden in ourselves, perhaps something quite different or alien, and this is why the chosen one may at first sight appear very unsuitable. S/he expresses qualities we have buried in ourselves, whether they are painfully unacceptable or idealised.[22] According to humanistic astrology, someone with too much 'earth' in their chart might seek a person with 'fire' qualities of intuition, creativity, vitality and adventure.[23] The chosen individual, who carries what we most fear or desire, becomes essential to our wholeness. To be complete we need to possess her. That obsessive feeling of wanting to eat the beloved alive is perhaps partly fuelled by the yearning to be whole.

The irony of projection is that while the lover experiences all the focus and meaning of her life as being with the beloved, in fact the beloved is an (often unwitting) actor in the lover's own internal drama. The beloved is chosen for the behaviour and feelings she catalyses in the lover, the qualities she draws to the surface, the buttons she happens to push. What is so magical about the person is that s/he illuminates the *lover's* internal landscape. As Raymond Durgnat writes of the role Jeanne Moreau plays in the film *Les Amants*: 'although she is seduced, in the sense that he lures her to follow him through the magical landscape, the landscape is herself, her own desires. His role is little more than that of a *porteur* in a romantic ballet.'[24] The power, the joy, is actually our own, but we rarely feel it as such. We need another to find ourselves, while we think we are finding them.

Ultimately, this can appear a rather sordid view of falling in love: we limp along appropriating others to fill gaps in ourselves, we latch onto them like vampires. Our own vitality and power in creating the situation remain unrecognised. Is it peculiar to patriarchy and capitalism that people have such large gaps that need filling? As people with more psychic scars, more unused potential, fewer outlets for self-realisation, are women in our society perhaps particularly prone to construct fantasies and seek completeness in another through these means?

However, we can also recognise that projection is a way of growing. It is possible to re-own, to reclaim what you are hooked onto the other person for. This process can be carried out quite explicitly in the therapy relationship, where the patient is sometimes encouraged to transfer feelings (which may be quite passionate) onto the therapist. In this case, as Perls points out:

> The therapist is supposed to have all the properties which are missing in this person. So, first the therapist provides the person with the opportunity to discover what he [she] needs – the missing parts that he [she] has alienated and given up to the world. Then the therapist must provide the opportunity, the situation in which the person can grow. And the means is that we frustrate the patient in such a way that he [she] is forced to develop his [her] own potential (my parentheses). [25]

Even in a personal love relationship, it is possible to recognise those magnetic, coveted qualities as one's own, and to work to express them more oneself.

Perhaps one way of understanding falling out of love is that the projection, which is often inaccurate, suddenly falls through. When the images which have been projected onto the beloved shatter, the person feels betrayed, 'as if "part of myself" had been taken away; and it has, but only because that part of myself, that image of self, was given to the other in the first place.'[26] Using another person as a symbol of our own potential can probably never stand the test of exposure to real life and actual contact for a great length of time. When the power given to a symbol is reclaimed, or recognised as inappropriate, the scales fall and we are left with just an ordinary-seeming person again.

In the meantime, however, the individual in love may have undergone enormous psychological and physical changes: the impact of such a powerful process of projection allows a suspension of normal beliefs, tensions and behaviour patterns, making space for new patterns to form. In the Seth books about the nature of human consciousness, Jane Roberts suggests that major problems can be shifted by any form of 'conversion':

> Under that general term I include strong emotional arousal and fresh emotional involvement, affiliation, or sense of belonging. This may involve religion, politics, art, or simply falling in love.
>
> In all of these areas the problem, whatever its nature or cause, is

. . . 'magically' transferred to another facet of activity, projected away from the self. Huge energy blocks are moved. . . .

Love, as it is often experienced, allows an individual to take his [her] sense of self-worth from another for a time, and to at least momentarily let the other's belief in his [her] goodness supersede his [her] own beliefs in lack of worth. Again, I make a distinction between this and a greater love in which two individuals, knowing their own worth, are able to give and to receive.[27]

The upheaval associated with falling in love may, then, be a signal or catalyst of major personal change. In societies which offer more structures to mark such changes (whether through politics, art, religion, rituals or rites of passage), we may wonder whether falling in love looms as large as in our own. A key element in the process seems to be the ability temporarily to transcend personal limitations and boundaries. The Psychosynthesis school of therapy suggests that an external ideal or figure can be a link to the higher Self which is reflected and symbolised in that figure.[28] You lose yourself temporarily in that figure in order to re-form. The psychological shake-up opens the way to a regrouping of the personality in a more coherent and unified form. In traditional language, the person 'drowns', 'dissolves', or is 'consumed' by the 'fires' of passion: again we find the implication of love as an agent of transformation.

Another angle on understanding falling in love has been to compare it to the overwhelming experience of childhood love for the mother, and to see it as some kind of regression to that early situation. This link is at the core of much traditional language about love, from the endearment 'baby', to the descriptive language about the loss of identity, the melting or dissolving, the all-consuming wanting, the return to an irrational or pre-rational state, the deep yearning and nostalgia as if for something which has been irrevocably lost. A woman in love can feel as totally vulnerable, as deeply intimate, as passionately identified with another, as a newborn baby with her mother. Perhaps it is some unanswered need for that time, or the premature loss of that childlike aspect of ourselves as we learnt the adult female role of caring, coping and servicing, which leaves a part of our being still crying out with open mouth for mother-love, and desperate to recreate it. As Melanie Klein puts it: 'However gratifying it is in later life to express thoughts and feelings to a congenial person, there remains an unsatisfied longing for an understanding without words – ultimately for the earliest relation with the mother.'[29]

If this need is part of the power behind falling in love, it might explain why intimacy and skin contact are sometimes more central to it than the act of sex itself. The yearning is perhaps not so much for orgasm as for symbiosis. This view would explain why the joy of falling in love is often very close to pain. Given the conditions of mothering in our society, few of us had a completely satisfactory early relationship with our mother, or were able to grow away from it in our own time. Recreating the same deep bond, it is hard for us to believe that the closeness will not turn sour or be withdrawn as happened with our original mother; perhaps we even unconsciously choose people who will fail us in exactly the same way that our mother did. This may be why the pain seems in some way precious. Perhaps we continually recreate the same scenario, hoping always that we can in this way free ourselves from it, that we can make a new ending.

Jane Rule argues that a relationship based on dependent mother-love is degrading and doomed to failure. She comments:

> I am always nervous about the suggestion that, as lesbians, we should mother each other, though I understand that the image comes from our first source of love. Our mothers are also the first source of rejecting power against whom we screamed our dependent rage. As adults, if we cry out for that mother-love, the dependent rage inevitably follows, and what is even more disconcerting is that, given total attention and sympathy, we are soon restless to be free, for we aren't any longer children.[30]

In this gripping re-run of our early emotional lives, it seems that men can stand in for our mummies, or women represent our daddies. What is riveting is the *internal* dynamic, the replay of the tragic drama. As Miriam tells Jackson in *Small Changes*:

> I wasn't a loved child, and I have those mechanisms of the woman who gets hooked on trying to make someone love her. You become the father I was never pretty enough to please. You become the mother who never found my best good enough.[31]

In her book, *Room to Breathe*, Jenny James states that for her the endless re-enactment is of winning not her mother's, but her father's love. She describes how, in one relationship after another, an inaccessible and desired person becomes unwanted as soon as they are won over and thus cease to recreate the right degree of childhood pain.[32]

But what is it that makes certain people 'right' to stand in for our mothers and fathers in this way? Is it, as some believe, the recognition of a twin soul reincarnated from the passion of a past life?[33] Or is that they are in the right place at the right time and imagination does the rest? There may be superficial parallels in personality and behaviour, but sometimes more invisible connections seem to be at work.

Here it seems relevant to examine how falling in love is experienced in the body. It is often associated with acute physical sensations, such as stomach churning, warm glows, tingles down the spine, and so on. However, these sensations are rarely investigated or correlated to our emotional experience.[34] Our ignorance of the body is so immense that I can only mention certain aspects of our experience which need to be discussed and understood at much greater depth.

Though I have said the experience may not be primarily a sexual one, it is certainly physical. We are to a certain extent aware of how the five senses are involved. Eyes are often the magnet for attraction, as in 'love at first sight'. The voice of the beloved is often important: in fairy stories a person may fall in love with the sound of another's singing. Taste and smell are perhaps more important than we consciously recognise. Techniques apparently now exist for odour 'fingerprinting' of human bodies: perhaps some people carry a smell which reaches us very effectively or echoes the irresistible smell of mother. The implication of recognising the role of sight, hearing and smell may be that we can be physically sensitive to a person before there is any contact. Our bodies may respond to a stranger in far more ways than we are consciously aware of. Touch is also important. Here a woman recounts a common experience: 'When I first met J., I was sitting next to her in a chair. My hand accidently brushed against hers and I felt a charge between us like electricity, as if there was a current between our two hands.'[35]

Here we have to stop and reconsider. Another vocabulary is entering the accounts. Why is it that one person's touch, given it is equally smooth or gentle or hot or cold, feels so different from another's and can galvanise us, or not? Why is it that one person's eyes say 'Hello', while another's reach into the soul and draw it magnetically? Here we are moving beyond the generally recognised powers of the five senses. What do we believe the eyes do when they 'mesmerise'? What do the eyes and voice do when they 'hypnotise'? The language of Alison Buckley's poem is illuminating:

In the first splash of meeting, first half-second
I looked; I saw she was open like a radar-scanner
picking up every prickly tingle from me. Smiles zoomed out

undulating quanta of warmth, racing each other
penetrating, and bursting inside my eyes
travelling light years inside my head.

Radar, electricity. A contact which zooms, races, penetrates, undulates like radio waves. This is precisely the kind of language used by esoteric anatomy to describe the phenomenon of the 'energy body' which is thought to interpenetrate and surround our physical body.

The theory is that each person has an energy-field similar to, but not identical with, an electromagnetic energy-field.[36] This 'electromagnetic' energy runs through the body along channels and radiates outwards from it. An inner layer of radiation close to the skin surface has been recorded photographically by Kirlian aura photography[37] which shows variations in the aura depending on the health, temper and state of mind of the person. The theory also suggests that people's energy-fields interact with each other. We can respond unconsciously to the energy emitted by another, and may be attracted or repelled by conflicts or resonances in the energy-fields.

This theory has some resonances in our everyday experience. There is the language of 'good vibes' and 'bad vibes' and of being 'drawn' to or getting a 'buzz' from someone. There are the metaphors of electricity from the accounts I have quoted, and many people will recognise the experience of feeling 'drained' by spending time with a depressed person. Some people may have experienced the movement of 'energy' in their body during yoga exercises, or may have met it as 'body energy' in bioenergetic massage or therapy; others may relate it to the 'meridians' of acupuncture.

This language could be used to give expression to the powerful rushes of feeling between lovers. One way of describing falling in love could be as a bonding between two people who have a particularly acute and needed exchange of energy to make with one another. This might explain the intense feelings of separation and difference combined with feelings of kinship: like two pieces of a jigsaw puzzle, each has what the other needs to make her whole. This 'fine' energy contact has been described as a sixth sense which imbues and informs the contact made through the other five. It sums up the feeling of wordless connection as a movement of energy between two people. It could account for the sense of undercutting normal ways of relating, as well as the sense of being physically potentiated, experiencing intimacy and close contact, without sex necessarily being the prime mover.

I am suggesting this approach as another of the theoretical frameworks which we could use for understanding the process of falling in love. It is not a popular approach, but it interests me personally as it provides a language for certain aspects of the experience which other theories ignore. We do not have to 'believe' in it, any more than we have to 'believe' in projection, but we can explore the usefulness of each framework. Nor do I see any of the theories described in this (personal and certainly incomplete) survey as incompatible or mutually exclusive alternatives. To say that two people have mutually interlocking energy-fields may be another way of saying that one has been building up tension which the other can release; or that one smells like the other's mother; or that they are formed so that it is easy for each to project onto the other; or that they fill holes in each other's personality. The same process can be understood on a number of different levels. To talk about 'energy' does not exclude looking at things in psychological and social terms, although we need to develop a more subtle framework to combine these understandings.

As an ineffable, intense and other-worldly experience, being in love has been compared to religious ecstasy. It has also been suggested that sexual relationships more often have spiritual overtones for women than for men. Béla Grunberger writes: 'As man's sexual life is focused on immediate instinctual relief, woman's love is also located in time, but she dreams of eternity.'[38] Socially we can explain this male/female difference, if it exists, as a result of our upbringing and conditioning around sexuality and relationships; but what is being referred to may be the greater facility women experience in tuning in to fine energy. Alexander Lowen defines the soul as 'the sense or feeling in a person of being part of a larger or universal order',[39] and sees it as the result of our body energy interacting with the energy around us in the world and in the universe, which gives the feeling of being part of something bigger than yourself. Perhaps the strong link which occurs when we fall in love can open us up to these wider connections. Perhaps it is an experience which opens the 'lines' between ourselves and the world.[40] In a culture which denies spirituality outside the confines of established religion, falling in love may have become unusually important as one of our few routes to an experience of the transcendent. It has been understood as a distortion of a deep urge to love the world which through social pressures gets funnelled into one person.

In this, falling in love typifies the contradictory nature of our experiences under capitalism and patriarchy, our efforts to be human in a world organised along inhuman lines. The positive is so entwined with the negative. Falling in loves makes us feel strong, but it also

62

makes us feel weak. It is liberating, but it is also obsessive. It tunes us in to our love and warmth, but also to our gaping need and vulnerability. It reaches out, yet it is highly individualistic. Even the much-vaunted melting and closeness has been open to challenge. Though spiritual disciplines may suggest that 'Love is the recognition of the same consciousness in another as in oneself',[41] others assert that true contact involves a recognition of separateness and differences.[42] From the perspective of political activity, falling in love has been seen as regressive, self-indulgent, privatised, time-wasting.

So how should we deal with it from a perspective of feminism? Should we struggle against these tendencies and feelings in ourselves as counter-productive? I don't think so. Rather, I feel we should take that power and vitality and work with them. If we were not damaged and empty, if our life-experiences had been different, perhaps our loving would not be shot through with need, pain and obsession. But we are as we are, and we have to start from there. Rather than denigrating falling in love, we could see it as a healthy response to a crazy world and perhaps one of the stratagems our organism uses to survive. Perhaps it gives a release where a release is badly needed. On many levels it seems to be a vehicle for the expression of the suppressed. We could see it as a distorted expression of real needs, but in some ways it may be a healthy choice for us: a lifeline enabling us to give and receive love in a way we usually cannot. The idea of love may have been misused, but to deny that we want and need intimacy with others is to avoid the whole issue.[43] We probably need both symbiosis with and separateness from other people, and what is important is for us to develop access to both, to open the channels so that we can move easily into each as we need, instead of lurching in juddering spasms from one to the other, out of control.[44] Instead of attempting to censor or dismiss these passionate feelings, we could work creatively with them. Perhaps the question is not why we have these 'incorrect' and humiliating experiences and how we can stop having them, but rather why that intensity and vitality of contact is confined to such a localised area; and how we can gain more access to experiencing and directing that vitality in other areas of our lives.

How can we do this? The first and crucial step seems to be owning our own power in the situation. We use the term 'falling' in love which disguises the fact that we have chosen to leap and have abdicated responsibility for our experience. The feelings, fantasies and sensations that possess us are in fact our own. We say that another 'makes' us feel unbelievable excitement, but actually the excitement is ours.[45] If we can feel it in one situation, we can feel it in another.

63

We need to cease thinking of others as the source or reference point for our feelings, and recognise our own role more clearly.

One way of doing this is to become more conscious of the stages and details of the process of falling in love. It is time to stop muddying our experience by talking about things which 'mysteriously happened' to us. What exactly *did* happen? Where did I feel it in my body? When have I experienced similar sensations? Who or what triggered it? What did they do? What did I do? What happens if I do something different? Gradually we can learn the paths into all these experiences for ourselves.[46] One area to clarify is the link for each of us with sexuality. What turns us on sexually? What makes us fall in love? What is the difference? We need to get more familiar with the body's language. As Jane Rule comments:

> Sex is not so much an identity as a language which we have for so long been forbidden to speak that most of us learn only the crudest of its vocabulary and grammar. If we are to get past the pattern of dominance and submission, of possessive greed, we must outgrow love as fever, as 'the tragic necessity of human life', and speak in tongues that set us free to be loving equals.[47]

*very nice*

Body awareness seems crucial. How can we retain a sense of our own power when we are draining out of our bodies to identify with another? One woman reports realising that 'the most important thing was not to make him love me but for me to love aliveness.'[48] Our experience of aliveness is in and through our body's sensations and processes: this is our ground, our sustenance, our inner richness, and we lose our power if we abandon it.

There are other aspects of the process with which we can get more familiar. What if I start a relationship with a slow burner rather than a flash in the pan? What do I gain or lose? If falling in love is a reaction to suppression, what exactly do I need to release: anger? sexual desire? grief? political energy? What other ways do I have of breaking out, of expressing what is held in? If projection is involved, we can ask: What *are* my 'fancies' about this person I fancy? When have I had similar fantasies? How do they connect to fantasies I have about myself? What does this person have that I need or believe that I lack? How can I bring those qualities into my life independently of them?[49] What does this person potentiate in me, and how could I potentiate it in myself? We might also ask: Is this person like my mother/father? In what ways does s/he love or fail me like my mother/father did? Do I want to change that and make a new ending?

If falling in love makes us feel spiritual, what else has the same effect? If we feel something similar when massaging or meditating or gardening or listening to music, we can watch those experiences. What are the situations, the ingredients, the states of mind that predispose us to feel that way? Thus we can learn how to choose certain experiences and not others. Falling in love is not unfathomable: the fathoms are ours, and we can learn to swim in our own depths without diminishing their power and beauty.

Another step we can take is consciously to broaden the scope of our loving feelings. Part of this may be to realise that we 'fall in love' in situations far from the socially recognised romantic or sexual ones. Because our culture does not validate such feelings, we tend to dismiss them ourselves. In accordance with prevailing economic and social pressures, we envision a hierarchy of relationships with the perfect couple at the top, while 'chance encounters with . . . children, old people, gas fitters, kite-flyers, just don't have a look in.'[50] Here a woman describes a situation which would never normally be graced with the title of 'being in love':

> 'Oh Johnny, it's you!' When my granny was dying, my brother looked after her and they developed a love relationship. When he visited her in hospital after an operation, she greeted him as she would a lover. There was an intimacy and excitement and interest and tenderness between them which looked to me like two people who are in love.[51]

We hear of non-sexual relationships between women which carry passion, fascination, delight and a peculiar resonance for the two friends involved. Mothers describe being 'in love' with their babies, intimately bonded by a magic line as strong as an umbilical cord. And it does not stop with people. A teenager may claim to be 'in love' with a horse. And what about moments of work which we can suddenly connect to, or the love-affair with a particular career or activity which may last stormily over many years? Or the times when ideas seize us and obsess us? Or the feeling of uplift on a mass demonstration when we feel intensely towards every other human being there? We can 'fall in love' with ourselves, or with a country, or with a movement. Perhaps recognising and nurturing those experiences can be one way of diffusing the passionate intimacy and contact of 'falling in love' into wider areas of our lives. Enormous power and vitality is involved: imagine what we could do with it. As *Ink* pointed out:

Puritans should note what while . . . resistance can take the form of the worker's absolute need for food and shelter, it is also manifested in the desire for excitement instead of boredom, love instead of politeness. The desire for love, conscious of itself and what opposes it, would become a determination to transform the whole of human behaviour and its economic roots.[52]

I would like to believe that it could. The first step may be to accept and know our own experience better, and to move outwards from there. We may be able to make the first step towards transforming our love from a bewildering passion for one person to a deep-rooted lust for all of life. We can at least try.

# 5

# Two Personal Experiences

Jo Chambers and Jill Brown

*1.* Jo Chambers
Struggling to Change, Changing with Struggle

I would like to tell you about my relationship with Jill; how it began, what I brought to it, what I wanted to get out of it, how it progressed, where we are now.

It began in a different way from previous relationships. With those, I had more or less fallen in love with women for no apparent reason, except that sometimes they reminded me of other women I had been in love with. The falling in love was always with women I hardly knew and always included a sexual attraction. Jill I had known very vaguely for about four years and I had never been sexually attracted to her. We then did some work together in the women's movement and I grew to like and respect her, her intelligence, articulateness, gentleness, commitment to women, her warmth, openness and integrity. She listened well and was interesting to listen to. During one particular conversation that I had with her, this sentence flashed through my brain: 'I could have a relationship with this woman, it's a pity that I don't fancy her.' (At that point I still equated 'important' relationships with sexual relationships.) I then, very slowly, began to fall in love with her. In other words, I had chosen the woman I would fall in love with because of who she was, rather than with who I thought she was or hoped she might be.

What did I bring to the relationship? Well, on the one hand I brought a consciousness of a) what I wanted from it, b) the areas of difficulty I had, c) where I wanted to change, and d) the tools to effect that change. On the other hand I brought certain rigid patterns of behaviour and feelings which play rather like a record with the needle stuck, instead of being behaviour and feelings appropriate to any given situation.

I believed then, as I believe now, that most of the in-love feelings we have for one another in a sexual relationship are irrational and inappropriate. I believe that in fact they come from very deep-seated hurtful experiences which have either been buried and forgotten or are continually replayed and dramatised, which influence enormously our behaviour and attitudes towards people in general, and those with whom we are in love in particular. For instance, there seems to be a lot of general distress around touching (and not touching) people. It would appear that most of us adults don't have enough warm, physical contact, and/or feel repelled or closed off from it. My specific history as a baby was that I was touched and cuddled and held close to fulfil the adults' needs for physical contact. Then I was pushed away and given very little physical warmth for fear I would become too dependent. In neither case was I being respected in my own right, because I was being used to meet the adults' needs; my needs were simply not taken into account. Repeated experiences of this kind, where I was not given the chance to express my anger and grief at this mistreatment, together with having been sexually abused as a very young child, contributed to leaving me with a lot of irrational feelings about the physical and sexual nature of relationships.

One of the reasons why I believed that most of our in-love feelings were irrational was that, regardless of who I was in love with, the in-love feelings were always the same. The needle was well and truly stuck in the same groove and I wanted to be able to unstick it. What I wanted from this relationship with Jill was the space to be able to acknowledge these irrational feelings, to express them and also to have them seen for what they were, that is, nothing whatsoever to do with Jill. I wanted to be able to say: 'Please love me forever.' 'Say that I'm the most important person in your life.' 'You're the only one who can make things all right.' 'I'm jealous of you spending time with X.' 'Please don't go to work this morning.' I wanted it to be OK to say these things to her, but for her not to act on them.

It seems to me that often we feel we can only get physical closeness through being sexual. I'd come to realise that that's what most of my sexual activity was about, wanting to have that physical warmth and closeness which I had been denied or deprived of when I was very little. So the other thing that I wanted in this relationship was to be touched and held and stroked, not in order to turn me on or to turn Jill on, but simply to be physically loved for my own sake and not for any other reason. Not that sexual feelings wouldn't come up, because sex and physical contact seem inextricably linked when we have in-love feelings about one another, but I wanted to be able to take a look at the grief and the anger and the fear of those very early hurtful experiences of being touched. I guessed that by being given what

I'd needed then, physical warmth and closeness in a respectful and loving way, those feelings would come up. I wanted to be able to cry away all the grief, shout out all the anger, tremble away the fear and laugh with all the embarrassment.

I had also experienced painful situations where my ability to love and nurture in a physical way had been severely undermined by the constant message of my love not counting, not being important enough. This, together with the general message from society that you don't touch people anyway, had led me to realise that I also needed to be able to hold and stroke someone just for my sake, that there were as many, though different, hurts around touching as there were around being touched. The goal in all this was to be able to give and receive real love without being constrained or straightjacketed by the scars of those early relationships.

I guessed that all this was possible by what I had learned from co-counselling; that people have a natural healing process of emotional and physical pain, and that it is possible to bring up old hurts, that is, feel them as if they're happening now, and cry, tremble, shout, laugh and sweat with them, until they become an ordinary memory with no pain or numbness attached to them. A counselling interpretation of human behaviour, which had made sense to me and which I had begun to use in a previous sexual relationship, was the idea that people are restimulated by situations and over-react. I'd like to explain that. If a situation bears enough resemblance to a previous one in which we were hurt, and that hurt has remained unhealed, then the previous pain will be reactivated (restimulated) in the present situation, and we shall behave and feel as we did originally, and react in an uncalled for and inappropriate way. Sometimes, a lover or friend just has to pay attention to someone else, and we feel ignored, slighted, uncared for, jealous. Regardless of whether or not they are doing it in an uncaring way, our response is restimulating of all those times when we were being ignored.

I want to make it clear that I don't see these hurtful experiences, or my attempts to free myself from them, solely in individual terms. Although the experiences are unique, I see them very much as coming out of my oppression as a child, as a female and, much later, as a lesbian. The way I see it, children have a genuine dependence on adults for love and nurturance, and that love is always conditional on the child's accepting, to a greater or lesser degree, whatever lies are appropriate to the 'roles' that child is born into, roles according to sex, class, race, religion, etc. Through my oppression as a young one, I ended up with some of the feelings and behaviour of a victim of sexism, for example, feelings that I am unlovable and don't deserve to be loved, that lesbians are disgusting, that I am powerless, that I am not a real woman. These are some of the rigid feelings that I brought to my relationship with Jill.

What was crucial to the success of our relationship was that Jill began to use the same counselling tools for change. She had already located areas which she wanted to work on, one of which was sex. After we had both agreed that we wanted our relationship to be sexual, we wrote down for each other in detail what we liked and what we didn't like. We made it conscious, not something that 'just happens', and we laughed a lot when we first got into bed with one another, allowing ourselves to feel the embarrassment and some of the fear. Throughout our relationship we have done our best to accept one another's limitations imposed by our distress, whilst at the same time we've tried not to slip into seeing those limitations as fixed, always holding out the expectation of change.

The factor that has been the single biggest influence on our relationship is Jill's pregnancy and move into motherhood. We began our relationship in September, and in February Jill became pregnant. I had known she wanted to become pregnant before I began my relationship with her, yet it was something I hoped wouldn't happen. I feared there would be no love for me when a child was born and I also feared that I would not have enough clear, unselfish love to give a baby, and had vowed not to have children for that reason. For a few weeks I vaguely imagined that my relationship with her would remain unaltered; that we would continue to see one another, the only difference being that a baby would be there too, whom I would love and spend time with sometimes. I felt committed to Jill and her unborn baby, but mainly because I had invested needs in her.

In one of those flashes of clarity where far-reaching decisions are made, I had a realisation of what commitment really meant and what I really wanted to do. I wanted to be a parent to Jill's baby, which meant sharing the responsibility and childcare, sharing the sleepless nights and the tiredness, sharing the decision-making. I wanted to do this, not because I invested needs in Jill or because it was 'getting it right', but because by doing it, however hard it felt, it would give me the opportunity to grow in my capacity to love, to think and to be more human. Being a parent meant life-long commitment. I had never committed myself to anyone before, through fear of being hurt, and I now wanted to face that fear and step right through it.

A week or so later, Jill severely rejected me. Her early pregnancy restimulated so much terror in her, combining with my clingy feelings of emotional dependence, that she pushed me away with a vehemence. The abyss opened. All the old feelings of terror and existential *angst* rose to the surface. I just managed to keep a hold of the fact that my feelings were old recordings of earlier hurts, and that of course I could cope with my life. I was able to take a look at some of these feelings in my regular co-counselling sessions, to cry and to get angry. It takes a considerable amount of crying and trembling for a past hurtful experience to become just an ordinary memory with no pain attached. But what some crying can achieve is clarity about what is hurtful in the present and what that present hurt is restimulating from the past. With this process I was able to stay in touch with the reality that I was a good woman to have a relationship with, and that in spite of some pretty 'off' behaviour, I always did my best. I also hung onto the fact that this was equally true of Jill, and that she would never have pushed me away if she hadn't been feeling terrified.

By mid-pregnancy, Jill was relaxed and entering a general state of well-being. We resumed our relationship, having made as conscious and as clear as possible all the factors in our behaviour towards one another which led up to her rejection of me. For four months I had the kind of happiness you get from requited in-love feelings. I felt very loved by her and very loving towards her. Occasionally I would allow myself to realise that the happiness I felt was completely dependent on her, that it was the feeling that all those unmeetable needs of 'please love me forever', and 'please make everything all right', were being met. I knew that they couldn't be met because they are reactivated needs from unhealed hurts, and the more you try to meet them the more you feel you want. I knew that they could only be felt and cried about. Sometimes I was able to do this with Jill, and that was part of the real loving of our relationship. We also went to the pre-natal classes together at the maternity hospital, and gathered information about pregnancy and childbirth. I looked into the possibility of stimulating my breasts for breast-feeding, but discovered that it had only been achieved by women who had previously been pregnant.

At about eight months, Jill's terror began to surface again and once more she began to push me away, though at no time during the nightmares that followed did she categorically reject me as she had done previously. She turned her needs and her love towards another friend who had children, who was a mother, who had given birth. It was not simply because of our respective distress that Jill was turning away from me, she was turning away from me as a childless woman with no experience of childbirth or mothering. Jill and I had reached the great divide over which she was about to cross, over which there appeared no bridges for me, and over whose other side there hangs a complicity of silence. A silence which comes from the oppression of women as mothers, the horrendous ways in which women in the West are forced to give birth, robbed of their power, their dignity and control, and the complete lack of acknowledgement of the work involved in nurturing babies and young children. A silence which comes from the way many mothers end up internalising that oppression, through no fault of their own, seeing the results of the oppression as personal problems only – 'If I'd done my breathing exercises properly it wouldn't have been so painful' 'If I'd given Becky a bit more to eat then, she wouldn't be making a scene now.'

Like any other divisions amongst women (sexuality, class, race, physical difference, etc.), that between mothers and non-mothers would not exist if women and children were given the respect and value we deserve, and I am enormously proud of the slow and painful steps that Jill and I, and other women like us, are taking towards a better understanding and eradication of those divisions.

With the birth of Bridget all my worst fears came true. There was no love or attention left for me, and this restimulated all my feelings of panic and worthlessness. I wanted to get as far away as possibe, but running away was an old pattern which I knew I could no longer use. This was what commitment meant, hanging in there with feelings of rejection, desperately trying to get it right, never being able to get it right, and going round and round in circles trying to work out what to do. From time to time, I had glimpses that I was actually doing my best and that I was of some use, and that Jill was in an equally horrible hell of her own.

In spite of all these feelings, I knew that Bridget was beautiful. There was no way that I could not love her, could not be delighted that she existed in the world, and I soon began to establish with her my most rational and loving relationship. It was not, however, what I'd hoped for, the real sharing, the becoming a real parent. This slipped away from me for a host of reasons which I am only just beginning to sort out. On a practical level, it seemed impossible simply because Jill was breast-feeding on demand, a twenty-four hour a day job. But the feelings about the practicalities were obviously influenced by what was happening on the emotional level. Jill was the woman I had invested all my needs in, the woman who had given me, during those middle months of pregnancy, what felt like uncon-ditional love, a mother's love. My 'mother' was pushing me away, how, then, could I truly mother another? It was a strain being in one another's company; how could I share the broken nights, when even my staying overnight was a torment to both of us?

It seemed right that Jill's needs as a new mother should take priority with our mutual friends, for the changes in circumstances and emotional and physical being that having a first baby brings are tremendous, and were little understood by some of us at the time. We gave what we could, but still competed for her attention, and lacked the resources whereby we could think consistently about her needs. Within all this, therefore, there was no space for me to say 'it's my first baby too', and the total lack of recognition, and the limited resources, and the pushing away by Jill, made it impossible for me to fight for that place as a real co-parent.

I now spend about thirty-five hours a week with Bridget, earning my living by a part-time job. When I am with her I mother her, though I would not call myself a mother in the sense of having that total responsibility of parenting. My commitment is still life-long, and I also support her financially, along with Jill and two other women.

As the weeks after Bridget's birth turned into months, and the tensions between Jill and I began to lessen, I alternately swung between despair of ever having her back again, and hope that I might. These irrational feelings vied for a place in my consciousness, trying to displace the very real love which I knew indisputably to be there, and which has continued to be there in spite of all the difficulties.

Hope began to outweigh despair after Jill agreed that it would make sense for her to resume a sexual relationship with me because of all the work we'd already done on it. I began to feel 'safe'. It was obvious that she now felt little need to push me away and was liking my company and it seemed just a question of waiting until she had those in-love feelings back again, of wanting to be close, sexual, which had disappeared for her about a month before Bridget's birth.

But it was a false sense of safety because it was totally dependent on Jill feeling good about me, rather than on me feeling good about me. In any case it didn't last long, for although Jill regained those sexual feelings, she fell in love with another woman. Jill's pushing me away and not have sexual feelings for me was one thing. Her having them for someone else and pushing me away was entirely different. In my sessions I cried and raged and raged and howled about the unfairness and the loss, as I pictured her in intimate love-gazing situations with another woman.

The result of all this brought our relationship under a new strain. More strong than ever was the feeling of wanting nothing more to do with her, of wanting to make a complete break. My committed and independent relationship with Bridget made this impossible, and I am very glad, for if I had been able to make the break, I would not have had to face the feelings. I almost certainly would have begun to look for someone else in whom in invest the same needs, where there would have been a tremendous pull to try to get those needs answered rather than challenged. In the past when a sexual relationship has finished, I have either withdrawn and become numb, or found someone else. I am still in love with Jill and I still have irrational needs invested in her. I think and hope that this will remain the case, until I have cried, laughed and trembled about them all in my counselling sessions, so that the pain of them disappears and I am left only with rational needs. I do not want to return to an old in-love relationship where sexual feelings are acted on uncritically, rather than attempting to scrutinise and make distinct what is rational and what irrational. I have no idea at present what a rational sexual relationship would look like, except that I think we would be far less sexual and much more physically nurturing.

Many of the expectations that we have of each other in relationships are both unvoiced and irrational, and cause a great amount of hurt, jealousy and resentment when they are not lived up to, or are not lived up to any longer. When they remain unspoken the other person can never know what they are, and consequently never has the chance to say whether or not she agrees to try to live up to them.

Jill and I have recently redefined our relationship in terms of what our goals are, when and how we want to spend time with each other, what expectations we have, and which of these expectations we agree to meet. We are in agreement that our relationship is a committed one, and that we continue to look at the distress between us and deal with it as intelligently and honestly as possible. Our long-term goal is to be warm, loving friends to one another, and in the short term for Jill not to reject me and for me not to give up. We have agreed that when we meet it should be for a particular purpose; spending loose unstructured time with one another is when there is the biggest pull to act badly towards each other.

It isn't easy, this relationship, but I am enormously impressed by the courage with which we face it. I love her and know that I am worthy of her love. I know that I am engaged in this struggle for a rational, warm, human relationship with one of the finest women I know, and that through this struggle I am indeed learning to be more human.

## 2. Jill Brown
## The Daughter is Mother of the Child:
## Cycles of lesbian sexuality

Moving house recently meant that some of my past became literally disturbed and, during the sorting and sifting, I took another look at my writing at the time of my first lesbian relationship, aged seventeen, in 1967. When the feelings of embarrassment had cleared I was able to see the struggle that I was in, as a young lesbian with no women's movement to validate my feelings. Alone, in a hostile world, I was grappling with such an intensity of feelings that, at points, I became overwhelmed by the isolation which my first lover and I found ourselves in. Reading between the lines of romantic love borrowed from our patriarchal English A level literature I began to see the ways in which I was internalising all the destructive and oppressive notions of lesbian relationships and becoming quite powerless under the weight of it all. What is also clear from that writing is the confusion of sexual feelings, a desperate need to be nurtured, and a striving to become vulnerable with another woman. In spite of feelings of confusion and fear of insanity the constant thread which ran through my first relationship, and which still continues with an increased clarity, was a need to reconnect with my mother through becoming close to another woman.

I felt for years, however spasmodically, and however vaguely, that it was within the area of relationships, within my lesbianism, that I was simultaneously most powerful and most powerless. In loving women and in being in love with women I became both whole and fragmented; pushed into isolation and pulled into closeness. In each relationship this conflict repeated itself; at its most acute it felt as though I was swinging between two contradictory parts of myself. It's hard to plot the first awareness of the contradiction which is held deeply within my lesbianism and within myself. Perhaps just the fact of being born the daughter of a woman in a world which is hostile to women and girl children is in itself the primary contradiction upon which all others are built. As my mother could only love me within the limits of her own unmet needs which came from her own deprived experiences as a daughter herself, then she, quite unconsciously, left me with feelings of great deprivation and longings to be fully loved by a woman. Her sudden death when I was eight increased the deprivation, and my feelings of loss became numb as I was never given the opportunity to express my grief. I experience the deprivation sometimes as a gaping ugly hole inside of me and other times as if the whole of my inner being were made of solid ice. In all my relationships with women I have had some awareness, to differing degrees of intensity, of the ice beginning to melt or the hole beginning to be filled as I have moved closer to a particular woman and she has let me in.

Over the years, on and off, I struggled sometimes clumsily, sometimes with great lucidity, to make sense of the conflicts within my lesbianism; to understand the yearnings I felt, the closeness I longed for and to try and express the untapped grief inside of me. Women came and went in my life, several women came quite close to me before the fear set in to stop the closeness and the vulnerability. When the fear was running high I pushed away from intimacy and dependency with a forceful viciousness. Although ostensibly it seemed as though I had repeated exactly the same behaviour in successive relationships – that of revealing myself only to the point of known safety and then shutting down to any further vulnerability – I know, in retrospect, that I was moving, however slowly and unevenly, to a better understanding of myself. Somehow and somewhere inside of me and through my connections with women, I believed that if my sexual feelings, my love for women, and my sexuality were better understood and if I were more in charge of that area of my life, then some of my fundamental feelings of powerlessness would radically shift which would, in turn, affect other parts of my life. It seemed that I was beginning to experience at a gut level the intrinsic way in which our oppression is maintained and perpetuated through our sexuality, and that our liberation could only be fully realised through the deeply revolutionary connection between the personal and the political. I knew, not with a sudden insightful awareness, but more through a progressive searching and struggling, that the more we took charge of our needs within our sexuality the more we would take charge and act powerfully in all other parts of our lives and the world. I knew that if my relationships became less like refuges and more creative and powerful then my life would lose its fragmentary nature.

Thirteen years later, and having had three significant sexual relationships with women, I reached 1980 and a decision that I could not and would not continue my relationships with women in the same way. Although I did not have a clear picture of the changes I wanted nor what a different way of relating with women might be, nor did I securely hold the tools for change within my grasp, I knew that there were certain aspects of my old relationships that I had to give up. I knew that it was imperative that I ceased to use drink as a way of numbing the fear which arose when I became close to another woman; that I needed to confront the fear and shame of being sexual with women and that I could only do so if I let myself experience the feelings; that I needed to distinguish between what parts of my sexual feelings were coming out of my oppression as a woman and as a lesbian and what parts connected with a primordial need to be nurtured and to nurture. I knew that I needed to give up seeing the other woman as a refuge for me, and my being her refuge from the hostile world; that I needed to express in detail, however falteringly and gropingly, everything I felt and thought during the times of greatest intimacy; that I needed to become both the little girl and the mother of another woman, and that through a process of greater intimacy and greater honesty, I would at last lose the painful feelings of isolation which I had experienced within or without a sexual relationship and that I would begin to break the stranglehold of internalised oppression which had always operated either crudely or subtly within my relationships. In short, I had to unlearn my oppression as a lesbian within the setting of a lesbian relationship. In that process I have had more and more to face the constant struggle of the little girl and the mother in me and to see how that connects with the self-same struggle in the other woman and I have learnt that in each lesbian relationship we have two daughters and two mothers all striving to meet unmet needs and yearning to have a well of frozen needs thawed out.

Running through all my relationships, throughout my life, there always was the desire to have a child. The desire to have a child certainly connected to that gaping hole in me and to unresolved feelings about my mother, for having a child in some way represented a clear relationship in which somebody else could be a part of me and yet separate. A child came perhaps to represent a hope that through mothering I could reconnect to that part of myself which I was forced to cut off many years ago. To be a 'whole' woman, through conception, pregnancy and childbirth, would somehow plug that gaping needy hole in me. This part of me seemed to be reinforced by my fear that as a lesbian I was not a 'real' woman. It was clear in my relationships with women that I had dealt with my lack of being mothered by being the mother of the other, and so it was not surprising that I would seek 'real' motherhood as a way to work out my own unmet needs as had thousands of women before me. The little girl in me was usually impossible to find, so frightened was I of exposing her needs which seemed to me, if revealed, so hungry, insatiable and ugly. Accompanied by the fear was the lack of trust that anybody could ever be strong enough to let me reveal those deprived parts of me and that the courageous mothering I needed in such a hostile world was not to be found. My involvement in the women's liberation movement over a period of twelve or so years had provided me with both the radical framework in which to understand the constructs of my sexuality under patriarchy and a powerful contradiction to my oppression as a lesbian through its confirmation and validation of my love for women. What was lacking for me was a way in which I could explore in detail the building of the constructs and a way in which I could release all the painful feelings which had gone into the woven fabric of my sexuality. It was as if the missing link between my sexual and emotional life and that of the world in which I acted, and was acted upon, was yet to be forged.

So it was against that background and with those particular decisions and awarenesses in mind that in the autumn of 1980 I began my relationship with Jo. Two other significant factors arose round about the same time which, during the relationship, took on an increasing importance both for Jo and myself and for my growing understanding of my sexuality. One was that the possibility of having a child was now tangible, as feminists in London had opened up the area of self-insemination, and the other was that co-counselling was beginning to present itself as a possible way forward.

I knew Jo as a woman who had consistently and rigorously given time to her own growth and who had a commitment to understanding her feelings, their origin, and thereby to changing the way she behaved, particularly in relation to other women. The seriousness with which she treated herself and her relationships was for me an exciting model of change and represented the possibility of sharing my ideas about changing old ways of relating. I entered the relationship with Jo with a new kind of clarity, different from previous relationships whose beginnings were precipitated by intense in-love feelings of yearning and wanting, particularly in a sexual sense. With Jo, the emphasis was more on a self-conscious planning for a relationship, rather than any spontaneous falling into a closeness with one another because of the feelings. I was not falling in love with Jo, yet I was very excited about the prospects of being able to change our ways of relating sexually and being able to explore all the tangled threads which join together in the fabric of romantic sexual lesbian relationships.

Although our herstories had, until that point, played themselves out in various and different ways, we came together with a shared commitment to give up old patterns of relating and to discover together a more rational basis for our relationship as women who had experienced ourselves as lesbians for many years prior to the second wave of feminism. The excitement of sharing a journey with a woman whose integrity and intelligence I greatly respected was intense, and yet the thought of having to leave behind those defences which had grown more sophisticated over time was terrifying. However, I knew even before the possibility of relating with Jo occurred, that I no longer had any choice but to give up the ways of relating which had kept me trapped in my own defences so that meeting with Jo was an opportunity to extricate myself from the painful restrictions of the oppressive constructs of my sexuality. We negotiated, in the best way we could, a clear relationship since we believed that spontaneity in relationships covered up a whole range of unspoken, unexpressed feelings which could lead to wrong assumptions and distortions of ourselves and each other. We planned what amount of time we would spend with each other, and what we would do within that period of time. If at times our rigour became rigid, it was only because we were aware that we needed to contradict all those pulls to invest an extra-ordinary amount of time, energy and feelings in a sexual relationship. I knew that, for me, the emphasis that sexual relationships had taken up in my life, particularly during their early stages, had always been disproportionate, and that other areas of my life had been neglected. It had felt, at times, that I was placed in a position of having to choose between being active and effective in the world and being in love with another woman. I no longer wanted to make that choice, and in retrospect wanted to understand why and how that choice operates for many, if not all, women.

A couple of months into our relationship, Jo made a suggestion for a way in which we could begin to share and explore a sexual exchange. I knew that I had been holding back from the idea of a sexual relationship with Jo because it seemed to be the most terrifying area, the one of greatest risk and greatest vulnerability. It was quite simply the fear of getting close, and the fear, this time around, felt so stark because I could no longer employ the old defences and I knew that I would have to go some way towards revealing my distress in this area. Yet, as before, I knew that there was no turning back and if I foreclosed that part of the relationship, I knew that not only would I be giving up on Jo and her own struggles towards a more rational sexuality, but also on myself. The suggestion was that we write down, as specifically as possible, how we would like to be sexual with one another, what we had enjoyed in the past, what we had disliked, and any new ways of being sexual we would like to explore. We wrote this away from each other so that we would not be in the position of feeling dependent on what the other wanted and so that, at least at the start, we would not be restricted by the other's needs before we could express our own. We then read each other's when we met together the next time, amidst feelings of embarrassment and a sense of relief that there appeared not to be too many differences between what we each wanted.

This simple process was extremely important in contradicting all the notions of spontaneity in sexual relationships and for me marked the beginnings of a definition of my own sexual needs and where those particular needs came from. In my sexual relationship with Jo, because we were able to give each other some attention about what each of us was feeling when we were sexual, I began to understand more clearly how many different entangled feelings and needs I had been bringing to all my sexual exchanges with women. Through my relationship with Jo and through my involvement with co-counselling, I had learnt that in order to understand, express and release our feelings, we needed a listener who did not let her own feelings interrupt our expression of ourselves. The theory of counselling which we used within our relationship states that in order to change we need to heal past hurts through the release of distress (crying, shaking, etc.) so that we release our intelligence to deal with new situations in an appropriate way. We need to free ourselves of the distress in our present behaviour which is related to hurtful situations in our past and which have created rigid patterns of defence. This is particularly difficult within a sexual context because of the emotionally-charged nature of sexual feelings and the intense vulnerability and fear of rejection involved. It was always our goal to do our best to allow space for one another to express whatever feelings resulted from being sexual with one another.

I needed to explore my relationship to orgasms, as I knew that our experience of sexuality was still restricted within the constructs of a male-defined, genitally-focused experience. It would only be through examining in detail the nature of orgasm that we could expand our sexual communication and experience the whole of our bodies as sensual and erotic. My particular relationship to orgasm was one in which I generally experienced difficulty in reaching one, and yet often felt a desperate need not just to orgasm but to get to the release of feelings which seemed to come after orgasm. I had often cried after orgasm, and had not been able to understand where the crying had come from but had felt it as a healing process far outweighing the orgasm in significance. I began to re-evaluate my orgasms and my sexual feelings in a new way. My relationship with Jo provided me with both the safety and the framework in which to understand more clearly the connection between my relationship with my mother and my sexual relationships with women. There were particular occasions during which that connection revealed itself with a startling perspicuity when I moved through feeling sexual, becoming orgasmic and finally releasing a great wealth of tears as I grieved for my mother. It was becoming increasingly obvious that sexual desires and feelings had more to do with early experiences of being nurtured than with pure erotica.

I was also beginning to learn that it was possible to move through feeling sexual and reach a more vulnerable state in which I could connect more to the little girl in me. Moving through the sexual area meant looking at my powerlessness as a sexual person which was the result of early sexual abuse by men and it meant having to look at feelings of self-disgust and shame which I had internalised throughout many years as a lesbian. Perhaps the internalisation of our lesbian oppression was the hardest thing for Jo and me to deal with in our relationship, in spite of our feminist understanding of our experiences. Since we both shared long years of internalisation, we therefore shared similar feelings of self-loathing, guilt and shame, so that we often colluded unconsciously with one another about those feelings which made it impossible for either of us to release these feelings or to see them as nothing to do with our reality.

Six months into our relationship the focus radically shifted when I became pregnant. The fact of being pregnant threw up such a wealth of confused feelings for both of us that I went into a period of withdrawal from any closeness with her during the first few months of pregnancy. The fear of being pregnant, although it had been something I had longed for all those years, seemed so intense that I could find no safety with Jo and the thought of relating sexually seemed a contradiction to my pregnancy. Lesbian pregnancy felt like a contradiction in itself and I experienced depths of isolation in those early months. As well as my isolation from Jo, I remember experiencing a distinct sense of separation from other lesbians in my life. I remember looking at their bodies, long before my body swelled and changed. I recall thinking that they were in control of their bodies and lives and that I no longer was. The feeling was of being taken over by another self, another force, a life which would pull me away from other lesbians into a world which they could not and perhaps might not wish to understand. I had feelings that I had betrayed them and fears that I could never get back to them, as if the pregnancy itself was tearing me away from my lesbianism because I would not be able to hold the apparent contradiction of lesbian motherhood. I was struggling with the conflict between motherhood and myself as a sexual being and with my internalised lesbian oppression which wrongly teaches us that we are not allowed to become mothers. Riven with conflict, I had sensations of being fragmented and torn in several directions at once; part of me desperate to connect with other lesbians, to say that I was still the same, and part of me needing to connect through my pregnancy to heterosexual women. It was as if I was being stretched and pulled between two poles of the contradiction and torn inside out. As a result I became disconnected from my sexuality and therefore deprived of closeness, of the thread of human contact which provides a physical, energetic nurturing and erotic communication.

Sadly, at that stage, I was unable to welcome the growing foetus within my body. In fact, the background against which all these difficult feelings were played out was one in which the reality of lesbian motherhood was an immensely powerful force. It presented such a contradiction to all the oppressive notions about ourselves as women and opened out the possibility of separating conception from sexual intercourse which has radical implications for our sexuality.

During the middle phase of pregnancy, when the intensity of the early fears and conflicts had subsided, I was able to make contact with Jo again and I began to experience a sense of completeness and power new to me. I felt very powerful physically, and it was as if the pregnancy, by then in full flower, had pulled together all the fragments which had previously been scattered. Regaining a sense of wholeness meant that I could connect again to my sexuality and I began to relate sexually with Jo in a way which was to a new and great extent unrestricted by my old defences. I was able to love and respect my body in a way that I had not experienced before, which meant that I was able to give and receive nurturance and sexual attention with a new-found ease. I understand the wholeness and completeness I felt then as being related to my incompleteness as a woman and as a lesbian. The pregnancy acted as a contradiction to this in that there was always a part of me which irrationally believed I was not fully a woman. Being pregnant confirmed my 'womanhood', and provided me with a whole sense of self. However the wholeness of the experience was double-edged in that although our fertility is a creative and powerful force it is often validated to the exclusion of all other aspects of our creativity – as a lesbian I was responding to this distorted confirmation of my femaleness.

During the last stages of pregnancy fear emerged again and my focus shifted away from Jo, away from my sexuality, and towards motherhood and a child. I became very strongly reconnected to

82

Carol, with whom I had had a sexual relationship and who was a mother herself. The combination of Carol's motherhood and her lesbianism gave me the perfect safety in which to continue the final phase of pregnancy and my relationship with Jo withdrew into the background. My daughter Bridget became, in those first few weeks and months, the most important person in my life; I was centred in her and her needs, so that all other relationships receded into the background and became secondary. My relationship with Jo, because of its sexual nature, appeared to be the most problematic as it became the one which I most needed to reject. It seemed to be in direct competition with my relationship with Bridget. Being so unsure and so unconfident of my ability to mother well, I lost again my defined sense of self and therefore the possibility of merging with Jo, of becoming dependent on her, became erased. Since Bridget had become my centre, and my body was directly connected to her existence through giving birth and through breast-feeding, I was unable to differentiate a sense of self with an autonomous sexuality away from her. The idea of being sexual filled me with disgust and horror and it seemed as if my being sexual would be in direct conflict with Bridget's needs. Somewhere in me there was a vague feeling with no detail attached to it that my sexuality would be hurtful to Bridget, which as a general level, no doubt, connects with notions of lesbians corrupting young children, but probably specifically connects to an early experience of my own, the memory of which still remains occluded.

My general state throughout the first few months of Bridget's life was one of numbness. I was unable to give out any attention, either to myself or to other women close to me. It seemed as if it took all my energy and all my thinking to deal with the presence of such a vulnerable and dependent person in my life, and during that time I was unable to express any of the feelings I had inside of me. Jo remained close beside me, committed to staying in the relationship with me in spite of all my rejecting behaviour. Again, I found myself in a false position of having to choose between two apparent conflicting parts of me: between being a mother, and being in a sexual relationship. Of course, there seemed no choice since motherhood was not to be abandoned. The point at which I picked up again on understanding and changing aspects of my sexuality, was in March 1982 when I began a new counselling relationship with Anne, with whom I had no other contact outside of counselling. Whilst Jo and I remained committed to our relationship, it had become clear that the issue of motherhood and probably the feelings born of internalised lesbian oppression were preventing us from becoming close in the way in which we had previously attempted. The counselling relationship with Anne offered the possibility of a clearly defined space away from other relationships in which I could continue to explore and change the painful parts of my sexuality.

As I emerged from the first, close, intimate period of the relationship with my daughter, it was vital that I secured for myself a relationship with a committed counsellor in which I could continue to work through my struggles in the world as a lesbian mother, and through the internal conflicts between the daughter and mother in me. I found the relationship immediately effective in that it provided me with the precise balance between safety and a space for me to bring to the surface the entangled confusion of feelings which had been building up in me during the preceding months, and which were indicators of much earlier and much deeper layers of distress. It felt as if I had found Anne at exactly the right time, that it could be with Anne that I could move through my powerlessness as a lesbian and with her that I could reach some of the feelings which had been laid in during my relationship with my mother and since her death. I knew that my mother's death had meant that I carried vast amounts of unresolved grief which I had brought to every relationship and that it had only been with Jo that I had begun to let go of some of that grief.

The fact that Anne and I had met as co-counsellors provided us with a clear framework in which to work with one another. Although this framework was the same one which Jo and I had used previously, the fact that it was the only way in which Anne and I were meeting gave the relationship more clarity and a finer structure. The framework is one in which we share the time equally between us, and during the time we both give clear attention to the other's feelings; the feelings can be expressed and discharged whilst the experience is then re-evaluated. At any one time one of us is staying clear of her own feelings, thus providing a non-judgemental and validating space in which the other woman can work as openly and freely as possible on her feelings and her life-experiences. Within the framework there is an agreement that our relationship does not get caught up within the web of socialising together, so that we are not using other socially constructed ways of getting close. Socialising together, whilst ostensibly very attractive (we have both experienced strong pulls to be together outside of a counselling setting), does not actually work in the sense that it confuses the relationship in getting close and becoming vulnerable with each other. Our counselling relationship is a life-long commitment in that we hold with the belief that any potential need to separate or terminate the relationship would come out of our distress and could be worked through within the framework of counselling. I had decided at this point to explore my sexuality within the context of my relationship with Anne and not to develop any other sexual relationships until my self-knowledge was clearer and until I was more in charge of my own sexuality.

It becomes increasingly clear to me that all women need a different kind of mothering from the one we have usually experienced with those who mothered us out of their own oppression. The nurturance which we need is one which shows a deep concern for our well-being, both physically and mentally and is not conditional on the needs of the nurturer. The best model of nurturance we have had has been that of our mothers or those who mothered us, yet that nurturance was always limited by the unmet needs of the nurturer. My counsellor, Anne, is able to model a better kind of nurturing as she stays outside of her own feelings, and I, when counselling her, do the same. This means that we do not become so caught up in issues of dependency at an unaware level. What seems to be thrown up time and again in my relationship with Anne is that we are both struggling with a desperate, hungry need to be nurtured yet we are afraid to ask for, or to receive, full nurturance because it seems to jeopardise our autonomy; to enable us to accept the nurturance, we have to become totally vulnerable. So we repeatedly find ourselves caught up in the conflict between nurturance and autonomy; in the false choice between being in love and being in the world and coping alone. Clearly, Anne and I share the same struggle in which the little girl finds it so hard to emerge and express the full extent of her neediness. Although we have experienced our sexuality in different ways, I as a lesbian and she a heterosexual woman, we both share that longing to be close to another woman and a yearning to reconnect to those first pre-verbal experiences of the mother–daughter relationship.

Receiving and giving attention in this relationship allows me the possibility of being loved and loving in a way which had ceased to be available to myself and Jo. The conditions were right both within the relationship and within the context of other parts of our lives for Anne and I to fall in love with each other. Rather than denying or concealing these in-love feelings from each other and from ourselves, we are able to recognise them openly and give them full expression; because without releasing them we cannot see exactly what they look like, or where they are coming from. The fact that I fell in love with Anne means that I am able to understand further the relationship between sexual feelings and the need to be close and physically nurtured. Feeling sexual about Anne gives me again a way back to my mother and those early experiences. When there is enough safety for me to allow Anne to nurture me, I immediately have the sensation of returning to a time when I had no language and no defences. Eye-contact and physical sensations become significant, and I am filled with a fundamental desire either to crawl inside her or to lie curled up on her stomach. These feelings are accompanied by an intense sense of physical weakness and powerlessness as if I am going to lose consciousness. During this kind of experience I need to cry and shake, which I interpret as the discharge of grief (loss of mother) and fear of losing my autonomy or fear of some kind of sexual abuse.

In this kind of exploration of my sexuality, through closeness and love with Anne, more and more layers of distress have been revealed. Within all the neediness of the daughter in me lies a considerable amount of fear of sexual abuse – resulting from painful experiences with men when I was very young – which creates strong feelings of mistrust in me which have functioned to keep me in an isolated position within the world, and have inhibited my effectiveness, especially in relation to men. It will be through working on early memories of sexual abuse that I shall be able to liberate myself from some of the more debilitating effects of our oppression, and re-connect with my own power.

A particularly crucial aspect of my relationship with Anne is around the area of my internalised lesbian oppression. As a woman who has expressed her sexuality until recently as a heterosexual, Anne has not carried the painful feelings of guilt and shame about being sexual with women; she therefore stands outside of my inter-nalised lesbian oppression. As my counsellor, she has been able to clearly contradict the painful feelings I have had as a lesbian woman, and I have been able to let go of some of the shame and guilt which I have carried inside of me since the time of my first lesbian relation-ship. I have now begun to develop a stronger sense of pride in my lesbianism as Anne has consistently both validated my love for women and loved me because of my lesbianism, not despite it. The process of freeing myself from the self-oppression that I have experi-enced as a lesbian allows me to make deeper connections not only with Anne, but with all the women in my life. The more pride I take in myself as a lesbian, the more I am able to resist the external attacks on my life since I am coming less from feeling that I deserve mistreat-ment in the world. The more I am able to release the hurtful feelings I carry as a lesbian woman, the more I am able to move towards a more rational expression of my sexuality with other women. The fact that

Anne does not collude with my lesbian oppression provides me with the space to explore in detail all the ways in which I have absorbed mistreatment and misinformation about myself as a lesbian.

The other aspect of my sexuality which I continue to work on with Anne is the one in which sexual feelings and erotica have become confused with our need to be unconditionally nurtured. With Anne I experience all the feelings of wanting to be sexual, and wanting to lay myself open to her completely through an erotic and orgasmic experience. Allowing these feelings to come up within a counselling framework means that I am less caught up with needing Anne to respond to me in a sexual way. Anne's ability to give me attention which is free from her own needs and feelings has meant that the expression of my sexuality has been revealed with far more clarity than ever before. I have been able to release some of the emotions which had become entangled in the pull towards orgasm. Instead of going on to the experience of orgasm when feeling sexual, I have been able to release large pockets of grief, fear and anger which have been laid in during sexual exchange in my past. Freeing myself from these kind of feelings within my sexuality has meant that I have been able to move towards a deeper closeness with Anne in which the possibility of receiving and giving full nurturance has become much more of a reality. Through this process I have been able to distinguish more clearly between the aspects of my sexuality which have been constructed by patriarchy and those aspects which are rational for me to own within my relationships. It has confirmed for me the long-held belief that our sexuality, if liberated from the painful constraints of our oppression, would look much more like a flow of sensual and nurturing energy between women which would not jeopardise, but rather enhance our autonomy in the process of that flow. What I continue to learn is that we cannot redefine our sexuality by an act of will or through a political decision alone, but that the redefinition will come through a real commitment between women in which each of us provides the other with both the space and the safety to let go of her defences and in which we hold out the highest expectation for each other to reclaim our sexuality as our own.

Working on my sexuality in a rigorously structured way is both a struggle and a triumph. A struggle because large parts of me still long for a situation in which I share all areas of my life with the person I feel sexual about, and that is often a lonely struggle; a triumph because I know that the needs that used to drive me into intense, romantic, monogamous relationships with women are diminishing, which means that overall I have more energy and more commitment for all other aspects of my life and feel a greater sense of my autonomy and a greater and more real sense of connection with other women. Jo and I continue to share the same struggle of changing relationships and despite all the difficult feelings which have come up between us, we have not rejected each other, nor have we ceased to hold out the highest expectations for each other and ourselves in the rediscovery of the power which was systematically taken away from us throughout our individual lives.

Although Jo and I have lost our sexual connection together our particular success lies in not only staying committed to our relationship, whatever feelings come up between us, but perhaps more importantly, never giving up on ourselves as lesbians. My relationships with Jo, with Anne, with my daughter Bridget, with all the women who share my life, reflect no more and no less the revolutionary, feminist process which, through politicising the personal, is breaking down patriarchal thinking and behaviour and opening up new possibilities of love between women.

# 6
# Sex and Childbirth

Lesley Saunders

Talking about sex and childbirth breaks an ideological silence. The usual way of dealing with the topic is merely at a technical level, discussing the frequency and timing of intercourse. We ourselves find it hard to talk about what sex after birth is like, either to our partners or to other women. We don't want to reveal this most intimate part of our lives to people who are going to make judgements of whatever colour.

Social science is, as we know, political – and powerful. It has grown out of an ideology which looks only at what can be measured; it compartmentalises and fragments our experience. The objectivity to which it pretends objectifies women: the notion (usually implicit) of getting back to normal after bearing a child is full of assumptions about what the ideal woman looks like, how she should behave, about monogamous heterosexuality, and fails to recognise childbirth as part of a process where normative prescriptions do not apply. In fact, we have to deal with the political dimensions of the process explicitly; and by politics I mean power-relationships. Clearly this encompasses much more than the sex act – this is one of the compartmentalisations we have to break down.

Since a lot of what follows is precisely this redrawing of boundaries, the issues cannot be treated in sequence or with some definitive 'line' – this is the way our experience has been falsely re-presented to us already. I try to do justice to the variety of the experiences and attitudes I have encountered in women, but within a particular framework. There is no easy answer to the question of 'consciousness' – a collection of random subjectivities does not in itself contain the necessary political cutting edge; but adopting a preconceived line about what the primary causes and structures of oppression are is one-dimensional, distorting. We adopt strategies specific to the demands we feel life is making on us, and according to our perceived or unconscious needs which may have a long and complex history. There are good reasons for our responses, and it is not a question of

89

whether we are 'right-on' feminists or not. This does not mean to say that the strategies are always appropriate – they may bind us to our oppression instead of challenging it. The dynamics are subtle.

I believe that the crux of this topic is gender oppression, though I do not exclude issues of class and race. Feminism, in comparison with orthodox Marxism–Leninism on the one hand, and alternative/growth movements on the other, is more successful in theory and practice at making connections between the different forms that oppression takes, and in breaking down the separate categories in which our experience of that oppression comes packaged – where 'feelings' are split off from and either subordinated to, or elevated above, 'politics'.

In this chapter I have not included any material which might distinguish between first and subsequent births, because it was too complex an undertaking.

I also tend to concentrate on what happens between men and women in long-term heterosexual relationships, which is the most usual set-up for women with children.

There is, of course, a distinction between sexuality and sexual relationships; I have dwelt much more on relationships because for most of us the boundaries are indistinct. I interviewed six women in depth, and drew on my own journal written before and after my second child was born. I have also used material gathered in the course of writing a detailed feminist analysis of childbirth practices; and the insights that come from just talking with many women about sex.

Because sexuality and reproduction are both processes, not single events or static attributes, I did not want to exclude pregnancy and delivery. There are many considerations I h. ve omitted – such as the beginnings of our experience of sexuality in our own mothers' wombs.[1] I hope that the framework I use, while leaving whole areas unfinished, makes space for these other speculations.

## I

A woman experiences profound changes in giving birth to a baby, especially if it is her first, in her body, her material circumstances, her relationships and her view of herself. Crucially these changes are mediated to us through the treatment we receive from various state agencies (hospitals, the DHSS, employers), the formal and informal advice we are given, the social images of motherhood enveloping us, the perceptions and reactions of people who know us, and the kind of research that is done on perinatal events.

When she becomes a mother, a woman is assailed by two sets of cultural assumptions: what she is/should be as a female (as opposed to male), and what she is/should be as a mother (as opposed to non-mother). Both models stem from the same ideology – patriarchal capitalism, in shorthand – but clash head-on in a series of contradictions. A woman's self-image is inevitably subject to change because of the radical process of pregnancy and birth leaving her exposed to the force of these double-binds within herself: they are enacted on the territory of each woman's body.

Reproduction – menstruation, pregnancy, birth, breast-feeding, menopause – is clearly the most conspicuous way women differ sexually from men, and is an integral part of female sexuality. For many of us it has been hard to accept, to feel, this connection, because we have been struggling *against* individual and cultural histories whose message is that sex should be a part of reproduction, and that certain social roles follow from this. We have had to fight to keep them separate so that we could have sex without becoming childbearers, with the often attendant monogamous property relationship with a man. But we also found that by being 'liberated' we were perceived as sexually available. Women can't win, in a sense, because in the process of rejecting one image, we find ourselves overtaken by its opposite, confronted by an impossible either/or option.

For some women, this dilemma between being sexual (and therefore available) and being a mother (and therefore untouchable) comes out of hiding during pregnancy: 'I felt particularly "safe" being pregnant – safe from being leered at or wolf-whistled at or attacked, and I wanted to be *seen* as being pregnant.' As we know, this safety is hypothetical. 'I wanted sexual contact but my husband saw me as somehow untouchable, the Virgin Mary syndrome. It made me feel quite strange.' The woman who felt safe while pregnant also reveals: 'My husband often jokingly made uncomplimentary comments about the shape and size of my stomach and although I wasn't seriously affected by these, I occasionally saw myself as someone totally *undesirable* sexually.' Our precarious feeling of safety (from men) is awarded to us precisely through becoming undesirable (to men).

What many of us want is to be desirable in our own right, to be let off the hook of continually comparing ourselves to svelte tigresses. We may feel a new and welcome sense of power in the capacity of our bodies, worries about contraception no longer exist, and we may feel healthier than we can remember. Others may feel unsure about our attractiveness, particularly if we feel tired and sick; we want to be reassured. Nausea, fatigue or anxiety may make us feel we just can't be bothered with sex in the usual way, or the risk of rejection by our partner may seem too great. Or we may experience pregnancy as a completion, a self-containment that leaves us wanting little in the way of deep sexual contact. Or it may be a negative experience: a woman may feel the baby inside to be a 'spy'; or that she hasn't sufficient privacy for sex, resulting from socially-induced guilt.

The responsibility for the changes which happen during pregnancy and for any adaptation to them, however, is borne by women – we are supposed to keep ourselves smart and not 'let ourselves go'. According to this mythology, we have to protect men from the reality of something for which they bear equal responsibility. At a deeper level, pregnancy is also a time when our sense of our boundaries can change drastically, for instance, 'inside' and 'outside' take on different significance because of the creature taking up our own physical space. There is for a number of women a sense of disorientation about 'in here' and 'out there'. A foetus is Other, but it is inside, the feeling is of being intimately connected with the Other that is unlike anything else, except perhaps during a particularly intense sexual experience with someone, although that lasts only a matter of minutes rather than nine months. And the baby has a life of its own, moves, grows, without any volition on the part of the pregnant woman. This can be both pleasant and distinctly weird. The woman no longer has a separate, knowable identity. She is both herself and more than herself, other than herself. She is never alone. Medical thinking distorts this dislocation by viewing the foetus as an internal parasite, feeding off the woman's body, subjecting her to 'abnormal' stresses and strains; hence pregnancy becomes treatable, its symptoms likely to be pathological.

Our sense of 'I' is increasingly modified and our emotions appropriately reflect this uncertainty. We behave in ways we do not recognise from our previous experience or image of ourselves. This is often labelled as 'instability' or 'emotionality' of the individual woman. We may become unaccountably weepy, or find ourselves suddenly identifying with news items about children or mothers we've never heard of; we may feel isolated ('I'm the one with the baby inside, no matter how close I was to my partner beforehand'); we may feel ecstatic, or desperate, or bottomlessly exhausted. Women who have had a sense of self-containment and self-knowledge before pregnancy can often be shocked at dependency needs asserting themselves. They may try even harder to cope without revealing what they really feel.

Women may feel all this in terms of a change in the power-relationship with their partners; wanting to be looked after is one way of getting something back. The ostensible justification for being taken care of is often not to redress the balance, not to get something for oneself to counteract a loss of control or greater vulnerability, but for the baby: women often cannot see themselves alone as special or as deserving good things. 'It was a fulfilment of my role. I expected to be pampered by my husband, and I took care of myself for the sake of my baby.' 'I liked the attention and feeling special. I wanted to be looked after – it was part of getting the nurture I wanted and had not had as a child.'

Feelings of powerlessness may actually be enhanced – the bargain has its unwanted side because we find ourselves in the familiar double-bind (as also with menstruation, post-natally or in menopause) of wanting our new physical and psychic state to be recognised but feeling uneasy about the notion of people making allowances for us, that is, acknowledging us on their terms instead of our own.

## II

A central preoccupation for most of us during pregnancy are the visits to the ante-natal clinic. Among the many destructive effects of the medicalisation of childbirth, two have a direct bearing on a woman's sexual identity. The first, which also has implications for becoming a parent, is the downgrading of her general abilities and sense of autonomy through the process of infantilisation by others. This reinforces, in specific ways, the loss of control we may feel, especially if at the same time we give up a job. Women puzzle over the fact that they are treated like children at exactly the time they have supposedly become truly adult, truly female. It is as if the baby inside us represents the mythical child within us; in order for us consciously to get nourishment for the 'child', as well as for ourselves as adults, we need to retain the choice of when, by whom and in what context. Instead, we are invaded by others' inappropriately parental ('fatherly') notions of what is best for us, by virtue of the foetus.

The second attack is sexual assault. The (male) doctor's total access to a woman's breasts, vagina and womb as she lies semi-naked looks suspiciously like a sexual power-game. Yet both the sexuality and the assault are denied: to admit one would be to admit the other. We are forced to deny it, too, by dissociating ourselves to a degree from what is really happening and by rationalising it in terms of medical practice. In effect, an unspoken contract has been enacted – we accept medical care from a position of weakness, thereby giving up the right not only to decide what will happen but even to *define* what is happening. Our physical and mental boundaries do not belong to us. Women doctors, for more complex reasons (to do with sexism in the profession, for one) can assert power of superior knowledge and detachment over us.[2]

The social imbalance of power between men as a group and women as a group means that the individual woman is already pre-programmed, as it were, to put her body at the disposal of a potential coloniser; various sanctions can be brought to bear if she does not 'co-operate'. These usually work by devaluing her as an individual and blackmailing her about the 'safety' of the baby. Her only defence, as an individual, is to walk out on her colonised body, to become alienated from her sexuality, by 'letting him get on with it'.

Women approaching the birth of a child are consequently having to handle many varieties of the double-bind syndrome in ways which feel disturbing and render us the more passive in relation to their real source.

## III

The birth itself is an epitome of de-sexualisation and infantilisation for many women. Making love and giving birth ideally and intrinsically have much in common, but the link between sexuality and birth has been completely broken down – it is obvious at once that making love in the sort of conditions we are customarily expected to give birth in would be a quite perverse and alienating act. I do not propose to detail the barrage of technological intervention and the bizarre attendant practices women undergo in hospital, and the kinds of blackmail and other sanctions used to enforce them. Others have done this adequately elsewhere, and others too have speculated about the ideological origins of these interventions.[3]

The point is not that we expect to have orgasms while giving birth (though some women do): most of us are too preoccupied with pain, the pace of delivery, anxiety over the baby, to be anything but taken up in the overwhelming process of our bodies. In giving birth we need to participate as we would sexually: to open up, let go, make a noise or be attentive and quiet. Being taken over by strangers and machines is diametrically opposed to this. 'Relaxation' or alternatively strenuous willed exertion (a performance model with a team of exhorting or critical outsiders) robs a woman of autonomy and intimacy simultaneously.

94

Much is subsequently laid on women about the quality of their labour and delivery – as much by some of the people seeking to change hospital procedures as by professional practitioners. Childbirth has become over the last decade an 'issue', and the campaigns of organisations like AIMS, ARMS and Birth Centres have challenged conventional practice and theory. But there is a danger of focusing exclusive attention on an event without looking at the reasons why its associated circumstances, including social and personal relationships, are contentious in the first place. Thus some of the alternative birth culture still manages to suggest that difficult labours and births result from individual sexual problems (or lack of centredness, unity with the ground of one's being, etc.). Undoubtedly we *can* do a great deal of help ourselves, but we should not have to pay the price of guilt for 'failure'. That guru of birth, Frédéric Leboyer, has an astonishingly misogynistic attitude coupled with a stress on psychic individualism; and alternative cultures generally which, while they certainly reclaim aspects of our experience, do not contain a political dimension, are susceptible to just this kind of scapegoating.

So, many of us bring from the birth a garbage bag of guilt and sense of inadequacy. Though some women feel that they come into their own with motherhood – the capacity of our bodies to bear and nurture a new human being is a source of genuine strength – it is very hard to disentangle the positive qualities from the web of associations spun by social and economic facts which elevate and restrict our strength into a static role. We have a location, our lives have a publicly acknowledged meaning. The rub is that it becomes the sole meaning and a falsified one. For most women, it means that role segregation within our lives is crystallised: there is less opportunity for sharing different kinds of work, domestic and waged, and more domestic work to do. This structure brings with it, whatever the conscious intentions of the partners, an increased imbalance in power and freedom. Domestic work and childcare are certainly unvalued by society economically, whatever ideological lip-service is paid to housewives and mothers.[4] Partners may increase our sense of devaluation by their personal contempt for our work and by their expectations that we should look after them after a hard day's work; or simply by the fact that men enjoy a higher personal standard of living than women.

*IV*

It is in this kind of context that sexuality must be looked at: the women's liberation movement has shown us that imbalance of power in the kitchen, in the workplace and at the pub cannot be shed with our clothes when we get into bed. In direct contrast, established assumptions in research about sex after childbirth strengthen our disadvantages:

> All but one of the couples had resumed sexual intercourse by the fourth interview [six months postpartum]. . . . Half the mothers reported some problem or difficulty with sex since the interview [seven weeks postpartum] in 27 of the 39 cases, the problem or difficulty was still continuing at the time of the interview.[5]

> After delivery, about one-third [of 119 primiparous women, i.e. first-time mothers] of subjects had resumed intercourse by six weeks and nearly everyone had done so by three months. Nevertheless, 77% of the women were having intercourse less often at three months postnatally in comparison with the month before they become pregnant. A few subjects described very marked and persistent reductions in sexuality and overall at a year postnatally about a fifth of the sample were having intercourse less than once a week . . . Factors such as nausea and vomiting during pregnancy, the mode of delivery and related obstetric and medical variables, breast-feeding, characteristics of the baby, did not appear significantly to influence maternal sexuality.[6]

To spell out these assumptions: that sexuality is synonymous with intercourse, as distinct from other kinds of interaction (oral sex, mutual masturbation, or more diffuse, goal-less forms of physical expression); that a woman's sexuality is bound up with her partner's activity, rather than being something for herself and by herself; that her partner's (always assumed to be a man) attitudes and actions are irrelevant, scientifically neutral, but that breast-feeding and so on can be explicitly designated as variables. Neither are these assumptions confined to academic studies.

Here are some comments from the women I spoke with about their sexuality after birth:

> 'Having intercourse was having something done to me.'
> 'Sex just seems a total invasion of my privacy. . . . I just want to continue intact. . . . My main physical bond is with my daughter – my breasts are for feeding her and not to be caressed by my husband. . . . I get enough feedback from my children and I don't

feel the need to be sexually fulfilled, or to give sexual fulfilment to my husband.'

'Although I often didn't want to make love with my husband, I used to fantasise and masturbate in private.'

'I just let him get on with it.'

'I had intercourse because I wanted the closeness.'

'I felt sexual very soon after the birth; I felt guilty about that.'

The reasons for our different responses, and the connections between them and the assumptions surrounding sexuality, are complex and subtle, interwoven with physical, personal and economic shifts, as well as changes in our relationships. A woman's sex life is but one of these and at the same time often the channel through which reactions to them are expressed: our feelings of fatigue, resentment, fear, depression and anger are inadmissible and unaccountable in the face of expectations of joy and fulfilment. 'I withdrew when we made love, as a defence. I was actually quite angry and distressed.'

## V

One of the major principles at work – and one which plays a negative role in our adjustment to change – is 'getting back to normal'. There is no getting back to normal. Even an early miscarriage or abortion changes us, and as mothers we should be asking how *we* can get back to normal when our circumstances have changed profoundly and forever. Moreover, the normality we're supposed to be getting back to is itself, as we know, very disturbing, presenting us with offers we can't refuse.

The effect of being pushed into an option we do not want is to compel us towards the opposite pole (or we may oscillate between unsatisfactory options in a crisis of self-doubt). We may retreat into our motherhood and there are sufficient ostensible justifications for doing so: the stereotype permits it, and the fatigue and lack of time that baby and housecare bring have provided many women with the get-out they need from the unpleasantness of competing (and possibly losing) in the sexual market-place. Or else, in fear of being submerged by one female role (the earth mother) we struggle back into our size 10 Levis, congratulate ourselves on having no stretch marks and set out to prove that we 'fancy it like hell' at the earliest opportunity. This mild parody discloses that there is no real choice about our self-image, and this lack of choice contributes to the dialectic between self-image and the responses we get from other people (mainly our partners).

Unravelling the interaction of self with society more closely in the context of responsibility without power, we must take into account once again the tendency for women to carry the emotional aspects of a relationship, as I have already touched on. It is our task to make it 'work', sexually as in other ways; and, of course, women with young children have all the more vested interest in keeping a partnership going. Women become the channels for the more disturbing, uncontrollable aspects of human experience, particularly sexuality; by a sleight of hand, a double susceptibility (ours and others') is fused into an individual neurosis: 'I thought I was frigid – I'd heard of frigidity, and thought that's what I was.'

Women are given the responsibility for dealing not only with our own emotions but also those of our partners:

> But remember: a man's adjustment to his lover becoming a mother is one of the hardest and most mysterious he has to make. It's more likely that he will be the one who, through utmost delicacy, will hold off. Call him back.[7]

Part of the way this responsibility is perceived is to do with satisfying a man sexually: the component notions are that men need sexual satisfaction *per se* in a way that women do not, and that part of caring for a man is to provide it, to be a vessel.

> About five weeks after the birth, my husband, who by this time must have been crawling up the wall himself – although he was very sympathetic and kind – and I started to make love. I thought, Whoopee, back to normal, at last, and then he very gently thrust his penis inside me. The pain was dreadful, but how could I complain, he was so gentle and loving but nonetheless it was agony. I tried to relax and he climaxed. He was kissing me when he noticed that there were tears streaming down my face. He realised why and we then talked about the pain I was still feeling.

It was not this woman's pleasure that was the priority – she notes earlier: 'Even just stroking my clitoris was painful.'

Other men make their assumptions more blatantly:

> The one thing that really put me off sex . . . is my husband's comment after we last made love – many moons ago now! He

98

complained that my vagina and womb felt absolutely enormous and that he could feel little stimulation or satisfaction just a great, gaping void! He didn't mean to reduce me to feeling completely inadequate, but he succeeded.

These comments are the underside of the casual preconceptions about penetrative sex being the norm.

Women very often find themselves carrying men in other ways, extending their new mothering role beyond the baby: 'I ended up, after the baby was born, being *his* big strong mother.' This kind of dynamic does not come from nowhere – sexual partners frequently have unconscious expectations of mutual parenting, even though a woman is not just looking for a father-substitute or a man for a girl just like Mother, at a conscious level. We want our partners to be something for us, this is why sexual relationships are so powerful. We set up mutual and unspoken rules which, if transgressed, make us feel betrayed. Women's responsibility for the emotional aspects is one of these rules. After a child is born, a combination of factors may force the game into the open with disastrous results. The woman is likely to feel sufficiently preoccupied with being a real mother without giving of herself to another adult in this role:

> J. said he felt hurt I didn't behave like a lover or make him feel like a lover. It's true . . . I have only a little left after being a mother – and I want it for myself.

Sexual demands from the man can easily be perceived as another task of mothering; and because of the guilt associated with trying to be a perfect mother, as well as the fact of our dependence (real and projected) on our partners, we tend not to see these demands for quite what they are. Fulfilling them becomes, for either or both people, a test of whether we 'really' care, or even of how competent we are in our role.

Men's problems concerning sexuality clearly bear on us when they are our partners or our obstetricians. Ambivalent feelings towards women and their own sexual nature will be projected through relationships which have a sexual element, including that of doctor and patient. These projections, in the context of inequality, cannot easily be thrown back where they belong. I do not want to take the space to deal at great length with male sexuality, but it is relevant that men may express extremes of hostility and affection through the medium of sexual interaction, and also communicate emotional needs this way. They are far from being merely reactors to the changes in our lives, as conventional thinking would have it, but it can be hard to get them to explore their feelings or express much that is helpful.

So a man may unconsciously both step up his demands to be sexually mothered as proof of his continuing status in the woman's life, and withdraw his parenting of her as an unspoken punishment. Communicating affection through sex may directly conflict with the woman's need to be mothered herself, in a non-sexual way. For other men, sex with a mother may border dangerously on sex with Mother and they withdraw inexplicably from sex after a baby is born. Women know we have protected male egos as well as our own vested interests and insecurities in being reluctant to discuss sex.

One of the grave disadvantages for women in handling this mesh of projections is that it divides us. We may label or feel defensive towards other women, trying to rationalise away the sexual threat they represent. Without exploring more fully issues of 'fidelity', it seems to me that jealousy and resentment are probably quite rational responses to role loss – the question of whether we freely want to continue playing this role, given its consequences, is an entirely different sort of question from whether we should be 'liberated' in a male-favouring framework. It is ultimately unhelpful, emotionally and ideologically, for us to be led into blaming or belittling other women, especially when women friends are likely to be the people to whom we most want to turn after the baby is born.

Confrontation with changes in role and self-image necessarily involves our physical health and material conditions as well. They are both causes and effects. Only a politically reactionary view could divorce housing and money, for instance (two of the most clear-cut ways in which society maintains inequalities) from how we cope and how we feel as individuals. Difficulties over money will be exacerbated by a sudden dependence on one income (usually the man's), which in itself encourages power-games within a relationship by limiting mutual independence and decision-making.

As for health, this is crucial to our confidence and sense of autonomy. Some women find that giving birth opens the way for a spate of active well-being; others are 'open' to ailments during the first susceptible weeks – thrush, cystitis, prolonged bleeding, mastitis, lack of sleep, are among the so-called minor problems which may make us feel very low. Many women have to deal with the after effects of episiotomy (cutting the perineum to enlarge the vagina during delivery).[8] Even when performed satisfactorily according to medical

100

norms, the operation may leave women feeling assaulted – it is the only operation which can be performed without the patient's consent or against her wishes – and unsure of their sexual desirability and sensation. Even worse, there are some women whose genitals are scarred for life by medical incompetence, and for whom pain or discomfort have as good as ruined their sex lives. They frequently have to deal with denials from doctors that there is anything wrong physically. The only remedy may be private and costly plastic surgery.

Fatigue, the relentlessness of broken sleep, also steals up on new mothers and may either mask or intensify these health problems. Clearly, the more emphasis is put on penetrative, goal-directed sex, the more a tired or ill woman is going to feel she is just not up to it, and she gets caught in a circle of withdrawal and anxiety on her part and demands (real or felt) from the man.

Post-natal depression is often cited as the cause of unhappiness, lethargy, lack of self-confidence and sexual interest. It is often seen as an illness to which some women are especially prone on account of hormonal changes during and after delivery, in the same way that pre-menstrual tension and menopausal symptoms are endowed with a hormonal basis. I find this problematical: 'post-natal depression' has been magicked into an identifiable entity, a label to package up the bundle of wholly defensible reasons why many women feel low after birth; often the concept is used as a form of social control. To state that hormones are a cause of post-natal depression seems to beg the question of mind/body dualism. Furthermore, all the other factors involved in becoming socially, as well as biologically, a mother cannot be reduced to a hormonal basis without severely limiting our political understanding and possibility of challenging them. Thirdly, and most importantly, an extension of the hypothesis leads to the conclusion that to be female is to be predisposed to be ill: the classic ideology of male as norm. For women to treat their bad feelings as purely hormonal is a self-defeating strategy[9]: we are left, as usual, to take the consequences of unequal power, in its overt or subtle manifestations, in our female hormones, our private lives.

The feelings we experience underline the problem of normality for women; birth is a huge physical and psychic process whose meaning is not publicly visible. We carry that significance as individuals, because the public meaning is a false one, and it falsifies our experience *to us*. Caring for a new baby means that we need support and love, too, and a recognition of our rawness and openness. Again, our material circumstances – money, housing, friends – are integral to how we feel.[10]

Physical problems may be temporary and right themselves with specific treatment; or they may be disguises for issues which require more far-reaching intervention. Life with a new baby makes it harder to make the distinction; it is as easy to blame problems on 'the system', ill-health or other people as to internalise them all.

## VI

Broadly speaking, there seem to be two distinct sexual strategies amongst women for dealing with the situations we find ourselves in: some of us react by needing sex, others by withdrawing from it, or we do different things at different times.

When the birth experience has been a bad one, it can produce feelings of loss and inadequacy, for instance, if the woman did not actively give birth. The subsequent craving to feel okay, to be filled up, may come out as a desire for sexual intimacy, deep contact on the same primal level as the hurt. Even if the birth was good, the birth of the baby may be felt also as the death of the pregnancy, so-called placental loss:

> Some months after my second child's birth, I had indescribably deep feelings when fucking. Orgasm only intensified them. I wanted to be filled up again – though not through the 'rational' process of conceiving. The man's penis seemed to put me in touch with my womb and I wanted to be immersed in those sensations forever, to be healed of something I didn't even know was hurting.

More generally, the anxieties ensuing from changes in role we may try to assuage through sex, as if it were a commodity that of itself can make us feel good.

We also genuinely want closeness, the feeling of being important in ourselves, confirmation that we are still sexually alive, and so on. Society is structured in such a way that it is difficult to get, and to perceive ourselves as able to get these things, except through a sexual relationship. The double-bind is that sexual relationships are more often than not ambiguous for us, and if we do get the things we want, they come with strings:

> 'I wanted to be accepted for what I was – a fat slob. I also wanted to be conventionally desirable. I got caught up in the whole thing of "making an effort" without at all wanting to.'
> 'I very seldom felt the urge . . . to make myself look good (for

whom?). Even if my husband tells me I'm looking "good" I just see that as a lead up to him wanting to have sex with me rather than as a compliment to me as a person.'

Some women effect a virtual substitution of babies for man; the sensual closeness they get from their children is satisfying and uncomplicated by comparison. Women who breast-feed often feel good about their bodies, but find difficulty in relating this to what breasts symbolise in sexist imagery. And the same goes presumably for vaginas. The closeness is most often mentioned in connection with breast-feeding and naturally diminishes as a prime source of sustenance for the woman as the child grows older, more independent. The bond that exists between a woman and her newborn baby is a primal, sexual one. (We cannot discount the similarity between the nipple/mouth and penis/vagina images in relation to women's and men's responses to breast-feeding.) As fast as it can, society transmutes that bond – a threatening one in patriarchal terms – into a social unit, the family. Required registration of birth (or the christening ceremony), legitimacy laws, social security regulations are some of the ways in which the woman and baby are normalised into society on its conditions. The post-natal examination is another marker on the route: it acts as a seal of approval on a woman's resumption of sexual activity, that is, it gives her permission to be penetrated. It is a medical/secular equivalent of religious purification rituals, where female sexuality has in effect been made public property in order to outlaw its dangerous aspects.

Most of the women I spoke to reacted by going through at least a phase of maternal sensuality as *opposed* to sexual feelings for their partners. they themselves made that distinction.

Replacement of husband by baby sometimes reflects a segregated and hierarchical family arrangement – the woman more readily identifies with her children than with her husband; the traditional female sub-culture provides her with a way of making sense of this arrangement. It implies that men are a different species, with different if not incomprehensible needs. While this can give a woman a sense of power in the emotional/domestic realm by ratifying her role as mother to the man, and allay any guilt about not identifying her needs and interests with his, it also keeps her in an objectively subordinate position where his interests are still the determining ones. Her sexual expression, for instance, if not identified with and measured by his, tends to be non-existent. His rights go unchallenged in real life.

Even when this traditional view is unacceptable to the woman (in notionally equal or open relationships), contracts between partners creep in by the back door. The result is suppressed anger and disappointment. Sex has an exchange value, it ceases to exist in a romantic void:

> 'The whole area of bed was contentious even before we'd get in; all the arguments we had were about who was going to get up to see to the crying kid.'

> 'Intercourse was payment to him for helping with the baby – I thought "If you won't get up and feed the baby, why should I give you my body?"'

> 'I closed my mind and let him get on with it. It was the usual tits and cunt preliminary, then fucking. It wasn't worth the hassle of refusing – I was tired, I knew the baby would be waking soon, and I didn't want a two-hour row about it all. Sometimes I'd turn away and pretend to be asleep, then soon there'd be this erect penis prodding me in the small of my back.'

> 'It was my duty, as a dutiful wife, not to say no. With other men I was desirable, as I thought, for myself. For my husband, it was what I was there for.'

> 'If I let go and showed him I felt turned on, it gave him more power to use me.'

> 'I ended up deciding I was going to use him for sex in the same way he used me – I'd get my pleasure without intimacy. I hated myself most of the time.'

Undoubtedly if such contracts were spelt out, many women and men would not countenance them; but they come to be made in this unacknowledged manner because relationships and sexuality are mediated through the social and political superstructure, not solely, or mainly, through personal intention. Contracts like these could not exist were women not made to bear isolated responsibility for childcare; if men's economic advantages did not give them personal power; and so on.

Alternative means of making family relationships and expressing ourselves sexually without involuntary contractual obligations are not immediately available to us precisely because they have revolutionary implications. We have put too much emphasis, it seems to me, on changing the way we feel sexually to fit into the structure and not enough on changing the structures that engender those feelings. The consciousness of being victims is only a preliminary one.[11]

# 7

# Is a Feminist Heterosexuality Possible?

## Angela Hamblin

> In trying to establish more autonomy and self-determination in
> my sexual relationships with men – I have to constantly fight
> against my own internalised controls – as well as confronting the
> cultural assumptions of the man and his resistance to change . . .
> it's surprising I have any sex life at all.
>
> Woman answering questionnaire

Feminists in heterosexual relationships have to grapple
with male definitions, male assumptions and male power in one of the
most intimate areas of our lives, involving some of our deepest
feelings, at times when we often feel at our most vulnerable. It is not
an easy task. Yet over the past decade an increasing number of
feminist women have been involved in transforming the basis upon
which we are prepared to share our sexuality with men. It has been,
for the most part, a very private struggle which, despite the support
which many individual women have given each other, has not as yet
been validated by the women's liberation movement as a whole. As
Anna Coote and Beatrix Campbell have commented,[1] perhaps it has
seemed too difficult 'to sustain a political and personal critique of
heterosexuality alongside a political and personal commitment to it.'
But the net result has been that, as heterosexual feminists, we have
found ourselves isolated – without a collective analysis or strategy –
thrown back into defining our relationships with men as belonging to
the 'personal' sphere of our lives, cut off from our 'political' concerns.

The dilemma which so many of us face is that we find ourselves
presented with a choice between two alternatives, neither of which is
acceptable. The first, a hangover from the 'sexual revolution' attitudes
of the 1960s, accepts a male-defined heterosexuality uncritically. It
ignores the crucial question of male power within heterosexual rela-

tionships and sees 'liberation' for women as liberation-from-the-fear-of-unwanted-pregnancy and from our so-called 'sexual hang-ups'. It sees the provision of contraception and abortion as the primary answer to women's problems. It never questions the assumption that sexual intercourse is or should be the primary goal for both partners, or that many younger women are being increasingly pressured into sexual intercourse (and consequently harmful forms of contraception or the risk of pregnancy) at an ever earlier age. It never even addresses the issue of an autonomous female sexuality, or why it is impossible for women to explore or express it within a traditional heterosexual framework. Instead, it accepts male power and control as 'givens' and attempts to get a better deal for women within this male-defined context.

The second alternative, springing from a feminist analysis, rightly rejects this view pointing out that all it has achieved is to make us more sexually available to men without giving us anything in return or even attempting to address the real underlying causes of our oppression. This view identifies *male power* as the central problem within heterosexual relationships and sees the oppression of women as an inevitable outcome. Consequently, the solution is seen by some women within the women's liberation movement to lie in total withdrawal by women from heterosexual relationships, thereby withdrawing female energy from men and undermining the institution of heterosexuality.

For women who are committed to both feminism and their own heterosexuality neither of these solutions is adequate or appropriate. The first denies our feminism, by insisting that we accept a male-defined sexuality, and evades the fundamental issue of male power. The second denies our heterosexuality by asserting that male power and control within heterosexual relationships are permanent and unassailable, thereby precluding the possibility that feminist women may establish a sexual practice between women and men which is not oppressive. What both these alternatives have in common is that neither allows for the possibility of change. The first accepts the *status quo* of male power as a 'given' around which it hopes to accommodate women. The second, whilst recognising the centrality of male power within heterosexual relationships, sees it as static and unchangeable. If heterosexual feminists are to find a viable way out of this dilemma we have to create a third alternative; one which not only confronts the issue of male power but at the same time is committed to challenging and changing it. Two of the questions we need to ask ourselves are: How does male power function in heterosexual relationships? and

106

How can we confront and challenge it in our own sexual relationships with individual men?

To find out how other heterosexual feminists have been tackling these issues in their own lives I drew up a questionnaire which was sent out to over 200 readers of *Spare Rib*.[2] The 61 questions asked women to describe their feelings and experiences around the areas of early experiences of sexuality and learning about sex; issues of power; penetration; pressure; force; pornography; fantasies; conflict; changes; what they want from a sexual relationship; what they want from men; celibacy; pleasure; orgasm; masturbation; self-image; cultural influences; sex with others; sexual environment; sexuality and sensuality; sexuality and friendship.

Eighty-four women completed the questionnaire. Many reported that answering it had been a valuable, if exhausting experience and some had found that it helped to clarify and bring together many hitherto disparate areas of their lives. The sheer volume (most women said it took between four and six hours to complete) and quality (the level of honesty and preparedness to dig deeper was quite remarkable) of the information sent in has been invaluable to me and has provided the basis of much of what follows in this chapter.

## How male power functions in heterosexual relationships

> The more you understand the fewer concessions you will make.
> (Redstockings)[3]

When we begin to explicitly 'name' and analyse how male power functions in our sexual relationships with men we begin to see a number of things more clearly. First, we become aware of a profound alienation from our own authentic female sexuality/sensuality, that is, a sexuality/sensuality which genuinely springs from and expresses our own female nature and desire and is not a response to any form of outside pressure, whether it be fear of losing a man, or a home, or financial security, or pressure to conform to some (male-created) stereotype of the 'liberated' woman, or fear of being labelled frigid, or the threat of, or actual experience of, male violence, or any other form of pressure which cuts us off from our own inner selves and forces us to behave in ways which are destructive and alien to us.

Secondly, we discover the means by which the development of our own authentic sexuality is crushed. (This is not to say that women cannot develop their own authentic sexuality but that in seeking to do so they will find themselves struggling against, and in total opposition to, the dominant culture.) Many women who answered the questionnaire described how they had never been allowed the space in which to explore or develop their own autonomous sexuality because, from the outset, a male definition of sexuality had been imposed upon them, predetermining how they were supposed to feel and behave, how males were supposed to feel and behave towards them, and what 'sex' was supposed to be. To describe this process, through which a male-defined sexuality is imposed upon us, I shall use the term 'the heterosexual ritual'.


## The heterosexual ritual

The heterosexual ritual, as we shall see, operates on a continuum which begins with male definitions of what constitutes 'normal' sex, leads on to the creation of specific sexual expectations upon which men act, results in both crude and subtle sexual pressure being brought to bear upon women, and ultimately legitimates the use of male force (violence) against women. All this takes place within a context of material inequality in which the majority of women are forced into economic dependence upon men.

Within the terms of the heterosexual ritual only penetration followed by penile thrusting and ejaculation is defined as 'real' or 'normal' sex, which at once asserts the primacy of the penis, renders the sexual pleasure of the woman irrelevant, and limits heterosexual practice to a series of repetitive acts which maximise the possibilities of pregnancy. It creates a male sexuality in which heterosexual men learn to seek their sexual pleasure, almost exclusively, from 'fucking' at the expense of all other forms of sensual/sexual bodily awareness, exploration or expression. It teaches men to experience this 'desire-to-fuck' as central to their male identity and leads them to believe that they have a 'right' to use women's bodies for this purpose.

This definition of what constitutes 'real' or 'normal' sex creates the expectations from which actual sexual behaviour follows. For instance, if the primary goal of 'real' or 'normal' sex is defined as heterosexual intercourse then the man assumes and expects:

That the appropriate way for him to express his sexuality is 'to fuck', and that all other forms of sexual expression are only preliminaries to 'fucking'.

That he has a 'right' to have sexual intercourse.

That he is not a 'real' man unless he has had/is having (regular)

sexual intercourse with a woman.
That fucking is what all women really want.

If the male sex drive is claimed to be, and defined as being, stronger than the female's and directed almost exclusively towards hetero-sexual intercourse, then the man assumes and expects:

That he has a right to women's bodies.
That it is 'natural' for him to put pressure on women to have sexual intercourse with him.
That if his 'desire-to-fuck' is thwarted it is legitimate and under-standable for him to use force to achieve his goal.

These are the assumptions and expectations which men bring to a sexual situation with a woman and upon which they *act*. This is not to say that all men act in precisely the same way but that the assumptions and expectations they have internalised from a patriarchal culture will be the same.

For women these definitions and expectations are imposed upon us in three ways – first, by constant reinforcement by the culture, secondly, by the actual sexual behaviour of men towards us, and thirdly, by our own internalisation of these beliefs. For instance, when women internalise the belief that the primary goal of 'real' or 'normal' sex between ourselves and a man is sexual intercourse we can come to believe:

That in sexual relationships with men sexual intercourse is inevitable.
That other forms of sensuality/sexuality which may give us more pleasure are not 'real' sex.
That if we express affection/sensuality it will be interpreted by the man as indicating our willingness to have sexual intercourse.
That we should expect to gain sexual satisfaction from sexual intercourse and if we don't we have a problem.

When women internalise the belief that the man has a stronger sex drive than us and that he needs to have this satisfied through sexual intercourse we can come to believe:

That we have an obligation to meet his sexual demands/needs.
That our own sexuality/needs are less important.
That it is 'natural' for him to initiate and control what happens

sexually between us.

That, especially in long-term relationships, we have a duty to satisfy the man's sexual needs by providing him with regular sex.

That it is our responsibility not to let things go 'too far' if we don't intend to have sexual intercourse.

That if we submit to sexual intercourse through pressure or fear, this is not rape.

That if we are forced into sexual intercourse against our will we are somehow to blame.

In reading through the answers to the questionnaire it was clear to see how this continuum – definitions→expectations→pressure→force – functions in our everyday sexual relationships with men.

### Definitions lead to expectations

Most women who answered the questionnaire reported that although they gained some information about sex from their parents or from reading books, by far the most pervasive influence came from school friends and the pressures of peer-group conformity. By the ages of thirteen to fifteen few girls were left in any doubt that 'sex' with a boy was an inevitability, and that 'sex' meant sexual intercourse.

If sexual exploration did not lead to sexual intercourse it was redefined as not 'real' sex. For instance, one woman described in great detail the sexual enjoyment she used to get from non-penetrative forms of sexuality saying 'that way I found out what made me feel good and that I could enjoy myself, but [she added] it would never go as far as *actual* sex.'

All of the women who answered the questionnaire reported their first experience of sexual intercourse to have occurred between the ages of thirteen and twenty-three years.

'I was seventeen. My boyfriend persuaded me to go upstairs at a party. It was all over very quickly and I got no satisfaction – I wasn't even that willing.'

'Boring! I'd had an orgasm with the same boy by manual stimulation and presumed that penetration would be even better! I kept thinking that it was amazing that I could have a baby by doing such a mundane thing.'

'It wasn't fantastic. I think the basic sensation was that it had been done, at last.'

Although these quotes describe the experience of the majority of the women who replied to the questionnaire, this was not universal.

'I was twenty-one. It was nice. We had all the time in the world. We took several nights over it (gentle semi-penetration). I had several orgasms before he had his first. Great.'

But whether we were part of the minority who had a good first experience, or part of the majority who didn't, penetrative sex had been firmly extablished as the norm. I asked women how they felt about penetration.

'When I was younger, I and my female friends considered that penetration was the definition of sex – until you have been penetrated by a man you hadn't "made it". All the men I've had relationships with have expected it – any sexual encounter was considered by them to lead ultimately to penetration and if it didn't they made it clear that they weren't satisfied. To me, penetration is only one aspect of sex – there are many others, all equally, if not more, fulfilling for the woman *and* the man.'

'Where at one time it was the be-all and end-all – I now cringe dealing with phallic tampons.'

'I like it. It gives me a marvellous feeling of being filled up psychically as well as physically. Just why I should need and like this feeling of being "filled" I'm not at all sure about!'

'Some men penetrate too soon. Some guys once inside me go on and on till it becomes painful. But I feel I must persevere. Why should I?'

The feeling of needing to persevere with it seemed to reflect an internalisation of the belief that sexual intercourse was what 'real' sex was all about, and that within it we would find our own sexual satisfaction. But frequently the internalised belief and the actual reality were in conflict.

'Often I want penetration but when it happens derive no pleasure from it.'

'In most cases it's wanted by the man far sooner than the woman; if she ever wants it. Sometimes it totally removes that feeling of desire in me – like a bucket of cold water.'

'Penetration is important. It's something I physically need even though I may have an orgasm through oral sex or manual stimulation. I still have a deep aching sensation that only penetration can satisfy. However, often men are too forceful or thrust too hard or deep and it's not at all enjoyable and I feel like a battering ram or just a vessel for the guy's sexual relief.'

'In the past it has happened that I have accepted it when I didn't want it, then felt invaded.'

So accepted does the idea become that sexual intercourse is what is expected from sex that there are times when both partners may engage in it without either of them really wanting to.

Especially at the beginning of our relationship I found it difficult to say 'No' when I didn't want things, although apparently my partner, though frustrated, would have accepted it. In fact, I got several urinary infections and sometimes used them to say 'No'. It appeared later that it had happened that neither of us wanted intercourse, but both went ahead because each believed the other did.

Another woman described herself as non-orgasmic until she was forty at which age she began to have orgasms through sexual intercourse: 'I now enjoy sex enormously.' But the same woman, when asked in another question to describe how and when she learnt to masturbate, answered 'as a teenager – I figured it out for myself.' This woman had been giving herself orgasms for most of her life but, like the rest of us, she had been taught to invalidate her own experience and define herself as non-orgasmic since her orgasms did not come through sexual intercourse with a man.

*Expectations – which lead to pressure and force*

We have seen how the definition of what constitutes 'real' or 'normal' sex not only creates the expectations from which actual sexual behaviour follows but also defines the terms in which we perceive and interpret our experiences. When men incorporate these definitions and build up expectations based upon them they believe they have a 'right' to sexual intercourse and a 'right' to women's bodies. It is from a basis of an unquestioning belief in their 'sexual rights' that men *act* sexually towards us.

He could come in late after being out alone all evening and expect me to be ready and willing without any prior communication. The

112

pressure was brought to bear by the view that he was 'normal' and I 'abnormal' and lacking in sexual enjoyment if, with a regular and close partner, I couldn't respond at all times. For me it was a vicious circle and I came to resent all sex with him simply because he expected it or thought he had a right to my body.

Feeling they have a right to expect sexual intercourse from women, men also feel they have a right to apply pressure to get it.

He had a nasty habit of creeping up behind me when I was half asleep and tired and he knew I had lots to do the next day. He would winge on for hours, so I'd give in, valuing my sleep. It did annoy me, but I couldn't get to sleep with all the whining so I often let him when I really didn't want to.

The sexual pressure which men bring to bear on us takes many forms.

I've felt pressured into sex – by persuasion, by arguments, by insults and by force. I had a fairly long relationship with a man who refused to have sex on any terms but his own which meant that I was constantly pressurised into sexual intercourse. Most of the time I resisted and was insulted by him for doing so. He gave me no space for developing my own sexuality in my own time but expected me to perform on his terms. It made me do a lot of thinking – was I really being unfair/unreasonable/unnatural, as he was always telling me?

Men, who feel they have a right to women's bodies, are constantly telling women who resist them that they are 'unnatural'. These men also believe that the woman has an obligation to satisfy their 'greater sexual needs'.

There were times when the man either claimed he hadn't had 'it' for weeks and I could give him something he desperately needed or he came out with the line 'All normal women want it' or 'Well, you're liberated aren't you?'

The image of the 'liberated woman' is used by men to pressure women into male-defined sex. It is not used as a positive image of a woman who asserts and expresses her own autonomous self-defined sexuality. Although it seems that men are very eager to have sex with

113

women, it is a kind of sexuality in which the man remains firmly in control at all times. Most men are extremely reluctant to relinquish control in heterosexual relationships and allow the woman the space and opportunity she needs to express (or even discover) her own sexuality. Some women had accepted the definition of the male's greater sexuality to such an extent that they felt it was 'natural' that the man should initiate and control what happens. Others had tried to break this pattern only to find themselves rejected.

> Several years ago I did actually take a more aggressive role in initiating sexual contacts but early on was rejected. I don't think the guys involved were at all happy about the role reversal.

Like the spectre of the 'liberated woman' the idea of 'initiating sex' has also been used by some men to pressure women into sexual interourse.

> My partner has complained because I leave him to initiate things too much. Sometimes I don't initiate because I fear that it will just make him want penetration too fast for me.

But one woman described what had happened when she had begun to initiate sexual contact two years earlier.

> I started being the initiator and now find it very easy. The advantages are that it gets off the usual sex-stereotyped path right from the beginning and sexist men get so disorientated, they either back off or become very willing to change at least some aspects of their behaviour.

Sexual pressure may come directly from the man or he may simply have to tune in to the definitions and expectations we have internalised.

> 'I couldn't bear to hurt him.'
> 'I've felt pressured by his frustration, even if he was willing to accept a "No".'
> 'It was usually an unspoken feeling that I'd let him get to the stage where he'd feel let down if I then said "No".'

The role of pornography in influencing the ways in which men perceive and act sexually towards women was also clear. Pornography supplies men with a steady diet of pictures and stories in which

114

women are used, degraded and discarded. When asked if they had ever been sexually exploited/abused in a relationship with a man, a number of women described occasions when they had been coerced (often by husbands) into dressing up and/or posing for photographs, engaging in humiliating and sometimes painful acts, and made to feel guilty or inadequate if they protested. Generally, there was considerable pressure upon women to accept pornography. One woman described her feelings about the abundance of pornography in the men's houses at university.

> I felt angry and was made to feel something of a freak because everyone [men] seemed to say it was "right-on" and I knew it was foul. There was a lot of pressure on me to keep quiet because women who complained about porn were dismissed as prudes, or screwed up about sex and their own bodies or just plain jealous.

Many men also apply economic pressure to obtain sex in situations where the woman is materially dependent upon them, either in the long term such as marriage, or in the short term such as being his employee/student/tenant and being dependent upon him for continued employment/academic success/housing. One woman described an experience in which her male boss had, over a period of time, compromised her by giving her small and then larger presents. He then insisted that she take a skiing holiday with him. When she refused he reminded her of all the gifts he had given her. She felt obligated and that she had no choice but to go with him 'So I went. I just laid and cried while he fucked me.'

The line between pressure and force becomes very thin to a man who feels he is perfectly 'normal' and is, after all, only exercising his sexual rights.

> He came home drunk, very late, got into bed and let me know what he wanted, whereas I'd been asleep and just wasn't interested. He went on and on until eventually I suggested I sleep in the lounge. I got up to do so and he pounced on me and beat me up. I ended up laid in the bed with him, him holding me down and finally falling asleep on top of me.

When we are forced by men into sex against our will it is a violation of our whole being.

> I felt sick. It was disgusting. He used me like an animal. I felt

115

disgusted with myself for trusting him in the first place.

And because we have been told over and over that men have stronger sex drives which they are unable to control, and that it is our responsibility as women to make sure that 'things don't go too far' we can easily blame ourselves when men sexually abuse us.

My feelings were strongly fear, together with a total helplessness, but also I was scared of my own stupidity for getting into the situation at all.

## Challenging male power in sexual relationships with individual men

> I claim that rape exists any time sexual intercourse occurs when it has not been initiated by the woman, out of her own genuine affection and desire.
>
> (Robin Morgan)[4]

When we confront male power in our sexual relationships with individual men we are up against not only the values of an entire patriarchal culture plus the expectations, pressure, (actual or implicit) and force of the individual man/men with whom we relate but also our own internalised beliefs and expectations, vulnerabilities and needs. It is a formidable and daunting task.

The very first step we have to take is to overturn the sexual definitions of heterosexuality which we carry around in our heads.

Men have no 'right' to our bodies.
Being sexual/sensual/affectionate with a man does not mean we have agreed to have sexual intercourse with him.
It is a violation of our 'right' to bodily integrity for a man to pressure us (by any means) into sex.
If a man has sexual intercourse with us against our will he has committed rape.
If a man subjects us to any kind of unwanted sexual attention he is guilty of sexual abuse.
We have no obligation whatsoever to meet men's sexual demands/needs.
In long-term relationships (including marriage) we have no duty whatsoever to satisfy the man's sexual needs by providing him with regular sex.

116

It is not 'natural' for the man to initiate, control and determine everything that happens sexually between us.

We will only engage in forms of sensuality/sexuality which enhance our pleasure and do not oppress us.

When we enter a relationship on the basis of these definitions the expectations which we shall then carry with us will be quite different. This is not to say that changing our expectations will by itself change the unequal power relationship. It does not, for instance, change the expectations and behaviour of the man. Neither does it remove the institutional power vested in the male in heterosexual relationships. What it does do is begin to change our consciousness and, within the women's liberation movement, consciousness-raising has always been the first step on the road to political action. But before we can begin to change these definitions we must first start to listen to our own feelings, give them space, respect them and learn how to validate and support each other. Because when we act, or allow men to act towards us in ways which are in conflict with our real feelings we suffer a violation. 'Going along with what the man wanted when my feelings were telling me something else' was reported by many of the women who answered the questionnaire as being the most common area of sexual conflict for them – within the relationship if they refused, and within themelves if they did not. When we allow things to happen which we don't really want, we feel bad inside. If we constantly find ourselves in such situations the consequent bad feelings can systematically eat away at our self-confidence and self-esteem, until eventually we can feel undermined in all areas of our lives.

We must recognise and name what damages us both spiritually and emotionally as well as physically and give ourselves and each other the strength to refuse this kind of oppressive sexuality. But we need to do more than this. We need to create the space and freedom for ourselves and each other to explore and discover what our *real* feelings are and what it is we would really like from our sexual relationships. This is something which as women, within traditional heterosexual relationships, we have never had.

## Exploring what we want

> We will not ask what is 'revolutionary' or 'reformist', only what is good for women. . . . To do that women will have to fight to say honestly what they want and why.

> (Redstockings)[5]

117

When women have the freedom and opportunity to explore and express what we really want from our sexual relationships, the creative sponaneous fun-centred sexuality which we describe is in total contrast to the dull repetitiveness of the heterosexual ritual.

'What do I want? Affection, generosity, respect, excitement, exploration (of bodies, of emotions) the chance to develop, the chance to direct and control what's happening.'

'Fun, friendship, pleasure.'

'Somebody who challenges me, makes me question things in myself, is daring in approach, open and direct.'

'A free-ness in sex – not a wild experimenting, but in ways thought of perhaps as "negative" – i.e. not having sex on occasions, sleeping separately at times. Enjoying sensuous contact. Wanting *me* not "sex", not "a woman", not a relief after a day's tensions – but *me*, to give to me and appreciate my body.'

'Spending a long time making love – slowly and sensuously without a mad dash for orgasm. Cuddling and kissing – feeling close and wanted for myself.'

Good communication and emotional responsiveness were very important aspects of what most women wanted from their sexual relationships, rather than solely the physical release which comes through orgasm. In fact, the quality of the orgasm seemed to depend upon the quality of the love-making which produced it and this was true whether we were making love to ourselves or with a partner. When orgasm was solely a physical response it could be an emotionally impoverished experience.

Sometimes, it can be like my body only responding to stimuli, while emotionally I'm hating it all. Orgasm then is like a flutter, a jerk, with none of the lead-up feelings that can make it so good – and afterwards I feel a kind of desolation.

Women's descriptions of their orgasms, and how often they desired them, were many and varied. A few women felt they needed orgasm several times a week, others much less frequently, and some described themselves as 'erratic' – 'five times in four days and then weeks off'. There seemed to be a connection for most women between their desire for orgasm and their feelings at different points during their menstrual cycle, although this was by no means uniform.

118

How often do I feel I need orgasm? I need it physically about once a month, generally in the week before my period is due. I need it emotionally when I have a desire to be very close to someone I love. But a really close, good, sexual experience, if it's really deep, can last me a long time – sometimes several weeks.

As we create the space to explore and discover our own authentic sexuality we also come to see traditional patriarchal male sexuality ever more starkly and understand the ways in which men sexually oppress us. For many of us this is a time of crisis, a turning-point in our lives, the point at which we must make sexual choices. Faced with this oppressiveness and rediscovering our own spontaneous creative female sexuality, one of the first choices we confront is: Do we really want to go on having sexual, or indeed social, relationships with men at all? For a considerable number of women the answer to this question will be an unequivocal 'No'. Some will choose celibacy, others will maintain social, but not sexual relationships with men. A number will reject all relationships with men. Their lives, their friendships and their love are for women and it is to women alone that they will make any future sexual commitment. During the past decade this has been seen by many as the politically 'correct' choice for women within the women's liberation movement. Heterosexual women have sometimes been viewed as on a 'continuum of consciousness' leading up to this choice and there has been sympathy and support for women coming up to and living through the agonies, the conflict, the losses, the long-term implications of making the choice to give up all contact with men. But there has been less sympathy and support for women who have lived through these same agonies and conflicts and have ultimately made a different choice. Those women who have chosen to maintain their relationships with men and struggle to transform them are often seen as taking the easy way out, selling out on feminism or even as 'collaborators with the enemy'.

When total separation from men is seen as the 'right-on' position for feminists to adopt, those heterosexual feminists who choose to remain in relationships with men can often feel politically isolated and frequently become apologetic or defensive about their position. If we are to get beyond this stage and develop a meaningful and effective politics of change for women within heterosexual relationships we have to create the space we need within the women's liberation movement for open and honest discussion. We need this space first, to recognise and confront the ways in which male power functions in our sexual relationships with men; secondly, to rediscover our own

119

authentic self-defined sexuality; thirdly, to make our own and support each other's choices; and lastly, to give each other the space and respect we need to understand the choices we make and sometimes the contradictions that go with them.

> I frequently feel contradictions, because I hate all men. I hate the way they oppress and sexually abuse us, and when I am deeply in touch with this part of myself I feel distant and alienated from all men, including my lover and my son. This can be very difficult for me (as well as for them) because, at the same time, I also love them.
>
> It sometimes feels to me that this part of me that loves them is the problem – if I could get rid of that and simply cut them out of my life and my heart, my life would be much simpler and less filled with contradiction. Yet, at the same time the part of me that loves them is a very important part of *me*, which I don't want to get rid of.
>
> There are a lot of contradictions but there are also positive things too – the affection, caring and closeness I have with them are also true – and I cannot give that up. I do not know how to resolve this contradiction and I think it's something all heterosexual feminists have to grapple with.

There may be many reasons why women choose to remain in heterosexual relationships and struggle to transform them. We may, for instance, be in a long-term relationship with a man with whom, through long and hard struggles, we have brought about real changes and be reluctant to relinquish the ground we have gained or the pleasures which the relationship now has to offer. We may be involved in wanting to influence our brothers or our sons (who, after all, will become tomorrow's men), our male friends or lovers. We may be committed to our own self-defined sexuality and prepared to fight for our right to have a sexual relationship with a man, if we so choose, which is good for us and does not oppress us.


## Making changes

When we have created and used the space we need to discover what we really want from our sexual relationships, we are then in a position to confront the men we relate to sexually from a position of strength and self-knowledge. Because if we are to transform our sexual relationships with men then the men will have to change. If we are clear in our own minds from the outset about the terms upon which we are prepared to share our sexuality with men then we enter the relationship on a different basis, firm in the knowledge of what we shall accept and what we shall not accept. If we find that some men are 'turned off' by our attitudes then we know that these men are to be avoided.

One of the questions I asked in the questionnaire was: If you could have a sexual relationship with a man 'on your terms' what would your 'terms' be?

'It's difficult to say what my terms are, because I don't think I've ever been given the chance (or given myself the chance) to work them out. "Space" would have a lot to do with it – space to find out what I want/feel good about. To *give* pleasure is also important to me as well as to receive and I'd like eventually to get to a place where it's what we both want/like. But *first _ we have to do things on my* terms because so far every sexual relationship has been on the man's terms until I've got so sick of it I've got out. I don't want absolute control of a relationship the way that men I've known have had – because that would just be a straightforward reversal of roles but I want enough control to be able to dictate what I feel and want. My terms would involve overturning traditional male concepts of sexual intercourse, not accepting things for the sake of it, not continually compromising and giving in because that's what is so often expected from the woman.'

'My terms – complete sharing, no barriers, sensitivity to my needs, *no power-trips*, no games, recognition of me as a person.'

'That sex would only be initiated when we wanted to "give" as opposed to the usual "take".'

'Ahh! My own bed for a start. In fact separate living place, meeting only when we both want to meet. Being able to say "No" to sex or an aspect of sex without being criticised or feeling guilty. Having other friends and/or lovers. Total honesty. Total equality.'

'I want closeness with a man physically, intellectually, and emotionally. A feminist sexuality is being able to satisfy your sexual appetite in the way in which *you* wish and not in the way men think you wish to do.'

Some women described the changes they'd brought about in their sexual relationships with men, but stressed that the man must be

121

motivated to change his sexist behaviour and that even then it is far from easy.

> 'Inequality *can* be changed but only if both people are willing to discuss it again and again; only if they are willing to re-evaluate their own ideas and challenge themselves, only if they are honest with themselves and with each other. It sounds pretty daunting, but I don't think it's in any way impossible, though it may cause a fair bit of pain getting there.'

> 'I have worked very hard on changing the balance of power in my relationship and feel I have things a lot more on my terms. At first he was resistant and I felt very bad but gradually my anger shifted him and he's now very supportive and sometimes surprises me with his level of awareness.'

It seems that most of the changes which have been made in long-term relationships with men have been possible where there exists a commitment to the relationship itself and also a commitment to the whole process of change.

> 'I think firstly he has to be willing and genuinely want to change – without that as a prerequisite nothing is possible. Also many men think they want to change, but deep down they resist all the time. Secondly, it has to be worth the effort of the challenging and confronting you have to do. There has to be sufficient *actual change* to make this worth while – you have to actually *get* something from it for yourself for it to be worth putting the effort into it.'

> 'Yes, I have tried, over the last ten years, to change my sexual relationship. It has not been easy. At times it has been hell. For years I was often in despair. I would not necessarily recommend it to any other woman. For some reason which I don't fully understand I felt driven to do it and this is what kept me going. I think it was a strange perverse kind of determination which refused to accept that I couldn't have what I wanted – in a way that would have meant that he (and men) had won. So I just had to go on battling.'

> 'At first, he reacted by not understanding what I was saying; by becoming celibate for months on end; by becoming self-punitive and self-destructive; by being constantly perplexed and "trying-to-do-it-better".'

122

'Eventually, I did get through to him and I get a great deal of satisfaction out of the warmth, closeness and intimacy which we now share – but this has only been possible through years of building up trust and risking being emotionally open and vulnerable on both sides.

'I would still like more freedom to explore my sexuality, my feelings, my desires. I would like encouragement and understanding of the difficulties, fears, conflicts and contradictions which *I* face, not solely a concentration on what he's doing wrong! Because it makes me vulnerable I find it difficult to ask for this and there is still an assumption that what I want is already known – at least to me – which is not always true.

'Ultimately, I think a rich sexual life comes from a rich emotional life – it has very little to do with sexual "techniques".'

In seeking to wrench our sexual relationships with men out of the crippling and oppressive confines of the heterosexual ritual, and establish instead a new form of sexuality which has our own authentic, creative, self-defined sexuality at its core, *we are actively engaging in the process of creating a feminist heterosexuality.* And in struggling to reclaim, assert and express our own autonomous woman-defined selves we stand united with our lesbian, bi-sexual and celibate sisters. In a truly woman-identified women's liberation movement there must be room for us all.

*Acknowledgement*
I would like to thank all the women who replied to my questionnaire and shared so much of themselves and their lives with me. I was deeply moved by your honesty, your courage and your thoroughness. I would also like to thank all those women who read and commented upon the manuscript during the writing of this chapter.

# 8

# Heterosexual Sex: Power and Desire for the Other

Wendy Hollway

A curious thing has been happening to me with various men lately: they don't want to have a sexual relationship when I do. But men are supposed 'not to be able to get enough of it', so the common assumption goes. The most obvious explanation would be that they're just not attracted to me. Well, they are! It's curious precisely because of the strong mutual attraction. Unfortunately, I don't think it's because these are feminist-influenced, anti-sexist men throwing off their conditioning about sex; and I'd probably think it was my fault if a couple of my friends weren't experiencing the same problem – for reasons that are strikingly similar.

In this chapter, I am going to give an account of the relation between sex and power in heterosexual relationships which explains why men in certain circumstances choose to avoid sex. It has very different implications for a theory of men's power from an 'all hetero-sexual sex is violence' position. It does not deny men's power in heterosexual relationships. But it doesn't deny women's either: it specifies how they differ.

I think it's politically important to theorise sex and power in a different way. So first I'll give my reasons. A friend of mine was talking about the sexuality issue of *Feminist Review* (no.11, 1982). It had sparked off all sorts of new questions and ideas for her. But why, she asked me, does feminism approach sexuality from the point of view of pornography and violence against women? It leaves out such a lot of our experience. This friend is a feminist, but not so familiar with the internal debates of the movement that she takes such positions for granted. It made me hesitate. I explained why I thought that one couldn't make a separation between sex and power. But in a way she was right. There are two issues that this equation of male power and heterosexual sex leaves out. The first is that it leaves uncontested all those subtle forms of men's power which regulate heterosexual relationships. A woman can be oppressed in heterosexual couples

124

even if her partner has never beaten her up, never even demanded sex when she doesn't want it. The second is that it cannot address the experience of women who seek and enjoy heterosexual sex, who are attracted to, and feel in love with, men. These women's experiences cannot be reduced to 'false consciousness' (which doesn't explain anything) nor can it be argued that they want men because they seek and enjoy domination (though some women do). I'll speak for myself: I feel equal in heterosexual sex as long as I feel equal in relationship to that man more generally. I have felt very powerful in heterosexual relationships and that has expressed itself in my sexuality. Moreover, I know that men experience me as powerful (particularly when they are attracted to me): 'too powerful' is often the message I get. But I'll come back to that question.

In summary, there is a whole area of women's experience of men in heterosexual sex which feminist theory and politics has not successfully addressed. It is almost as if the more widespread assumptions about love and sex are so taken for granted that we keep missing the basic and fundamental question: why do some of us feel so strongly about men that our feminist analysis (the oppressiveness of sexual relationships with men and all that) just does not succeed in determining our feelings and practices? And if women like me feel like that after years of struggle, what about other women that we would like feminism to speak to – women more materially dependent on relationships with men than middle-class, employed feminists?

The question of women's desire for men is a huge one. I want to focus on sex because it is such an important definer of all those intense feelings. More particularly, I want to look at why men[1] feel similarly intense, irrational and vulnerable, and what effects it has on their relationships with women. Feminists do a lot of talking and thinking and writing about our gender and sexuality. If we're not careful, it ends up looking as if all this desire and contradiction is part of being a woman. And that can get read back through old sexist assumptions as further 'proof' of how irrational and needy we are: woman as pathology, man as normality. It's perfectly clear to me that it's not like that at all.

What does 'sex' mean that it produces all these strong feelings of desire, jealousy, dependence, dedication and fear? How do these affect the power relations between men and women who are involved with (or potentially attracted to) each other? How is it the same and different for men and women?

The sections of this chapter run as follows: The 'greatest need' (1) indicates the intensity of feeling that is underneath men's sexual

125

attraction to women. In (2), I show how these feelings have been assumed to be a part of women's, not men's, sexuality. By referring to several coexisting sets of assumptions about sexuality, I show how women's and men's sexuality is differentiated in such a way that men's vulnerability is protected by displacing those feelings on to women. In (3) I use the psychoanalytic concept of defence mechanisms to explain this. In (4) I indicate an answer to why men feel so vulnerable by showing the link between men's desire for the mother and the desire for a woman. Men's power can then be seen as something not inherent, but at least in part as a resistance (5). The perception of men as powerful is also promoted by women's desire for the Other and subsequent misrecognition of men as a result of their own vulnerability and also their assumptions about gender difference. In (6) I show how men's desire for the Other/mother is particularly felt in heterosexual sex, and how they thus experience the woman involved as powerful. When in other respects a woman and man occupy equal positions (and where the man cannot compensate in other arenas, as he has been able to do traditionally), the woman may well be experienced as 'too powerful' (7). I conclude by pointing out some of the implications of the argument (8).

## 1. The 'greatest need'

What do men feel like when they are 'attracted' to a woman? Is it just an urge as society would have us believe, located in their anatomy (in their erections, to be precise)? One man I talked to put it as follows. He generalises, but as men are wont to do that to protect themselves I was pretty convinced that he was talking about himself. Besides where else would he have got such knowledge? Certainly not from how men are supposed to feel:

> Martin: 'People's needs for others are systematically *denied* in ordinary relationships. And in a love relationship you make the most *fundamental* admission about yourself – that you want somebody else. It seems to me that that is the *greatest* need. And the need which, in relation to its power, is most strongly hidden and repressed. Once you've opened yourself, once you've shown the other person that you *need* them, then you've made yourself *incredibly* vulnerable.'[2]

Because I knew Martin quite well – indeed, I'd been in the position of being very attracted to him and had experienced him as astonishingly

126

strong, self-sufficient and independent of women – I wanted to find out more about this question of vulnerability.

> Wendy: 'Yes, I agree. But I think there's a question about how much you show yourself to be vulnerable.'
>
> Martin: 'But you *do*, just by showing that you're *soft* on somebody. When you're not *admitting* it and when you're going round looking very self-sufficient. But it seems to me when you've revealed that need, you put yourself in an *incredibly* insecure state. You've shown someone what you're like. Before you've managed by showing them *only* what is *publicly* acceptable. And as soon as you've shown that there is this terrible *hole* in you – that you want somebody else – then you're in this absolute state of insecurity. And you need much *more* than the empirical evidence that somebody likes you, or whatever. You become neurotically worried by the possibility that you're not accepted, now you've let them see a little bit that's you, that it'll be rejected. The insecurity gives someone else power. I don't mean any viable self-exposure, or anything like that. I just mean any little indication that you *like* the other person.'

The intensity with which Martin speaks, the implications of the terms 'love relationship', 'wants', 'incredible vulnerability'; all these suggest that he is talking about a once-in-a-lifetime love. It comes as a surprise, then, when he explains that he's not talking about a 'viable self-exposure' (a wholesale declaration of life-long love perhaps?), but rather 'any little indication that you like the other person'. And this liking is bound up with attraction: he also refers to it as 'showing you're soft on somebody'.

For me, this example – and it is by no means unique – raises two questions: First, why are the feelings – the wants and needs resulting from being attracted to someone else (in Martin's case, it was to women) – so strong, so non-rational? In other words, where do they come from? Secondly what effects do those feelings have on men's relationships with women whom they're attracted to (or have a sexual relationship with)? The following two sections address these questions.

### 2. The sexism in assumptions about difference in women's and men's sexuality

'Sex' does not just mean one thing. In fact the significance of sexual

127

practices is that they stand in for so much which can go unsaid or misrepresented as a result. It's rare for two people to be explicit about what they want and mean when they make love/have sex for the first time. The needs and fantasies expressed through sex make us feel too vulnerable, or too guilty maybe. Yet people assume that 'sex' is simply about bodily pleasure and doesn't *mean* anything else. This comes from the assumption which sees sexual urges as natural and direct, unmediated by social meanings. Although more recently in western culture the idea of sex as a biological urge has been applied to women's sexuality too, it is still more characteristic of views of men's sexuality (Bland and Hollway, in press)[3]. So the meanings of 'sex' are different for women and men. For example, the curious phenomenon that I described at the beginning of this chapter – men refusing sex with women where there was a mutual attraction – would not have seemed so curious in the case of a woman. Men are assumed to want sex anywhere for its own sake. One man friend of mine summed up his sexuality in such terms: 'I want to fuck. I *need* to fuck. I've *always* needed and wanted to fuck. From my teenage years, I've always longed after fucking.' It would be unusual to hear a woman say that. Traditional assumptions rather place women as wanting sex within the security of married life and motherhood. For contemporary feminists it is not as clear-cut as that, but for some it's still very much about relationships:

> Dot: 'The one time I did fuck with Charles, it felt really *good*, like there was an awful lot that was important going on. But I didn't have an orgasm . . . I had lots of highs . . . maybe the tension between us was too great, or something. I don't know, but I was very *turned on*. When I think about that, I get a kind of quiver which is not about how successful it was sexually – if you can separate out these things. It was . . . it was the idea of fucking with *him*, rather than with someone else. If I'm caught off my guard thinking about it, the image I get makes me physically shudder with excitement. . . It grabs me at an *uncontrolled* level. That reinforces my hunch that it's the *idea* – that it's what's invested in the *idea*. I was in love with him. It's not fucking itself, it's something to do with the rights it gave me to see myself as having a relationship with him. I didn't have any of course.'

Despite the teachings of a permissive era that sex without a relationship was fine because women could be into sexual pleasure too, Dot's

128

sexual responses, even at the level of her physical arousal, were a product of 'being in love'. What sex meant in that case was that it gave her 'rights to a relationship'. She reflects the obsolescence of this assumption in her final comment 'I didn't have any of course'.

Despite this recognition, and her participation in 'permissive' sex while growing up, her feelings and fantasies about wanting a relationship were still aroused by having sex. Men often see women's involvement through the same lens. One man described it in the following way:

> Jim: 'I remember I had a strong thing for many years that you shouldn't actually sleep with someone unless you were actually in love with them in some way. And if you did it to someone you weren't in love with it was somehow pretty horrid and pretty nasty. One reason was feeling that sex was kind of dangerous. If you had sex, it meant that you were committed in some way and I didn't want that. Also that it said something – if you *just* had sex without a relationship it was letting them down because you somehow thought that they'd expect a relationship and it was a pretty shitty thing to do to have one part of it without the other. I still feel that to some extent – that somehow it was cheapening sex. It was very prissy – that this thing was so beautiful that you couldn't actually spread it around too much.'

Despite feeling that it is 'prissy' (and indeed it is not consistent with men's claims about sex), Jim feels that the beauty of sex had to do with it being in a relationship. He's not explicit about it, but it's fairly obvious that many men (and most likely Jim) do desperately want and need relationships with women. Yet despite sideways references to his own experience of the specialness of sex within a relationship, he implies that it's *women* who want the relationship; that it's because of *women's* needs that he didn't indulge in sex without a relationship; it was *women* who wanted commitment. Why did he not want commitment? His explanation below situates the sexual relationship where it belongs for him – in the realm of 'strong emotions'. However, there too his account avoids his own strong feelings by projecting them on to the woman:

> Jim: 'I was frightened of strong emotions, that's basically it. Because I remember, again a person at school, the tremendous

relief when I ended the relationship, of not actually having to carry that – of not actually having to be responsible for those things.'

Wendy: 'And was it that the girls wanted to be more intimate?'

Jim: 'Yeah – that really frightened me, because I was frightened of making that kind of commitment, that kind of involvement, I thought I'd be let down, because of what happened the first time, when I was so unreserved about how I felt. I think that really affected my life incredibly, that first time when I fell in love.'

Wendy: 'Why was having a relationship with this girl such a burden?'

Jim: 'She was very strong and very emotional – that's pejorative – but I mean she had strong reactions, so that I didn't actually feel safe that I wasn't going to be knocked out, or sucked in, by her.'

'Responsibility' turns into 'commitment' and 'commitment' turns into 'involvement'. Her involvement turns out to be his involvement. His fear of involvement is linked to the first sexual relationship he'd had, before he'd learned any defences against the strength of his feelings towards women he fell in love with/made love with. With a woman who was strong and emotional the fear was greatest, because he could not be sure of his defences, his own ego boundaries. During a different conversation, Jim used the same term 'sucked in' to refer to the pleasure, intensity and danger he felt when he made love with the woman he was in a relationship with at that time. 'Sex' is capable of meaning the same things for men as it does for women: intense feelings of involvement and need, the danger to one's separate identity; wanting to have somebody for ever and fearing that they will let you down.

However, gender makes a difference to the recognition of what 'sex' means. Men can represent themselves according to a set of assumptions in which they are not in need of a relationship – in fact, not in need of anything that would make them vulnerable. After all, according to the idea that male sexuality is a 'natural drive', men are only in need of sex and they can, supposedly, get it anywhere.

'Permissive' sexuality gave new legitimacy to men's wish to have uncommitted sex with women without feeling irresponsible. In the following extract, Sam illustrates the points that I have made above – the same slippage and projection, the fear of feeling strongly. His principle that it is all right not to feel any responsibility is legitimated

130

by permissiveness. It is motivated by his fears of his own 'sentimentality':

> Sam: 'I'll tell you something – I don't know what it means, but I'll say it anyway. When I say to somebody, who I'm making love to, I'm close to, when I say "I love you, I love you", it's a word that symbolises letting go. The night before Carol went away, she was saying it, and then I started saying it to her, when we were making love and um, what frightens me in that word, is . . . it's an act of commitment. Somebody suddenly *expects* something of me. They've said something that's somehow . . . the first word in a long rotten line towards marriage. That when you fall in *love* you're caught up in the institution. And it's been an act of principle for me, that I can *love* somebody and feel *loved*, without feeling any responsibility. That I can be free to say that I love somebody if I love them. Be free to feel. I can feel it quite unpredictably. It can hit me quite unexpectedly. And I think I worry about it because I can be quite sentimental.'

To the extent that this is possible in practice, Sam can eat his cake *and* have it, so to speak. His feelings, which can hit him unexpectedly, particularly when making love, are worrying. So his wish to say 'I love you', gets projected onto her declaration, where it can be comfortably located as somebody *else* expecting something of *him*. Of course, he still wants to feel loved – isn't that the crux of the matter? – but with no strings attached.

I have referred to three different assumptions concerning sexuality in the course of commenting on the meaning in the accounts that I have used. These are (i) that men's sexuality is a natural drive with any woman as its object; (ii) that women want sex within a relationship and men can get caught in commitment; (iii) (characteristic of 1960s' 'permissiveness'), both women and men just want physical pleasure from sex and neither wants a relationship.

The point that I want to emphasise is that women and men occupy different positions in these 'discourses'.[4] In the first case men are subjects, the possessors of biological urges whose 'natural' object is women. In contrast, women are subjects of the second. According to this, they are subjects of the wants and needs for relationships, rather than one-off sexual encounters. Men experience themselves as objects of this wanting and fear being 'hooked' when they sleep with women. According to 'permissive' ideas, in principle women and men are equally subjects; that is, the assumptions are 'gender blind', they

131

are supposedly subject to the same sexual urges and wishes not to commit themselves. In the previous analyses, I have shown how men position women as wanting commitment rather than position themselves there.

## 3. Defence mechanisms

Gender difference thus means that women and men experience their sexuality differently. I have shown, in the case of Jim, why he was motivated to take up this position. He was enabled to defend himself against his own strong emotions by displacing them on to the woman. This is best understood through a psychoanalytic perspective.

According to Freud, material is repressed through defence mechanisms. These do not operate only within a person, but between people. The clearest example of a relational defence mechanism is projection: the feelings which a person is uncomfortable with, and therefore cannot recognise in her/himself, are projected onto another. Jim is motivated to suppress his strong emotions and sees the woman as being the one who feels strongly, wants commitment, and so on. This makes sense of his fear of involvement (which is actually to do with getting too involved) in terms of her needs. He is thus purged of his own – they have been externalised.

However, a psychoanalytic account does not draw the implications about the power differences which result from these dynamics.[5] Gender difference means that women are suitable vehicles for men's projections: they have already been constructed in such a way that they manifest the characteristics that men are suppressing. Likewise they experience themelves as wanting commitment and materially are more likely to be in the position of needing it, because this is how they have been positioned historically. Thus women's and men's positions are complementary, in the sense that these gender differences make it likely that both men and women will see men as wanting uncommitted sex and women needing committed relationships. The way that gender produces different identities leads to a collusion between women and men which makes change in these areas difficult. None the less, the effect is consistently oppressive to women: it reproduces a power difference where men are supposedly free of needs and invulnerable. Women are left carrying this for both. No wonder we sometimes feel powerless! Despite collusion, the resultant contradictions have created a significant space for change.

If men's sexuality were wholly accountable through these gender positions (subject of natural drives, object of women's wishes for commitment), why would they ever stay with women, need women, feel strong emotions, and feel lost and desperate when women leave them? The answer is that 'sex' does mean more than natural urges for men too, but their subject position in that discourse offers them the possibility of repressing their strong needs of women. They take up this position unconsciously, as the slippage from one meaning to another in Jim's account illustrated. As psychoanalytic theory would insist, the slippage of meanings, the inconsistencies and illogicalities, are not arbitrary; they are motivated. As Martin's account illustrates, they are motivated by the extreme vulnerability which is the consequence of needing a woman that much – a consequence which is not eradicated when the feelings are projected onto her.

## 4. Desire for the Other is desire for the mother

We want to feel loved. Sex is just about the only practice permitted to adults where wishes for comfort, support, loving can be expressed. Lacan summed up the origin in each person's history of this desire in his phrase 'desire for the Other is desire for the mother.' It may sound a little far-fetched. In the following extract, Jim's account of what he wants from a relationship with a woman makes the same point in a way which is recognisable to most of us:

> Wendy: 'What was it that you wanted out of your relationship with Jeanette?'
>
> Jim: 'Well I think support, actually. Knowing that there was somebody who was going to be on my side. That I could talk about things that were affecting me and they would automatically be important to her. And that she would be able to give me strength in that way. Very classic. Like my parents' relationship in a way. But it was me who set the agenda, set the whole thing up. I remember her saying – well I was into classical music, so Jeanette pretended she was until she got confident enough. She wouldn't actually challenge me. There's a gaze of uncritical, totally accepting love that I find really attractive. "I'll love you for ever whatever" is a really powerful gaze. And that's a mother's gaze.'
>
> Wendy: 'Is that how your mother relates to you?'
>
> Jim: 'Absolutely. Whatever I do, she'll support me, she has supported me. It's quite incredible. And that makes my relationship with her very easy.'
>
> Wendy: 'And did you get that from your father?'

Jim: 'No, that was very different. Well, I always felt he loved me, definitely. But he was much more – well he got annoyed with me when I didn't do it right.'

There is no reason to suppose that this 'desire for the mother' is not the historical origin of desire for the Other in both men and women. However, according to Freudian theory, the passages of boys' and girls' entry into culture and to gender create a difference not only in the object of that desire but in the intensity of that desire. Girls supposedly transfer their desire onto the father, and in doing so displace their desire for the mother, who none the less remains the primary giver of love and caring. Boys repress their desire for the mother but do not normally displace it from one gender to the other,[6] it is usually relocated with full force in the first sexual relationship that a boy has.[7] As Jim's comments illustrate, sex is the most powerful expression of this desire – the site where men want and need most and therefore feel most vulnerable. It is not arbitrary that Jim uses the same term – 'sucked in' – to refer to his relation to women's emotionality and his feelings while making love with the woman he loved. Men 'enter' women when they make love. There is a metaphorical slippage between the womb of the mother (the ultimate in protection and security and the antithesis of separation) and the vagina, wherein they can feel engulfed in the love of the Other/mother. Women's vaginas thus can be dangerous places – dangerous because men's identity depends on separation from the mother; a maintenance of fragile ego boundaries which are most vulnerable, as Martin testified, when 'attraction' to a woman heralds desire for the Other/mother.

## 5. Men's power as resistance to women's power as the mother/Other

The links of meaning between the mother and the woman with whom a man has sex (or is attracted to) is significant only in so far as it has political effects. It is a mixed blessing to understand that women do in fact have power over men. One of the puzzling things about feminists' analyses is that they stress men's power and women's lack of power as if they were immutable principles. I am astonished when my mother, in her matter-of-fact, apolitical way, talks about men in terms which leave me in no doubt that she feels more powerful, competent and in control than they are. Why is it so elusive to many of the women I know? In this section, I want to suggest some answers to this question. First, men's strategies of resistance to the vulnerability they feel through 'needing' a woman are precisely ways of exercising power: a

134

power conferred on them by the positions available to men through the system of gender difference. Secondly, women misrecognise men and women because we too are subject to (sexist) assumptions in which men are produced as 'strong' and women as 'weak'.

Martin's comment in the first extract I used indicates that his way of coping with his extreme vulnerability to women he is attracted to is to put on a front in which he is strong and self-sufficient. Yet because he feels so vulnerable, he cannot believe it doesn't show ('but you do show yourself to be vulnerable, just by showing that you're soft on somebody'). As a result, he cannot see himself as others see him. However strong he appears to women, he experiences himself as dreadfully vulnerable. The meanings attached to his identity are inextricable from his desire for the Other. It is ironical that Martin is one of those men who is systematically misrecognised by women as the ideal in dependability, strength, resourcefulness and so on! Women see the façade and do not see what it is covering up, particularly if they are attracted to him. How does this misrecognition come about? In the following extract, Clare gives a graphic description of her misrecognition of Phil, the man she lived with for many years:

> Clare: 'That guy! I didn't even know he was so dependent on me – I had no idea, not a clue.'
>
> Wendy: 'That's so often the way men play it. But it's also often the way women *read* it.'
>
> Clare: 'Oh, exactly. It's two-way. His behaviour was very stereotypical, really. He was very . . . I thought he was a *competent* person, but he didn't think he was at all. He was outwardly confident – domineering – which actually made me feel incredibly oppressed.'
>
> Wendy: 'How long did it take you to realise that?'
>
> Clare: 'Oh a long time. I didn't realise he was dependent on me till I left him – literally, I had *no idea*. And when I look back on it, I realised that I *should* have known. I realised that the signs were there, and I hadn't read them. I felt him as – dominant, and domineering and confident. And he felt *lacking* in confidence. The very signs that I took to signify confidence were actually exactly the signs of his *lack* of confidence – like talking too much, being opinionated . . . and things that I couldn't *bear*. And when I read it back as lack of confidence, I could see. But when I was in a situation, reading it as confidence, I could never get that. Quite a lot of things changed in our relationship. When I first met him, he had a degree and he encouraged me

135

> . . . but I got far higher qualifications than he did. So that also
> made him feel unconfident. And I hadn't realised that either.
> We did things like – both applying for Open University teach-
> ing. I got it, he didn't. It didn't occur to *me* it was a problem. Of
> course it was a problem for him.'

Phil's displays are equivalent to Martin's 'public acceptability'. True,
masculinity is meant to involve being confident, dominating, self-
sufficient (all the signs that Clare systematically misreads).

What is interesting is that Clare knew in retrospect that she had
misrecognised Phil. However, she goes on to say that she falls into
exactly the same patterns with her present man. Learning about men
is not a process of rational acquisition of experience. She
misrecognises the men she is attracted to (just like men misrecognise
those women whom they desire). For both, recognition of their own
power disappears at the advent of desire.

> Clare: 'Why is it, then, that I can't get hold of that knowledge
> about Ken? Why can't I see it? – because I can't. I still don't feel
> as if I know it – I don't, not in my gut. It's very silly. It's
> obviously that I don't want to see it. But I am extremely
> powerful, when I stand back and think about it, I know that. I
> know where my power lies. If I were somebody else, I could see
> it. But I have great resistance to recognising it in myself.'

Desire produces misrecognition. Through the sense of vulnerability that it inspires, the other is seen as relatively strong. The
fantasy is that he/she can fulfil those needs which, though so long
repressed, go back to the infant–mother relationship. The sense of
vulnerability may not itself be a sign of misrecognition of oneself, but
in the way that it floods other feelings about oneself, and evidence of
realistic capabilities, it creates a distortion. However, the *content* of
these misrecognitions depends on gender. The way that vulnerability
is a product of desire for the Other may well be the same for women
and men, but the positions that can be taken up in order to resist the
Other's power must be different because of gender. It is for this
reason that men's and women's power in sexual relationships cannot
be said to be equivalent. It is not a question of 'equal but different'.

Women's power as the Other/mother in sexual and couple relationships is politically contradictory because it motivates men's resistance. Men's experience of women's power is not equivalent to
women exercising it. Ironically, it is a power that women do not

necessarily recognise because of our misrecognition of ourselves and men (although unawares we may use it in the way we 'mother' men in order to keep them needing us).

## 6. *'Frightened of getting in deep'*

Broadly speaking, the sites of men's resistance to women's power are twofold. First, traditionally, men have used the same site – sexuality – to resist the woman of their desire. By having multiple or serial sexual relationships, men dilute the power that they experience one woman having over them.[8] But it's not entirely satisfactory. As Sam said:

> Sam: 'The thing that has caused me the most pain and the most hope is the idea of actually living with Jane, and that's in the context of having tried to live with three other women before. And each time the relationship's been full of possibility. I don't want to live on my own. There's too many *things* all wrapped up in coupling. There's too many needs it potentially meets, and there are too many things it frustrates. I *do* want to have a *close, central-person* relationship, but in the past, the negative aspects outweighed the positive aspects dramatically. Or my inability to work through them has led me to run.'

He then specifies further what led him to run:

> Sam: 'I'm very frightened of getting in *deep* – and then not being able to cope with the demands the relationships's making. You see a lot of these things aren't really to do with sexuality. They're to do with responsibility.'

Whose? Isn't it the same slippage again? From responsibility to commitment to involvement to fear of being let down. Multiple or serial relationships enable men (and women) to avoid facing the fear.

Secondly, in juxtaposition to the private world of the home, which is also the site of women's sexual/mothering practices, men have asserted the superiority of their position in the public world. If they depend on women at home it is not so bad if there is always work to do which comes first, or meetings to go to, or buddies to meet in the pub. The woman's sexual power can be countered through her material dependence, or her emotional dependence, or her incompetence/ unconfidence in the 'real' world. When men are attracted to women who occupy all the same positions in the world as men do, women end

137

up having a 'double power': there is no site of resistance for men, no place where they are uncontestably in power.

## 7. *'Too powerful'*

So let me return to my original question and summarise my conclusions as to why (some) men avoid sex even when they are attracted to a woman. Put simply, the feelings that they are keyed into by having sex in those circumstances makes a man feel extremely vulnerable. I want to emphasise that it's not the 'power' of a woman's sexuality as such. That would be to naturalise it in much the same way as many oppressive cultures do. It would also be to carry over the sexist rationalisations that men have used to claim the power of their own sexual 'drives' or their penises as natural. Rather a woman becomes the 'object' onto which older desires are hooked. The power of women's sexuality is as 'psychic' object not as 'real' object. But in practice the two cannot be separated (until a man has either done some hard work on those feelings, or displaced them into a different object).

*pessimism*

There are an infinite number of strategies whereby men can deal with their vulnerability. I don't want to generalise to 'all men'. Most men don't resist sex: they are too driven by their desire for the Other. Usually, as I have argued above, the power is balanced by all the other arenas in which men can so easily operate. Men's power is as 'real' objects as well as 'psychic' objects for women.

However, when none of the usual inequalities operates to produce a power which counterbalances their vulnerability, they may have to refuse a sexual relationship. The boundary is drawn to exclude sex because it is there that desire is strongest and therefore there where vulnerability and the threat of losing a separate identity is greatest. Emotional involvement is not necessarily banished with sex however. He phones up because he cannot bear to lose contact. He might need me after all. But instead, he asked me if *I'm* all right. Displacement of his needs onto the 'needy' woman convinces him he's fine and it's me who's suffering. He wants to carry on being friends (because I'm the only one 'who really understands'). Another will stand on the doorstep for half an hour (after midnight) saying 'I'm going now', but never quite bringing himself to leave. Another will reach out physically to touch me (before he's censored the spontaneous gesture), then, when I respond, he withdraws.

What is it like to be on the receiving end of these contradictions? Women have often felt that it was our madness, or paranoia, or confusion, or our failure to reach the right standards of feminity. Now at last I recognise those double messages when I receive them straight in the gut. I see it clearly: it is not that he doesn't like me or doesn't want me. But, yes, it is that he will not have a relationship with me. One tells me quite openly that it would be a disaster because he'd need me too much and then I'd go. For another, it was too good. For a third it would change everything and so he's safer with his present part-time relationship.

We must also be scrupulous in recognising how these double messages, power plays, contradictions, fears are used by us in relationships too. Desire for the Other is not only men's bane. However, there are two differences. One is that women have taken on the need to change these harmful practices more seriously than men have, and can often be very honest and courageous about them. The second is that we have never been exonerated from these needs anyway. It is only the sexism of assumptions – the way that established 'truths' about sexuality are gender-differentiated – that have provided a cover for men's actions and feelings.

It is not impossible to change these dynamics. Just because women have a head-start doesn't mean men can avoid them. Some men are strong enough in themselves not to feel engulfed by their desire for the Other/mother. I think what it takes is that every man has to 'separate' from this mother. Most don't. Rather, they displace the desire onto a safe woman 'object'. If he can make it feel that she's needier than him (not so difficult, given patriarchy) he won't even know that he's vulnerable. Well hopefully it won't escape us so easily!

## 8. Conclusions

The main point that comes out of this analysis is to show men's vulnerability. Many of our mothers know it. How often have we heard them say 'All men are little boys. They need mothering.' Such a recognition was obviously not sufficient. However, I think that it's important that feminism reclaim this knowledge. Making political this knowledge gives us a different view of men's displays of self-sufficiency, their resistances, their distancing and rejections, their 'more important' commitments. However, the point of inserting this recognition within a feminist politics is obviously not to do what it did in my mother's generation: to keep women firmly within the domestic sphere where women's power and men's resistance goes to reproduce gender difference and women's oppression.

Changing these dynamics – both men's and our own patterns which pull us into a collusion with them – is not a simple matter of political fiat. Understanding is not synonymous with changing. One man recently, confronted with what amounts to the analysis here, acknowledged that it was very accurate, very perceptive. But it didn't make any difference. He couldn't change his feelings about it just like that: neither the desire nor the resistance motivated by the vulnerability that it produced. Changing desire is not a question of political 'will'. We have to take seriously methods such as consciousness-raising, therapy, and being open to feeling and expressing our contradictory wants and needs. Here I simply want to register that this knowledge is a necessary but not sufficient condition of changing gender difference.

I want to stress that there is a relation between knowledge and power. It is relevant for feminist politics to theorise men's sexuality as well as our own. Most particularly, it is important to understand power in such a way that our own powers become apparent to us and we are not trapped in a discourse which sees power as being solely the property of men – a possession which we can never acquire by virtue of our sex. In this chapter, I have used a notion of power which sees it as being part of all social relations. It is produced not only through differences in material resources, but in the meanings through which we understand our relationships, and in the effects of gender difference in conferring power on men. However, these meanings are multiple and contradictory. By recognising these contradictions, we are not stuck with a political analysis which sees men's power as monolithic and unchangeable and which keeps women in the victim role. Power is productive, and wherever there is power, there is resistance. Heterosexuality is a site of power and of resistance for men and for women. As women we can share and analyse our relations with men in such a way as to challenge the sexist assumptions whose effects I have shown here.

140

# 9

# From Where I Stand: A Case for Feminist Bisexuality

Deborah Gregory

This is a revised version of an article originally written as part of a project on radical implications of women's sexuality. At first the task at hand seemed relatively simple. We talked about our own diverse sexualities, saw what they had in common, where they differed. We tried to distil some essence of female sexuality as it had been constructed and experienced by at least this one group of women of various ages, nationalities, classes, political perspectives, sexual herstories, and so on. We hoped to be able to put forward a notion of a woman-centred sexuality which would unite lesbian, heterosexual and bisexual women, and which would include celibate women, since we all recognised immediately that sexuality is as much about our thoughts and feelings as our overt sexual behaviour.

After several weeks of most interesting discussion, we selected specific topics. I decided to write something about bisexuality and non-monogamy. At least I knew something about my own bisexuality, and about my own experience of rebuilding a relationship from a monogamous, heterosexual marriage into a non-monogamous, bisexual (on my part), living-together-separately.

As I didn't want my contribution to reflect only my own experience, and had no idea how common my experience was amongst other feminists, I constructed a questionnaire which I circulated at the Third London Regional Women's Liberation Conference in 1980. I also introduced a workshop at that conference for bisexual women. I subsequently participated in a workshop on bisexuality at the Haringey Women's Centre. I have discussed the issues extensively (endlessly, compulsively) with nearly every woman I know at all well. In addition to receiving completed questionnaires, I have had letters from a number of women on the subject of their own bisexuality.

Now I find myself in the position of having learned so much I no longer know anything. When women talk about their sexuality, they talk about various social, emotional, physical and spiritual needs, desires and forces which contribute to their identity as a female person. When women describe their sexuality, how it feels, how they feel, how they live out their sexuality, it seems to me they say roughly similar things, regardless of the gender of people they would potentially choose for sexual partners.

They also say very different things. These similarities and differences simply refuse to line themselves up neatly with such categories as lesbian–bisexual–heterosexual. They refuse to align themselves with differences of class, race, or any other instantly recognisable pigeonhole. When you talk about specific sexual practices – such as vaginal penetration, oral stimulation, masturbation, soft all-over caressing of the body, whatever – if you eliminate gender-specific pronouns and references, most of the time you cannot tell whether the speaker identifies as lesbian, bisexual or heterosexual. When women describe their sexual fantasies, fears, desires or joys, those categories simply do not explain the content of the descriptions. They do not designate different kinds of women.

I think of a heterosexual woman as one whose sexuality can be most safely and deeply and fully expressed with a man and not with a woman. I think of a lesbian woman as one whose sexuality can be most safely and deeply and fully expressed with a woman, and not with a man. I think of a bisexual woman as one whose sexuality can be safely and deeply expressed with either a man or a woman, but fully expressed with neither. The sexuality which is expressed – how women behave with their sexual partners, what they think of and how they feel about their sexual behaviour – cannot be defined nor encapsulated by the terms 'lesbian', 'heterosexual' or 'bisexual'. Individual differences within each category far outweighs differences between groups.

We have to go beyond individual experience, if we are to understand that experience. So I start with the one thing I know for certain: the invisibility, hostility, and self-doubt experienced by *all* women who attempt to control their sexual destinies.

## Assumptions

Bisexuality seems to be in disfavour everywhere except in Lonely Hearts columns. The dominant culture views it by the same heterosexist norms which condemn lesbianism as a perversion, and woman-centred heterosexuality as non-existent or grotesque. The women's liberation movement views it as either non-existent (where do I fit into the current 'lesbian–heterosexual split'?); destructive (dabbling in women from the security of heterosexuality); or as frivolous. It seems acceptable only to the sexual liberationists, who see sexual activity solely as an expression of pleasure, sociability, and personal growth, divorced from any boring political analyses, within a general framework of 'more is better'.

There are many more feminists than ever I supposed who identify privately as bisexual. Few of them seem pleased about it. Many feel they are bisexual by default, as they seem to be neither lesbian nor heterosexual. Many fear their feelings for particular male lovers are a contradiction of their emotional and political commitment to women. Some previously heterosexual bisexual feminists would rather be lesbians and see lesbianism as a more desirable sexuality but one from which they are currently excluded by remnants of attachments to particular men, to the dreams and fantasies which haunt them, or by remnants of fears connected with embracing a lesbian existence. Some women who formerly identified as exclusively lesbian now have male lovers, and find their lesbian identity challenged by this experience. However, most women who identify as bisexual are not failed lesbians. Many feminists view their bisexuality not as a transition period to either lesbianism or heterosexuality, but see themselves as having *made* the transition *to* a positive acceptance of their bisexuality.

This is an area in which confusion abounds (I think every woman who answered my questionnaire used the word 'confused' at least twice), so before going any further I would like to make explicit a few of the assumptions which underlie my thinking. There are four.

First, I am assuming that all women suffer from heterosexism. Whatever our sexual orientation, male sexuality is the standard by which we are defined, judged, treated and mistreated. Women of different sexualities (like women of different classes or races) are in different positions with respect to the dominant culture, so we are oppressed differently by men and by patriarchal institutions; but we are certainly all oppressed. *Conventional heterosexuality is not a place of safety for women.*

Secondly, I am assuming that no sexuality is 'natural'. Heterosexuality, bisexuality and lesbianism all tend to be presented as *the* natural sexuality by their supporters. I think this is impossible to demonstrate, given that sexuality is socially constructed. We have learned our sense of ourselves, generally as well as sexually, within a context of enforced heterosexuality and male supremacy, which makes any talk of natural sexuality particularly misleading. Furthermore, appeals to nature generally function as subtle normative statements and should never be trusted.

Thirdly, I am assuming that no sexual activity or practice is political in itself. What is potentially political and radical is the sort of relationships which make these practices both possible and necessary. It is less a question of what is done in bed and with whom, and more a question of the connections between what is done in bed and what is done everywhere else. Large-scale changes in relationships between people can only be realised in a context of changes in the structures and institutions which make relationships of any sort possible.

Fourthly, I am assuming that there is not an irreconcilable contradiction between opposing men as a class and accepting the possibility of close emotional/sexual relationships with some particular man. I assume that feminists hate male political power, social maleness, rather than biological maleness in itself. Many women who are bisexual don't sleep with any men at all nor do they contemplate doing so, but they recognise within themselves – and do not want to reject – the emotional openness to the possibility that they could feel sufficient rapport with some man to want a sexual relationship with him. I assume there is a big difference between 'unlikely' and 'impossible'.

*Identification*

Most women I have talked with make a clear distinction between their sexual activity and their sexuality. For most bisexual women, ticking off the sex of their current and recent sexual partners would not convey the substance of what they mean when they say, 'I am bisexual'. Many lesbian women have had sexual relations with men, and this does not make them identify as bisexual. Many bisexual women have or have had sexual relations with only or mainly women, only or mainly men, or they rarely have sexual relations with anyone. So what meaning, and what importance, does a bisexual identification have for us?

Bisexuality has to do with how we think and feel about ourselves in relation to other women and to men. In order to flesh out what this means, I need to talk about a 'lesbian component' and a 'heterosexual component', and then I hope to be able to talk about the bisexual whole which is constructed from these fragments. (I am using 'lesbian' and 'heterosexual' loosely to mean 'in relation to other women' and 'in relation to men'. Talking about components sounds disgustingly like hi-fi adverts, I know; alternatives gratefully accepted.)

Bisexual women share with lesbians the joy of identifying with the femaleness of our woman lovers and, by extension, with women generally. There is both pleasure and relief in the feeling, 'I know you. I sense what you want, I sense what you feel, because you are like me, I feel those things, too.' Acceptance and love of your own body is connected to acceptance and love of other women's bodies. Love-making with another woman is, according to many bisexual women, simpler than with men, more harmonious, more sensuous, more relaxed. There are longer periods of arousal when sensuality and sexuality flow into each other; there are generally fewer anxieties about the acceptability of one's body, performance, sexual–emotional needs, or about whether your lover will give you an orgasm. There is a feeling of continuity with other areas of our lives, the sense that we are still within the world of feminism when we are in bed with another woman.

Of course, not all women have such ideal sexual relationships with other women. Relationships with other women can be disastrous, both emotionally and sexually, in spite of sharing lesbian separatist, radical feminist or other politics. To idealise lesbian-feminist relationships is to make them invisible and unliveable. What in the final analysis makes a woman identify as lesbian, or identify with her lesbian component, must surely be a sexual-emotional-spiritual desire for contact with specific other women, not merely a sense of shared oppression. Generally, the experience of loving other women sexually has made bisexual women feel more attached to women emotionally, more attuned to women, more secure in their identification with other women. Most women who answered my questionnaire related their lesbianism to their feelings of solidarity with all women.

However much bisexual women feel gladdened and nourished by their sexual attachment to women and their sexual identification with women in general, they do not feel complete in that lesbian identification. Our sexuality – the emotional field surrounding our sexual identification – encompasses a heterosexual component. This may be directed toward a particular man (perhaps a long-standing partner). We have a certain relationship which makes sense in our life, and which we value. We see ourselves as attracted to a particular person, and the fact that he is male is not sufficient to make us discontinue the relationship. This is something which we share with many heterosexual feminists.

145

Many bisexual women who do not have a long-standing relationship with a man still have sexual relationships with men. Some of these women have previously spent many years in exclusively lesbian relationships and are as surprised as anyone else to discover themselves in relationships with men. Unfavourable responses range from simple incomprehension to enraged accusations of betrayal. Why do women who do not identify as heterosexual choose to have sexual relations with men?

First of all, many women say they do not particularly look for a man. Most of us feel closed and hostile to most men most of the time. It is not maleness itself which attracts us, nor do we seek something from men that we find lacking in women. Often we look for the same emotional and sexual qualities, the same spiritual and physical qualities, in men as in women. And the truth of our experience is that sometimes we do find those qualities in a man. We do not ignore the fact that the bearer of these qualities is a man: not our own awareness, nor the ways even the most androgynous man behaves, nor the ways in which the world is structured would ever let us do that, *nor do we want to*. Simply, we would rather confront the difficulties than avoid them. We do not experience all dealings with men as servicing them and draining ourselves at our sisters' expense. We would experience more draining of psychic energy by cutting off from our own possibilities than we do from accepting them and working from there.

A number of women say they find it easier to assert themselves with male lovers, without feeling guilty about being too dominating. We tend to have high, perhaps unrealistic, standards of feminist equality in our relationships with women, and often find it hard to come to terms with ways we need to assert ourselves in sexual relationships. We have developed a firm political basis from which to do battle with men; we feel entitled to assert our own reality, our own interests over theirs. Between women, the dimensions of power and control are often more ambiguous; this is sometimes overwhelmingly threatening. Many women have had to fight so hard to be a person that the thought of surrendering any crumb of our hard-won autonomy to someone else is devastating. It is often easier to hang on to our identity and autonomy with a man, who is clearly different from us, and whom we know we can fight, than with a woman who is so similar, so close.

*Making love*

What is it like to make love with a man when one also makes love with women? What is similar, what is different? The answers are various.

Some women generally prefer sex with women but do like to sleep with the man or men they are close to. Many women replying to the questionnaire said they prefer casual sex with men – that is, relationships which are more friendly than romantic, and fairly circumscribed in time and place – rather than deep involvements. Many said it feels wrong to have sex with women outside the context of a deep, loving, committed relationship. Others say they find sex with women more comforting and sensuous, sex with men more erotic.

Many women, perhaps the majority, feel they are still in the first stages of exploring their sexuality, with both women and men. As one woman wrote, 'I hate the idea that everyone is either gay or straight. I don't want to have to make a choice. I don't want to *define* my sexuality, I want to *explore* it.'

Most women found it hard to put into words specifically what it is they do with lovers – men or women – and responded to questions with general statements. Some said they do entirely different things in bed with women and with men, and connected this with being sexually 'aggressive' or 'passive'. Some worried about being 'too aggressive/domineering' with other women, 'too submissive/passive' with men, or just the reverse. Others say they do pretty much the same things with men or women, kissing, stroking, licking, sucking, reaching orgasms from clitoral stimulation provided by fingers, mouths, genitals, accompanied or not by vaginal penetration.

Many women find penetration by a penis oppressive and humiliating, and refuse to do it. Most said that they find it irrelevant or obstructive to their orgasms. Other women do like it, but less for their sexual satisfaction than for a feeling of closeness and oneness with their partner. Some women like penetration with male partners, but with women never think to miss a penis. Some mentioned a dislike of semen or a dislike of available contraception as reasons for preferring sex with women.

I have found it difficult – initially, nearly impossible – to make love with a man the way I wanted to, as I knew it was important to me that the man would be as vulnerable to me as I was to him. He had to be able to receive my caresses, to let me make love to him as I would to another woman. I would only feel close to a man who could accept that sex was about me expressing my sexuality as much as about him expressing his, and that my sexuality did not consist in my responsiveness to him. Had I not found any man equal to that challenge, I would today identify as a lesbian.

I think a lot of the erotic interest of male lovers has to do with the challenge they pose in terms of their total difference from us, the gap between their perceptions and ours. (This may also be true at times with other women.) We find the sorts of confrontations we have with men stimulating and energising. Much of what goes into a bisexual woman's heterosexual component is a need to express aggression, to challenge, to overcome the limits imposed by the partner's reality, a need to express the passion of ferocity. There is no logical reason we couldn't do those things with a woman. I cannot offer an explanation for why we tend not to look to women for combat. My guess is that it has something to do with our earlier experience of achieving individuality in struggle against male dominance and our later experience of achieving individuality through positive bonding with other women. I want to correct the impression I may have given above that lovemaking between women is all gentle, easy-flowing sensuality; while lovemaking with men is all about the taming of Tarzan by Jane. Lovemaking between women, however, is full of challenge and the interplay of distinct, sometimes conflicting egos. It is not all sweetness and light, because women do not generally want all sweetness and light. Nor do all men want to bang away at a warm, wet hole. Within the women's liberation movement we tend to emphasise the brutishness of typical phallocentric sexuality and the sensitivity of lesbian sexuality because those aspects of reality are seldom discussed anywhere else.

Nearly all the women in the discussions and in their responses to the questionnaire said that sexual experience with other women made them feel better about themselves as women, as sexually potent people. Many women experienced orgasm with a sexual partner for the first time with another woman. They also experienced a loving, more thoroughly honest connection with a sexual partner for the first time. They felt more confirmed in their positive feelings for women. Even women whose sexual relationships with specific women were disappointing and unsatisfying feel attached and committed to the lesbian component of their sexual identity. Women whose background was previously lesbian also say that their decision to confront men sexually in their personal lives, or their decision to validate their sexual feelings for a particular man, has not changed their basic perception of themselves as woman-identified women.

Rather than feeling tied to a male-defined identification because they accept their heterosexual component, bisexual women say they feel more than ever woman-identified. We know we are not operating from a position of fearful rigidity, or from the sort of dependence which had formerly pushed some of us into intransigent separatist positions which felt politically correct but emotionally all wrong. (I am not claiming this is a characteristic of separatist positions, only that some women say this was characteristic of their own separatism.) Women say they became 'less prepared to put up with men's lack of sensual sensitivity, less interested in tolerating the game-playing, need for mothering, power-tripping', and found they did not have to shut out part of themselves in order to do that. They refused to service men sexually.

We do not have to assume that a penis is an infallible sign of stunted humanity. We can remain attuned to the possibilities, even when we declare war on the current realities. The whole point of why bisexual feminists embrace our heterosexual component is that we see it as more about *us* than about men. We would feel diminished and crippled without that part of ourselves.

Ultimately, it is for each woman to discover which aspects of herself she wishes to express sexually, and what forms she wishes to give to that expression. It would be a pity if we thought that the meanings of sexual expression are entirely the property of the dominant culture. That would force us to abandon the search for control over our sexual practice. We are not only the objects and receptacles of cultural meanings, we are also their originators and creators. This is part of what consciousness-raising is all about.

From what we have learned within our world of women we conduct our heterosexual activities from a position of strength based on ultimate indifference to men. This is not taking energy from women to give to men. We are taking something for ourselves, something which we can share with other women. Bisexuality is obviously not the only position of strength from which to operate with men, but it certainly is *a* position of strength for us.

## Autonomy

Until a bisexual woman questions, confronts and accepts herself positively as a bisexual woman, she is likely to feel like two separate people walking around in the same body. She is likely to feel always slightly cut off from the people around her, slightly out of place everywhere. Put off by the claims of separatists and heterosexists, yet identifying with the rejection each group feels at the hands of the other, she often feels more defined by what she is *not* than by what she *is*.

I think that one of the most interesting features of a bisexual identification is that no one lover can confirm our sexuality, no one relationship can represent it. Apart from wearing a badge or a sign, or visibly being part of a three-way relationship with another woman and a man (not likely to appeal, I should think, to many women as a long-term prospect!), there is no way to project a bisexual sexuality. This makes it particularly necessary for bisexual women to be clear about their own identity, as it is likely to be only that sense of ourselves which does make the identification possible and real.

When we have a strong, positive bisexual identification we feel like much more than just the same physical space occupied by two realities. Besides 'confused', the other word used by most women in answering my questionnaire was 'whole'.

> 'For the first time I felt like a whole person.'
> 'Bisexuality has meant a further development of my personality, I am wholer.'
> 'My sexuality has caused me problems because it was too broad to be acceptable to me, as I was trying to force it into narrow definitions – first heterosexual, and second, lesbian . . . I cannot switch off one half or the other of my nature, *nor do I want to*.'

It seems to me that bisexuality has a built-in potential for personal autonomy. For me, and at least some other bisexual feminists, it is our bisexuality which is one of the starting-points in our quest for personal autonomy within sexual relationships. Whether or not we choose to have relationships at all, or whether we have relationships which are monogamous or not, there is an element in our sexuality which, by its very nature, keeps us from identifying ourselves completely with our lovers. Though our bodies and hearts be faithful unto death, our sexuality can never belong to anyone but ourselves.

At the moment my thinking about personal autonomy is based on two lines of searching. One is my own experience of developing a kind of non-monogamous relationship which works. The other is a fantasy of developing a kind of emotional celibacy which would allow women to have sexual relationships with other people while keeping intact our personal integrity.

### Relationships

Issues of personal autonomy and freedom within sexual relationships (however is it possible to be autonomous and be in love at the same time?) are difficult and delicate balancing acts for all women. We are learning all the time how to extend our possibilities, whatever decisions we make about the importance of sexual relationships at various points in our lives. For me, 'the personal is political' means, among other things, that we seek to make ways of living our sexuality in such a way that our female identity is confirmed and our bonds with other women strengthened.

What kinds of models can we use, what kinds of criteria can we use, to pursue the lives we would like to lead? At the moment I see two sets of related but different considerations. First, there is how we see ourselves as people, specifically as bisexual women. Then, there is how we can make relationships that confirm and extend our sense of ourselves.

When we consciously embrace our bisexuality, we affirm that our full individual sexuality can only exist in so far as we locate it within ourselves. By definition, it is not something which can be given to or constructed with any other person. We can only share parts of it with others. That means we can never surrender responsibility for our own lives to any lover or partner. Even when we would like to, we cannot submerge ourselves wholly into any relationship and still remain true to our own sexual identity. A consciously bisexual woman is forced to believe in her own autonomy. The challenge of our sexuality is to find ways of living which express and enhance that autonomy without doing violence to other aspects of our identity.

Women's decisions about what sorts of relationships they want to pursue are in one sense never freely chosen. We cannot totally abstract ourselves from our past histories or from the social and political realities in which we live. Nor can we decree that everybody else be available to us in the way we have autonomously decided we want them to be. The fact that the world is full of wonderful women doesn't mean that any of them will want to be my lover. The trouble with claiming my autonomy is having to allow for everyone else's. Even in a feminist Utopia there will be conflicts of personal interest. A truly radical attitude towards sexuality cannot be prescriptive, it can only be explorative; otherwise autonomy becomes meaningless.

The choice I have made is to live non-monogamously with another person. I live in a terraced house. I have a room, my son has a room, his father has a room, the cat has to sleep in the dining-room. The man I live with is the same man I married sixteen years ago, but we no longer live as a married couple. We still have a few friends in common, but I spend most of my time with women. We usually try to have a meal together once a week. Some weeks I see a bit more of him. Sometimes we sleep together for companionship. Sometimes we sleep together for sex. Sometimes we don't sleep together much at all.

151

Whenever we do, it is on my invitation and in my bed.

For the past nine years we have lived together as separate individuals. We both are free to have other sexual relationships as part of our separate lives, and that is no longer an issue between us. That was not difficult for us to work out in theory, as it followed easily from the other kinds of changes we made in our relationship once I discovered radical feminism. In practice, there were many difficulties. It is one thing to demand freedom for yourself, quite another to allow it to your partner. It takes some experience to know what your own needs and limits are, what the other person's needs and limits are, and how you can reconcile the contradictions between them. Accumulating that experience can be terribly painful. We have both cried a lot.

I like the way we live together now. I don't know if we shall always live together, and don't really care. If I need to leave, I shall. If he needs to leave, he will. Often I feel I would rather live alone. The time we spend together is usually happy and satisfying now that the major battles are behind us. But my sense of myself, the dynamic for my work, the meaning of my life does not come from him. It comes from my interactions with other women. My constant companions are women, my intellectual colleagues are women, my peers are women, my inspiration comes from women, my heart goes out to women, I live and breathe women. Though I love and respect him, he is just another man, just another member of the oppressing class, and when he acts like a man, I fight him. Although he shares parts of my life, he has no rights over me. No man could ever define my femaleness for me. Every woman helps me understand my femaleness. I stress all this because it was stressed by every woman currently relating to men who answered my questionnaire. None of us doubted that women come first for us.

I know many women would not like to live the way I do. They do not want to give the time and energy required to make non-monogamous relationships work, or they simply do not want more than one relationship at a time.

Now I want to make a prescriptive statement. I think that all bisexual women (in fact, all women) should consider that they live non-monogamously even if they do not choose to. I think all of us should consider that we are separate, independent women, responsible for our behaviour to all others, but accountable finally only to ourselves. If our commitment to a couple relationship is stronger than our commitment to our own lives, neither the relationship nor the life will ever be worth the sacrifice.

152

*Celibacy*

If we are to pursue our lives as actively autonomous and potentially non-monogamous women, we are going to have to give some serious thought to the clock and the calendar. If we take all our relationships, our work and our activities seriously, we are probably on the edge of not being able to take ourselves seriously for sheer lack of time and energy to remember who we are. If we are constantly sharing ourselves with others, it is hard to get back to the core of who 'we' are.

This is why I put a high value on the concept of celibacy. Since I think of my sexuality as belonging to me and sometimes shared with others, I sometimes need to have it all to myself. Since different aspects of my sexuality are brought out with women and with men, and with different women and men, I sometimes need to retrench a little and think about what it all means, the sex itself, as well as the relationships. I also need to spend time with myself. The more time I spend with others, the more time I need alone. When we talk about being sexually and personally autonomous we sometimes conjure up an image of a woman who doesn't need anything or anybody. I don't personally aspire to total emotional self-sufficiency, and doubt whether many women do, though our notions of what we mean by autonomy have still to be developed. It seems to me that if we are to realise our potential for autonomy, at the same time embracing a commitment to deep relationships, we shall need to operate from a position of separateness, a kind of emotional celibacy.

The goal I aspire to is a sense of being connected to all other women, by birth right and in a common struggle. Additionally, I want to recognise and acknowledge the personal love, desire and affection I feel for some women, and, when it seems right, to express that love, desire and affection in sexual relationships. I also want to be able to include my sexuality in the close relationships, however few and far between, I have with men.

I cannot feel connected to other people unless I can experience my separateness from them. That positive sense of separateness and uniqueness, even and most particularly in the moments of connection, is what I am calling emotional celibacy. That is the base I want for myself from which it can feel safe to pursue relationships.

For me, then, bisexuality implies a fundamental separation of ourselves from all our relationships. It implies that our sense of sexual definition and personal fulfilment can never come through any one sexual relationship. It implies a primary and essential bond with women, as our individual female experience and identity is inextricably tied to the position of women in society. It implies that each woman's sexuality is unique.

## Political implications: coming out

Coming out is still an area of confusion for me. Women who answered my questionnaire said different things about this. Some felt that bisexuality is a challenge to heterosexist ideology.

> 'I see bisexuality as very important politically (though risks of betrayal do abound) but it means to me admitting your full commitment to women on every level (which perhaps a committed heterosexual would be holding back from somewhere) but also believing that men can change and must be confronted.'
> 'I feel bisexuality is similar to lesbianism in its refusal of hetero-sexist norms, its rejection of male-defined sexuality, its love of femaleness and independence from maleness.'

Other women felt that bisexuality is uncomfortably amenable to being defined in male terms.

> I feel I'm a lesbian feminist first who occasionally gives some energy to men in a way I hope is meaningful. Men are not any priority for me. I would have to understaɩ d how bisexual feminists define their relations with men in respect to their relations with women before I would feel any degree of commitment politically and emotionally to the label 'bisexual'. It still feels like a cop-out.

Still others felt that the importance of coming out bisexual is that of being more honest in building our politics on our day-to-day reality.

> 'I now don't feel so confined or defined by my sexuality . . . Bisexuality is a reality of my feelings and I don't want to deny that, but to question it.'
> 'Since bisexuality does not completely reject the possibility of some kind of sexual-emotional congress with men, I don't know if that makes it a weaker political statement than lesbianism, and I don't really care. It's me, and *I* am not a political statement.'

The problems involved in demonstrating the emergence and radical potential of a woman-centred bisexuality are different within the women's liberation movement and in the outside world because of the different assumptions, values and social structures that operate in each sphere. Even the notion that sexuality has an important political dimension and is therefore an appropriate area for feminist analysis and action, so commonplace within the movement, is practically unheard of anywhere else.

If you show up at certain kinds of events, look a certain way, behave a certain way, it is assumed you are a lesbian; and if you admit to having any sexual relationships with men, it is assumed you are heterosexual. It is very difficult to explain that you are bisexual against the apparent evidence of your heterosexuality or lesbianism, and often feels inappropriate in the context, especially when what you are talking about is more your feelings than your current sexual relationships. Too often, we retreat into silence or slogans.

Yet for our private changes to be politically significant, they *must* be made public. The difficulties and dangers of affirming a positive bisexuality are shared to a certain extent with lesbians and non-conforming heterosexual women. All women who publicly challenge prevailing notions of female sexuality are prey to mental abuse: derision, marginalisation, isolation, ostracism; physical attack and harassment; economic sanctions; loss of security and status; threat of or actual loss of our children; imprisonment, torture and death.

The problems are different for bisexual, lesbian and heterosexual women because their lives represent different aspects of the challenge to heterosexism and male supremacy. But it seems to me that the difficulties all hinge on taking control over the representation of our sexuality and our sexual relationships – at the same time as we make changes in our lives, we need to be able to communicate the substance and meanings of these changes to other women. Otherwise we are not challenging male supremacy, merely accommodating to it. There must be some way of showing the world that my life as a bisexual woman bears no relation to those dreadful 'Attractive couple seek bi-girl for fun and frolic' advertisements!

How we do this, I still don't know, beyond the stock answer of consciousness-raising at every opportunity. I hope women will say more about how they represent their sexuality in public. Within the movement as well as 'out there', it feels easier to come out amongst people you know and trust, in circumstances which permit you to go into a little detail, to make your life credible. It was important to me to do that within the movement. I wanted to demonstrate that you could have a radical feminist passion and sensibility and still be neither a separatist nor an apologist for men. I needed my public life to reflect my private life. That is, ultimately, what coming out bisexual means for me, affirming the truth of my feelings and creating politically effective ways of making them viable. I like what one woman wrote about how her sexuality and feminist politics were connected:

> My sexuality today is a mixture of old patterns and new insights . . . a glorious mish-mash which my feminism is committed to nourishing and developing. Feminist politics must make all our sexualities liveable.

*Acknowledgement*
I want to thank all the women whose honesty, courage and love poured out in the discussions and on to the pages of my questionnaire. I fear their lives, which they described so fully, are thinly represented in this paper. I hope that women will be stimulated to further thought as much by what I have had to omit as by what I have been able to include.

# 10
# Women Alone

Tricia Bickerton

The ideas in this chapter are based on a workshop I ran for three years at the Women's Therapy Centre, London. The workshop was entitled 'Women Alone', and it usually ran for three evenings and a day. In the group I used a number of experiential exercises which enabled women to work on the various issues arising from the theme. There was also homework that looked specifically at the question of nurturance and caring. Surprisingly, many of the same issues were raised and I have tried to give an overall context and general understanding to what was expressed.

I would like to take the opportunity to express my appreciation to the women who risked sharing painful and often contradictory feelings about being on their own and I hope the chapter will be of value to other women in this situation.

Many women are on their own, by which I mean without a sexual partner; not necessarily without sex, but without a primary, intimate relationship in which there is a long-term commitment. Of course, heterosexual, lesbian and bisexual women may all be without a partner, but this chapter will focus mainly on heterosexuality. This is partly because of my own sexual orientation, and partly because the workshops mostly attracted heterosexual women. The few lesbian women who attended spoke of similar experiences and feelings in relation to being alone; nevertheless, it is important to distinguish the differences. This applies also to women of different classes. The women quoted are usually middle-class, which does not mean that what they have to say is not also meaningful to working-class women, but it would be inaccurate to suggest that their experience is the same. The ages of the women are very varied, from those in their fifties who have been married, with or without children, to relatively young women with little sexual experience. They include childless women, mothers, women who live alone, and those who live with others.

I begin the chapter by looking at some of the social factors that have led to many women being on their own, and at the external pressures that continue to make it feel difficult. I explore the connections with early childhood – both how present unhappiness at being alone can resonate with past experiences, and how these past experiences can sometimes prevent women from forming the close relationships they want. Finally, I illustrate some of the positive gains of being a woman alone and suggest possibilities for enriching this situation.

At present it seems likely that many women will spend at least part of their lives alone, not because their partners are killed in a war, or die from a terminal illness, but because sexual relationships are less likely to be life-long. Many couples, whether married or not, are choosing to separate when their relationships no longer feel satisfying. New relationships are sought, but this engagement in serial monogamy means that for one person there may be a gap between one partner and the next. This is often the woman.

During the last ten years or so many women, and in particular middle-class women, have struggled to achieve a greater financial independence. They have become more involved in the workforce, and as such are less economically dependent on men. Even for mothers, the possibility of being financially dependent on the state has created an alternative – albeit a difficult one – to being a dependent wife. Contraception and abortion have allowed women the choice of engaging in sex whilst remaining single. Pregnancy no longer leads inevitably to forced marriage and motherhood. What was once exceptional to the vast majority of women, has now become an option for many. All of these factors have meant that women are no longer destined to become wives and mothers for lack of any other alternative. It is possible now to choose to be alone; to become a single parent; to live with and love women; or to have a number of relationships with men, without signing a lifelong contract, even though such choices may not be easy.

Women, if they are seeking relationships with men, are doing so not so much for material security as for the fulfilment of sexual and emotional needs. This kind of intimacy, the promise of happiness in a romantic, sexual relationship, is perhaps desired even more intensely now that a man is not so absolutely necessary to economic survival. Women are making demands, not just for sexual pleasure, but for emotional support and understanding within a relationship. Unfortunately, men are not necessarily able to meet these demands and many women despair of finding an equally caring partner. This is not surprising given that men generally grow up to expect nurturance as a right, but are rarely taught how to give it. Women often complain that, despite feminism, men have not sufficiently changed themselves. This particular imbalance of past expectations compared with present changes has meant that men and women can no longer continue to base their relations around the old stereotypes of male and female, but have great difficulty in creating a successful alternative.

To be alone therefore often seems a preferable choice, given the problematic nature of present sexual relationships. At times it has even assumed an ideological status within the women's movement, indicating a strength and independence in not compromising with a man. However, despite these changes, most women still wish it were different. It may sometimes seem less painful to be alone than to be in an oppressive relationship; but it nevertheless is painful. This is not surprising given the weight of continuing patriarchal pressure.

Harbouring fantasies of the perfect, romantic relationship or the warm, connected family are such crucial aspects of our culture that to be alone is to feel excluded from the norms, to be marginal and outside of everyday life. This is particularly apparent at weekends, festive occasions and holidays. Despite the existence of alternative living structures, people still have a tendency to spend these crucial times with their respective sexual partners or families. It is very alarming to dread what appears to be a celebratory event to everyone else, since to express the fear is to admit a terrible failure. For the woman alone there is always the question of whom to spend time with.

Other people's expectations continue to have an influence. Most parents still want to see their daughters happily married and imagine this to be a proof of success. A general surprise and curiosity is expressed at the lack of a partner – questions have to be contended with: 'Has she met anyone yet?' 'When is she going to settle down?' It is very easy for a woman to conceive of herself as a disappointment in her parents' eyes, that her other achievements are somehow irrelevant. Although the daughter is no longer literally passed from father to husband, the unconscious association remains. Of course, there may be a genuine, if distorted, worry and concern that she will not be able to cope without a man, since this is a general assumption most parents grew up with.

Remarks are made at work, and even women friends who are in couples sometimes wish the woman on her own was attached, especially if she seems to enjoy her freedom. She has a disquieting effect, and poses questions they prefer not to consider. For heterosexual feminists in particular these questions are generally around the issue of compromise. To be alone and independent may seem enviable, even exciting, if one feels trapped but unable to desert a restricting relationship. What is at stake, of course, is how far any woman is prepared to deny herself and her needs in order not to be alone.

The women's movement has gone some way towards creating the possibility of a woman carving out her own destiny and identity without the necessity of a man; but old attitudes persist. After all, for a woman to express the possibility of finding fulfilment without a sexual relationship with a man is tantamount to saying that men are not necessary. It is no wonder that women who are alone are considered to be a threat to the established order. A man alone is viewed as adventurous and freedom loving. For a woman it is the inability to find a mate. The word 'spinster', which condemned a woman without a sexual partner as a frigid and barren member of society, still reverberates. It is therefore difficult to resist the ideological and cultural pressures, and to maintain a strength and a positive feeling of choice in the face of what seems like pity and rejection. Although heterosexual women can try to comfort themselves with the knowledge that few men have the capacity to give much of worth, this strategy does not go very far. It is only too easy to imagine that, if you are on your own, it is because you are sexually unattractive, or even worse, because you are unlovable. Many women secretly believe that there is a problem at root with themselves.

> I keep thinking there's something wrong with me, that I've done something, or that I'm not doing something right. Perhaps I'm too desperate, or then again perhaps I'm not desperate enough. People tell me to stop worrying and then it will happen; but it doesn't happen. Am I frightened of relationships? Is it because I don't want to risk being vulnerable? Or am I too demanding? Should I expect less? Why am I on my own? I must be at fault somewhere.

There is often the expression of such feelings of failure and inferiority. The feelings are a mirror of patriarchial society's definition of womanhood, the need to maintain women's identity as dependent on men and children. This being so, it is especially hard for a woman to discover her own self-esteem as separate from another, to enjoy her aloneness, to care for and nurture herself.

It is, of course, much better if women can direct this sense of blame against the sexual and cultural norms rather than against themselves. For obvious reasons it creates a more positive attitude. But the problem does not always end there. What many women discover is that the difficulty in feeling confident and separate alone is not only linked to the immediate social pressures, but it is also located in the past. This usually becomes evident during the process of the workshops, and it therefore helps to explore feelings assimilated during childhood. It is often the relationship between mother and daughter which is crucial to understanding a woman's lack of self-esteem.

A daughter is generally taught to believe that her life depends on another. She is ill-equipped to imagine a life on her own. How can the adult woman begin to understand her own needs, let alone go some way towards meeting them, when her very identity has been formed on the basis of serving others? She is unpractised in caring or planning for herself. This was particularly apparent in the group whenever it was suggested that the women should write down ways they could spend the week nurturing and mothering themselves. There was a tense silence, often a real resistance to beginning to think of anything vaguely nurturing. And if something was written down it was often sabotaged during the week or carried out dutifully without pleasure. What seemed particularly significant is that the exercise relied on discovering an ability to mother oneself, but it is precisely the real mother who often emerges as the source of lack. It is difficult for a daughter to feel separate and autonomous when she senses her mother is pushing her away. The more her dependency needs are dismissed, the more dependent and deprived a daughter may feel. Of course, many women will grow up seemingly capable, coping and independent, but continue to feel more or less unconsciously like a small child clinging to Mother in the hope for comfort. It is such past rejections which can prevent women from regarding their present aloneness with confidence. The nature of being on one's own arouses feelings of loneliness which resound in the psyche and recall some of the early feelings of loss or distance. No wonder there is a constant yearning for a sexual relationship that will fill the gap. Perhaps in someone else's arms there will be a totality of love, a unity and lost perfection.

This is not to say that the adult desire for a sexual relationship is reducible to a woman's socially-determined dependency on men. A group will sometimes express the idea that this is so when one woman despairs very greatly at her lack of a partner. It is meant to give solace, a way of saying that there is nothing amiss with her in being alone, but unfortunately this can have an adverse effect. It makes it even more difficult for heterosexual women to acknowledge their need for a relationship since to do so seems to question their ability to be

161

independent. Of course, such needs may be distorted by the relationship between men and women in our society, but in fighting the social norms it is important to maintain a sense of what women are struggling towards. To what extent is it possible to have the experience of being known and connected without the involvement of the body? The desire for sexual love is often the desire for a total acceptance, somewhere a woman can express all her worst feelings, her twists, distortions and idiosyncracies and still be cared for.

Why is it difficult then for some women to form close, sexual relationships? Rather than assuming that the problem is created only by immediate social circumstances and leaving it there, it is worth considering other, more individual reasons. Yet again the past is invariably revealed in the present. Defences necessary to a child's survival may continue to operate inappropriately in adult life and act as a block to achieving intimacy.

The merging of the two bodies in a sexual relationship necessitates a letting-go, barriers are broken, and a sense of vulnerability increased. For the woman whose memories of being touched are painful or faint, it can feel terrifying to get too close. There may be an expressed wish for a relationship and a loneliness, but the fear of losing even an artificial independence may seem that much more disturbing. It is safer to maintain a distance than to risk reliving the pain.

Sometimes the resentment at not having a sexual partner emerges as a bitterness related to early relationships. Of course, it has the effect of pushing away anyone who comes too close. It often seems preferable however to maintain a passive and hard-done-by attitude than to expose the years of anger. It is difficult when a woman experiences herself as a victim of the lack of a sexual relationship to realise how much she may be participating in the situation. The unexpressed anger towards others can stop her acting on her own behalf. How much a woman is prepared to risk and reveal of herself is likely to affect how much she will receive.

It is not untypical for women to fear their own negative, hostile emotions and to imagine they will have a devastating effect on others. For the woman alone there is often the fantasy that she is undeserving and destructive and must therefore keep a distance. She may even attribute her being alone to what she assumes is her badness – a punishment for not being good enough. To become acceptable some women are driven to perfect themselves, to achieve more, or to become more attractive in the hope that it will create a lasting relationship. Of course, this is a never-ending task which only serves to make any real contact impossible. Such defences, however, may seem necessary to prevent collapse.

The loss of previous relationships may also keep a woman in the apparent protection of being on her own. Ending a relationship, whether chosen or not, can stir up an intensity of feeling from the past. There is also a period of mourning, a gradual disengagement from the relationship. At such a time a woman is unlikely to connect with anyone else. After the initial period of turmoil, however, when it seems as if all the psychic structures are disintegrating with the disintegration of a close relationship, there is understandably a resistance to exploring any further. Perhaps it is too painful. After all, life has to continue and it is problematic to maintain work, children and responsibility when feelings are constantly threatening to erupt. Many women, having recovered some semblance of normality, wish to forget. It feels safer to close the wound, and to be alone. Of course, there is the added fear that whatever difficulties existed in the last relationship may be repeated. One woman confirmed this fear, even though some time had lapsed since her marriage ended:

> I felt so terribly hurt and rejected, that even though it happened eight years ago, I don't really want to make another commitment. I spent days, weeks, months, feeling dead, aimless, unmotivated to do anything. I woke every morning with a terrible ache in my chest. When I cried it was overwhelming, sudden, unpredictable at all sorts of occasions. I really couldn't cope with day-to-day responsibility. I keep a distance now which doesn't feel very fulfilling but at least it assures me of some protection. If I really get involved, who's to say I wouldn't be left and have to go through it all over again.

What is feared in becoming attached is the risk of losing the relationship. But there is often a fear of losing oneself too. Many women have recently created independent lives, live alone and pursue interesting work, but nevertheless feel there is something missing from not having a close, sexual relationship. Yet it is precisely the dependency that a committed relationship entails that seems so disturbing. For most women it is a question of how to be both close and separate, how to be dependent and yet remain independent. Having struggled so hard to achieve an intellectual and economic independence, it feels like giving up a hard-won sense of themselves to admit dependency, particularly on a man. One woman felt the women's movement had reinforced the strong, independent aspects

163

of herself, making it even more difficult to come to terms with her need for support and nurturance. 'The movement,' she said, 'is like a continuation of my family. There I had to be strong, just as now I feel other women expect me to be.'

Indeed, there is often an expression of disgust and fear when women approach what they assume are the weaker aspects of themselves. It invariably feels humiliating to admit to the loneliness and the overwhelming need. Pride dictates that it is more important to maintain dignity and a coping façade, rather than seek out comfort. Such vulnerability might create an alarming dependence and invite rejection and loss.

Of course, the possibility of a woman losing herself in a sexual relationship is not just a fantasy. It is the effect of a socialisation process which provides women with little sense of their own identity. For this reason it is often a very positive experience for a woman to be alone. It may be the first time in her life she can discover what she wants, her own needs, without taking someone else into consideration. Women often describe the pleasure of going to bed alone, reading a book, deciding when to turn the light out. The challenge of a woman being able to control her own life and decide her own future is an exhilarating and exciting task. It may be painful, but it has its rewards. If the definition of herself has always been in relation to another, then who will she be as a woman alone? She may discover new possibilities, talents and horizons. Without a sexual partner, and an assured sense of company, she is forced to ask for support and to make new relationships. Indeed, perhaps she becomes stronger and attempts to do things that once seemed easier to avoid. She is free, as it were, to create herself.

In the search for a new identity, confusion and uncertainty are paramount. A period of celibacy may feel like a peaceful haven in a prolonged battle of sexual relationships. Even when such time however is preciously needed and consciously determined by a woman, it is difficult to admit wholeheartedly that she is doing what she wants. There is a guilt attached to being alone, a feeling of selfishness – but also self-pity. It is easier to conceive of oneself as a victim, rather than to face any responsibility for the situation. 'How is it possible,' one woman asked, 'to choose so much pain and loneliness?'

It is possible and often necessary as part of the struggle for a life which is less compromising and more in a woman's control. After all, if it is not possible to be alone, then it is usually not possible to be close. No matter how many friends, lovers or children we have, everyone is, at the end of the day, on their own. Without any experience of separateness, sexual relationships are reduced to a child-like desire for parental security, with all the conflict that this entails.

Our patriarchal culture so denies and degrades the reality of aloneness for women, that it feels like travelling a new journey without a map. Perhaps it is precisely because women have been regarded as children, to be protected and economically maintained, that it is difficult to find an adult status. There are few reference points in a society which creates the image of woman as sexual object or mother. The models that do exist tend to reinforce the ideas of deprivation; the single parent, struggling with little money or support; or, at the other extreme, the glamorous career woman, ruthless and self-assured, who sees sex as a desire to be satisfied regardless of feeling. Neither image suggests dignity and self-esteem.

The degree to which it feels creative to be alone is obviously partially dependent on age and circumstances. What may at one point feel like a phase of movement and discovery can give way to a generalised feeling of being stuck. It was possibly easier to be alone during the 1970s, when there were great hopes of radical change. In the present climate of cuts and unemployment women and men are once again looking towards the family for security, a shelter from the storm. There is less sexual experimentation and fewer alternative living units so that to be a woman alone is to feel more under attack. Whatever changes have occurred, it is still difficult to choose to become a single parent. Beginning to reach the end of childbearing age and wanting a child increases the pressure to find a committed relationship.

For women in our society, growing older is often associated with feeling unwanted. One woman in her late fifties was particularly fearful of the idea of spending her old age alone. Having felt she'd wasted years in an unhappy marriage, she wanted some experience of love and companionship at the end of her life.

Of course, creativity is also dependent on the resources that the woman alone is able to mobilise. There is a danger of feeling that without a sexual relationship there is no one to turn to for support. This is rarely true: most women have friends or relatives they can turn to. This was consistently revealed in the group when women were asked to write down ways they could receive nurturance from people during the week. This could vary from asking for a cuddle or a massage, to a Saturday night out with a friend, or perhaps some time and attention. The exercise usually proved to be even more threatening than the one involving caring for oneself. The women were reluctant to assert their needs, and found various justifications for not doing it in the week. Despite the difficulties, however, most women gained powerful insight into their own psychology and were surprised to find that there was some support, if only they could ask for and accept it. For many women the act of sharing their experience can be decisive in lessening their isolation. This was certainly one of the functions of the workshop and is a way in which women can create alternative means of supporting each other.

It is also crucial to feel that there is some element of control: this is why many women came to the workshop in the first place. They wish to unravel the parts of themselves that might be contributing destructively to the situation. It always feels more powerful to know how the past may be affecting the present, since this is an area in which there is some possibility of change. That doesn't necessarily mean finding a sexual relationship. What it does mean is acquiring a more realistic sense of one's own possibilities and a greater degree of choice.

No doubt there will continue to be more women who will spend at least part of their lives on their own. As this happens, new images and models will probably grow, alternative means of support will be created, and experience gathered and shared. To be a woman alone will hopefully become a more positive experience: not a gap between relationships, but a time of essential growth.

# 11
# Duty and Desire: Creating a Feminist Morality

## Sue Cartledge

The first years of my life were spent on a battlefield between Duty and Desire. The Protestant ethic – tempered with love – ruled in my family. It was clear what we ought to do, from great matters (chastity, fidelity, honour thy father and thy mother) to small (wash your hands before meals, don't drop litter). The rules were not there for utilitarian reasons, to promote the greater happiness of yourself or others. They were moral absolutes which should not really be questioned. If there was a conflict, the right course was clear: Desire should always be submerged to Duty.

The rules certainly had a powerful hold on me. Particularly as they were backed up by fear (I half-believed in hell-fire and I fully believed in the anger of adults). And also by guilt (Jesus died on the Cross for me: how could I possibly cause him – and my mother and grandmother – yet more pain?). But the desire for happiness was strong as well. What I wanted to do kept irrepressibly bubbling up and cracking the surface of what I ought to do. On the whole I followed my desires secretly. I was too afraid then for open rebellion. As I turned into a teenager my secret, guilty determination to have what I wanted was succeeded by more and more open questioning of the rules themselves. Perhaps Desire and Duty need not conflict? Perhaps I could drop the whole idea of Duty and make Desire itself the rule? Or at least rewrite Duty so that it coincided more closely with Desire?

When at the age of eighteen I finally decided, after much mutual moral agonising, to sleep with my boyfriend, it seemed at the time as if the battlefield had been abandoned. Desire had won a decisive victory over Duty. From now on, not only would I have what I wanted, but it would make me happy, it would make everyone else happy, we would write our own rules and the conflict evaporated out of the window.

167

Fifteen years later, the battlefield I abandoned is dwarfed by the vastness and complexity of the one I entered. The extracts in this chapter are from journals I have kept over the last nine years. Rereading them, it is clear how, sometimes years apart and through all the changes in relationships, living situations and sexual orientation, the same themes recur. The battle between Desire and Duty has continued to rage, though in more subtle and bewildering forms. Duty is no longer absolute and unquestioned. We write and rewrite our own rules. But we still break them and feel bad about it. With no parents to punish us, we punish ourselves. And when my desires clash, not with parental tablets of stone, but with the real, living, human desires of another person – probably my nearest and dearest – what should happen then? Even more complicated, when my own desires are at war with each other, who is to be the internal referee?

Marxism, feminism and psychology have thrown a different light for me on many of the problems. But, rewrite the terms, the conflicts still remain. And many remain, irreducibly, as *moral* conflicts. The questions, How should we treat each other? How should we act? and How should we live? are still real. I don't think they are easy to answer, but I think it is terribly important that we keep trying. God the Father – earthly and heavenly – is gone. In his place there is only ourselves and each other, and for ourselves and each other, only we are responsible.

When my desires appeared to conflict with the needs of my husband, I felt responsible for the pain I was causing:

> 1973: Martin keeps ringing me up, and leaving 'presents' (notes, cheques, records). Still turns to me when he feels depressed. And I still feel 'responsible'. I got a letter from his mother which said, 'Do you know what you are doing to Martin? I wonder what will happen to him – feel he has had it. Poor old Martin.' This really upset me.

Hadn't I always been taught to put others (especially men) first? If a clash of desires caused pain, it must be my fault. The women's movement has clearly identified and described this aspect of patriarchal morality. As women we are brought up to be 'unselfish' and more aware of other people's needs than our own. This is the pattern on which countless women have moulded their lives. However, martyrdom is not so simple. Suppressed desires have a way of resurfacing as resentment. A woman learns 'to give to others out of the well of her own unmet needs'.[1] But the well starts to boil with fury, runs out in gullies of bitterness, dries up.

> 1974: When I came back I started to cry with frustration. Then I shouted at Stefan – all kinds of things came out. That we always did what *he* wanted, made love or not when *he* wanted; that I didn't have the strength of will to decide what I wanted to do, and do it; that we might as well give up making love because it drove me round the twist . . . . The pattern seems to be, that I don't have enough confidence in myself. I let myself be over-ruled by what Stefan wants. And yet I don't have the generosity to do what he wants gracefully. I am full of smouldering resentment.

The traditional, self-sacrifice model of dealing with conflicts between our needs and other people's has been largely abandoned. A greater understanding of psychology has demonstrated its ineffectiveness – repressed desires resurface as depression, illness, bitterness, madness or whatever, but generally cause mayhem in the end. Psychotherapy and the various 'growth' movements stress that, far from suppressing our needs, we have to discover what they are and try to meet them. Not only does this help ourselves, it actually helps other people too! (What a relief to those of us who haven't quite shaken off the injunctions to worry about others.) After all, who wants the burden of being the grateful recipient of someone else's martrydom? Other people are tougher than we think: it helps them more to be challenged openly with our wants than if we try to protect them. Okay, so conflict may ensue: but conflict is healthy.

In my own life, attempting to put other people first – or not even other people, but more abstract notions of duty, obligation, 'unselfishness' – has been on the whole destructive to me and unhelpful to those I was close to. Struggling to 'be good', I remained, of course, as selfish as anybody else. In recent years the concepts of therapy have certainly helped me reach a more sensible balance between my own needs and other people's.

But I still doubt whether the conflict can be dissolved completely. Is the opposition of needs *always* a false paradox? Rejecting the tradition of putting everybody else's needs first, there does seem to be a danger of swinging to the other extreme, disregarding other people and elevating our own wishes into a gospel. I am still enough a child of my upbringing to believe that other people's needs matter (and indeed this belief is deeply rooted in feminist and socialist, as well as Christian traditions). I am no less important than the next person, but neither am I more important. I was struck when I read Natalie

169

Barney's biography[2] by her resolution, made at the age of eighteen 'never to suffer'. Apparently she never did. But many of her lovers did: at least one allegedly died of a broken heart. Or did they not *really* suffer, or not more than they would have anyway? Did Natalie's treatment of them really liberate them from the stifling sense of obligation that a faithful lover would have laid on them? In her book *The Sadeian Woman*,[3] Angela Carter describes the character of de Sade's Juliette, sister of Justine. Justine is the eternal martyr, virtuous and doomed to suffer. Juliette, on the other hand, is monstrously selfish and prospers happily: 'She is a woman who acts according to the precepts and also the practice of a man's world and so she does not suffer. Instead, she causes suffering.' Angela Carter goes on to draw a parallel between Juliette and a false model of women's 'liberation': pursuing the goals of men. 'Their liberation from the goals of femininity is a personal one for themselves only. They gratify themselves fully, but it is a liberation without enlightenment and so becomes an instrument for the oppression of others, both women and men.'

Refusing 'womanly' martyrdom, we do not wish to embrace 'masculine' selfishness. At times our needs and desires really *do* conflict with those of other people, often those we love most. Sometimes we *do* treat each other badly. Getting our needs and other people's in balance is obviously the ideal: simple to say, but far harder to work out. In the rest of this chapter I want to write about some of the ways in which conflicts occur and how, as feminists, we try to resolve them.

Traditionally, sexuality has been seen as *the* site of moral debate, and especially so for women. To refer to a woman's 'morals' was to say something about her sexual behaviour. The morality involved was crude in the extreme. What was at issue was not the quality of relationships and our treatment of each other, but simply what we did or did not do with our bodies. Homosexuality, premarital sex and adultery were in themselves immoral, without any need to enquire further into the circumstances or details of behaviour. The 'sexual revolution' in some ways perpetuated this equation. If sex, outside strict confines, had been in itself immoral, then the breaking of the sexual rules became a revolutionary act. From being on the whole a bad and dangerous thing, sex became a good and healthy thing. But simply to reverse the overall judgement leaves unanswered a million questions about sexual behaviour and relationships. Sexuality is a crucial area of moral debate, not because sex is naughty, but because it is a focus for powerful feelings. As it is constructed in our society, sexuality carries a heavy emotional load. Not only love and companionship, but jealousy, our need for security, our fear of loneliness and even our search for identity are all bound up in our sexual relationships. And when one person's deepest needs and longings encounter those of another, the potential for conflict and heartbreak is equal to the potential for joy.

1975: I had a dream two nights ago, and woke up in the night. The dream was about Martin. It was after we split up, and he had come to see me for a weekend. It had been difficult, embarrassing – I had been cold to him. We were parting at the end of the weekend, and he looked very sad. He said he had tried to love me, as much as I would let him. But I wouldn't let him.

Love out of balance – when one person wants the other more than they are wanted – has always raised for me painful and apparently almost irresolvable questions about how to behave. As the one who wants, how much is it fair to impose your needs on the other? And as the one who is wanted, how can treating someone else kindly be an adequate response when what they really want is your heart and soul? How should you exercise this power over them – a power you did not even ask for?

The issue is complicated even more by the fact that the links between desire and power often ensure that we are attracted to other people *because* they are unavailable. Their inaccessibility heightens their desirability, while those who love us faithfully stifle us with their predictability, and we devalue their love because we are sure of it.

In my relationship with Martin I felt crushed by the burden of what seemed to be his excessive dependence on me. The more he clung, the greater his needs, and the more it appeared that I and I alone was the one who must meet them, the more I withdrew and became cold, unloving and rejecting. And at the same time I felt consumed with guilt at how I was treating him, wrecking his life, as it seemed.

1974: I had another dream about Martin last night. He had gone out in a bad mood, and I went after him to look for him. I found him in a pub: a smooth bar. Martin was wearing an old sweater and leather jacket, slouched in a seat with a glass in front of him. There was a general air in the bar of pity and distaste for the miserable character he looked. But as soon as I came in he brightened up, drained his drink, became cheerful and confident, nodded to the barmaid and came out with me.

The guilt pursued me in my dreams for several years after we split up. Looking back, I would now judge that Martin was indeed too dependent on me; but also that I overestimated both his dependence and the extent of my responsibility for him. As a result I set up within myself alternating moods of guilt and resentment, based as much on my own fear of being held responsible for someone else's happiness, as on real pressure from Martin.

A few years later, in my relationship with another man, I had for the first time the experience of being the one who wanted and needed more, who seemed to love more. My reaction was to set myself impossibly high standards of 'correct' behaviour – never to intrude my emotions, never to show anger, always to be cheerful and loving when we met.

> 1976: I feel a riot of conflicting emotions. One quite simple one is that I want him – I just want him. I want to be with him and hug him and sleep with him. I also feel angry with him for never getting in touch with me, the anger and sinking heart of rejection. I feel if he *really* wanted to see me he'd be able to – and am angry at the realisation that he doesn't really want to. I know that what I feel for Greg isn't really love, but selfish wanting, like a spoiled child. If I really loved him, I'd be understanding without any effort, prepared to let go if loving demanded that.

As far as I remember none of this 'riot of conflicting emotions' was ever revealed to Greg. In my anxiety not to burden him with my dependence, I denied myself the expression of my feelings, and spared him the discomfort of having to face these. Given that we had a sexual relationship which lasted (though intermittently) for eighteen months, I think I had the balance wrong. He could have tolerated hearing – perhaps even needed to hear – that I was hurt. My fears of the consequences of telling him might or might not have been realised, but a new level of understanding would have been created between us.

I was confused, and still remain confused, though perhaps a bit less so, about the amount of emotional response we can and should expect from a lover. A few years ago I wrote down in my notebook a quotation from Jung:[4] 'Emotional relationships are relationships of desire, tainted by coercion and constraints; something is expected from the other person, and that makes him and ourselves unfree.' I suspect that I took the quotation out of context. Rereading it now, I feel that we must be able to expect *something* from a lover without making both of us 'unfree'. Too often, of course, we expect *every-thing*. We load onto our lover the whole responsibility for our emotional fulfilment. Writing in 1919, Alexandra Kollontai[5] gave an incisive descriptive of this process: 'To be rid of the eternally-present threat of loneliness, we "launch an attack" on the emotions of the person we love with a cruelty and lack of delicacy that will not be understood by future generations. We demand the right to know every secret of this person's being.'[5]

Kollontai locates the genesis of this grasping, needy possessiveness in bourgeois society. With half a century of psychology between ourselves and her, modern feminists would share many aspects of Kollontai's general analysis, but feel impelled to add more complex explanations of the formation of individual emotional needs. The notion of sexual 'rights' to another person is indeed a capitalist concept, and sexist as well: sexual fidelity is demanded more of women than of men. But if our upbringing left us 'needing' to own another person, body and soul, then we shall indeed feel terribly insecure if they withdraw. Such feelings cannot be wished away through political analysis.

For many of us, the point at which conflict between our needs and other people's are most acute is over the issue of non-monogamy. Certainly the two most miserable, guilt-ridden periods of my life were those when, after a long monogamous relationship, I had started to sleep with somebody else.

1973: I have certainly learned something in the last five months. I started as a kind of naive Reichian, thinking one or two carefree additional affairs would solve everything without creating problems of their own. Instead, being with Stefan has shaken my relationship with Martin to its foundations, as well as taking on its own momentum and growing far beyond the limits I had drawn for it. At first I assumed it *should* be – and therefore was – possible to love Martin and Stefan at the same time. After that I could see that it was terribly difficult; and wondered whether it would 'work'; whether I should 'give up' one or the other. Now I don't think the decision to give up one would be realistic.

My clearest memory of those months is of trekking from one flat to another, diaphragm in handbag, trying to appease both husband and lover, endless rows, and feeling somewhat like a bone between two emotionally-demanding dogs. My journal reference to Reich was not merely academic. Martin and I read *The Sexual Revolution* (on the recommendation of friends who were already experimenting with non-monogamy) and were excited by Reich's ideas. No doubt this was mainly because they seemed to offer an escape route from the doldrums of our relationship. But we felt that our motivation was ideological. In this we were in tune with the times. Monogamy and couple relationships were under attack on the Left and in the women's movement. As the 'Red Collective', a group of men and women, put it in their pamphlet:[6]

> We have to understand the exact bonds which unite the couple, and begin the long struggle of changing the ways we have been formed into monogamous, coupular women. What the struggle will actually entail for any individual obviously cannot be predicted.

The attack on monogamy was not on the pragmatic grounds that it did not work (though much of the emotional force of the attack came from the wish to break the chains in our own relationships). It was ideologically wrong, for all sorts of reasons. One of the strongest of these was that monogamous sexual relationships were privatised and 'coupley': they set up barriers which kept other people out, as well as imprisoning the couple. They elevated one kind of relationship above all others, and this narrowed the scope of other kinds of friendships. This strand of criticism is still a powerful one. Writing in *Heresies,* Pat Califia comments on what she sees as a 'sentimental' trend back to couples and romantic lovers: 'Rather than being critical of the idea that one can find enough fulfilment in a relationship to justify one's existence, feminists are seeking membership of a perfect, egalitarian couple. I question the value of this.'[7]

Probably the main reason for this 'retreat' to couples is the enormous and agonising difficulties (emotional, practical and moral) that most of us have experienced in trying to put the ideology of non-monogamy into practice. Early optimism led to a great deal of diving in at the deep end and subsequent floundering and heartbreak. What happens when one partner is keen to have other relationships and the other prefers to be monogamous? Whose wishes should be given greater weight? Is all the onus on the would-be monogamous partner to swallow her feelings or even try to change them? What responsibility does the other have to take account of those feelings? Is there indeed any negotiable ground upon which compromises could be worked out between monogamy and non-monogamy? The process of negotiation is itself problematic. How do you discuss with a lover your wish to have another lover without putting her in the position of being asked to give or refuse her permission? A position in which she loses either way – for if she agrees she loses her exclusive rights to your affections, while if she refuses she bears the burden of denying your freedom and your desire.

Even where both partners agree on non-monogamy, the solution which is honourable and realistic for them may be unacceptable to their other lovers. When interviewed on British television,[8] Simone de Beauvoir described how she and Jean-Paul Sartre agreed at the start of their relationship that each would always be the most important person for the other. Their love was 'necessary'; but this would not preclude them from having other 'contingent' affairs. And her use of the word 'affairs' for these other lovers is significant. For it is clear from her autobiographical writings that some other lovers, both hers and Sartre's, resented their automatic second place, and that this resentment was a constant destructive factor in these relationships.

There are, of course, worse and better ways of trying to work out the problems of non-monogamous relationships. Joint discussion, honesty and sensitivity are obviously an improvement on the traditions of secrecy and manipulation whereby one partner (usually the man) maintained his power and choice at the expense of others. But a 'sensitive' approach is also emotionally demanding and time-consuming, and needs constant attention to everybody's feelings. In a recent feminist film[9] three women described how they tried to deal with their triangular relationship: 'We were trying to find a balance and then next day everything would have changed.' It is difficult to reach any emotional depth, even in just one relationship, without a commitment of time and care. The time left over from the necessities of jobs, children, housework, may in fact impose a practical limit on the possibilities of non-monogamy.

> 1982: Becky and I thought it was important to discuss what we felt about monogamy at the beginning of our relationship – in the hopes of avoiding problems later. Becky said that for her it depends a lot on how strongly she feels. If she doesn't feel very emotionally involved, she is not very bothered by a lover having other relationships. Her commitment to non-monogamy would only be really tested with someone she cared about very much.

In my own life, I have still reached no decisions about these questions. How can the pain and problems of working out non-monogamous relationships – which in practice usually turn out to be less a true attempt at non-monogamy than a transition from one monogamous relationship to another – be balanced against what has seemed the virtual impossibility of maintaining sexual and emotional fidelity to one other person? The problems to be negotiated in a long-term sexual relationship – the maintenance of each person's sense of identity, the drawing of the boundaries between self and other, how to avoid boredom – have for me become overwhelming after a few years and I have ended by feeling that the relationship has blighted and deadened my emotional life.

1974: On the coach coming down I was thinking back over the years since I met Martin. Long stretches of them I could not remember at all – hardly a thing about how I felt, what I was doing. And I said to myself never again will I put up with such *unconscious* life.

And yet, I am haunted by the conviction that it is 'better' to maintain relationships for a long time, preferably forever. I am not sure how much this may be a product of not-yet-shaken-off conditioning, and how much a genuine belief that the continuity and depth of a shared lifetime is preferable to the variety of experience of changing relationships. Is it a relic of a Puritan upbringing to believe that what is most difficult can also be most rewarding?

> It's simple to wake from sleep with a stranger,
> dress, go out, drink coffee,
> enter a life again. It isn't simple
> to wake from sleep into the neighbourhood
> of one neither strange nor familiar
> whom we have chosen to trust.[10]

1980: Cathy and I are locked in a fruitless argument about morality. She accuses me of selfishness, consumerism towards other people, that wanting to sleep with others is behaving like a man (worst of crimes). And I scream back that she is a narrow-minded moralist, what could be more male than her possessiveness, wanting to tie people down and own them?

Behind these rows about feminist morality, of course, lay our pain about our relationship. Given the emotions involved, the chances of reaching agreement on moral issues were slight. However, I do not draw the conclusion that such rows are simply about hurt feelings, and that the moral issues can be reduced to the expression of conflicting feelings and attitudes. We do need to debate where to draw the line between tolerance of each other's behaviour and a license to walk all over other people. We do need to work out how much another's pain should weigh in the balance of our own actions.

The line between widening our sexual relationships and sexual consumerism is indeed a difficult one to draw. Feminists have tended to draw it with a particular bias: against casual sex; in favour of 'meaningful relationships' and knowing somebody well before you sleep with them. This bias has come under attack recently, particularly from some American feminists who feel that our early attempts to open up sexual relationships and reject monogamy have given way to a new repressive feminist moralism:

> It's turned the other way now, and sex has to occur in a certain way for it to be good. And the only legitimate sex is very limited. It's not focused on orgasms, it's very gentle and only takes place in the context of a long-term, caring relationship. It's the missionary position of the women's movement.[11]

What Gayle Rubin is objecting to is not so much that some women prefer 'gentle' sex in the context of long-term relationships, but that (she feels) this is represented as the only legitimate sex. The debate is not only about how we personally feel we should act, and how we prefer those close to us to act, but about how *everybody* should act. Moral debate implies we are discussing not only our own choices, but general rules. Is there room in the women's movement both for those who prefer monogamy and for those who are prepared to state (as did a recent contributor to *Heresies*): 'I like promiscuity, group sex, casual sex, recreational sex'?[12] How much sexual and moral pluralism is possible within feminism? There isn't a pre-set answer, of course. But there are obviously better and worse ways of working towards answers. Hasty condemnation, judgement and the policing of other women's behaviour only leads to defensive reactions. The personal is indeed political. But the force of this statement should be to liberate us from the prison of impossible, private struggles and increase our understanding of the structures that condition us and the changes that might free us – *not* to hold up all our actions for public censure. We have to find ways of discussing moral issues seriously, taking our own and each other's choices seriously, and facing the inevitable conflicting views, without alienating each other so that every discussion proceeds rapidly to confrontation.

One problem for feminists in discussing questions of morality has been what I see as an unresolved and little-considered paradox in our own theory. On the one hand, we have devoted much effort to understanding the ways in which women are the victims of oppression. The more we are oppressed the more we are victims; the more we are unfree, the less choice we have, and therefore the less responsibility. At the same time an equally strong thread in feminist tradition has been the assumption of choice and responsibility for ourselves and each other, an endless delving and soul-searching for correctness in motive and action. Feminism has sometimes even been seen as a form of *ethics* as well as a form of politics.

What is the sensible path through these somewhat contradictory views of the extent of our own moral responsibility? First of all, I think a recognition of our conditioning, by structures both external and internal, is helpful in freeing us from the traditional feminine trap of guilt.

> 1981: I feel, if my heart is broken, it is I who have broken it (twice). And yet, guilt is not the point. Could the past have been different, could we have done better? Of course we could – but not the people we then were – these people could not, were not equipped to.

As one contributor to *The Politics of Sexuality in Capitalism* describes, we tend to blame ourselves and each other rather than the situations we are in: 'My logic left me flailing about within the relationship, not sure who was to blame. I didn't manage to think it was the relationship between us, its emotional basis and exclusivity, its centrality, that made us feel in infantile ways.'[13]

Obviously there is a limit to the amount which we, as individuals or collectively, can change ourselves in one generation. We cannot reconstruct ourselves overnight as beings free from possessiveness, jealousy, pain, loss (and do we want to, anyway? As beings with only rational emotions, would we have lost something in the process?) What is desirable, even assuming we could all agree on that, is bound to be limited by what is practical.

However, a realistic appreciation of the limits to change imposed both by surrounding circumstances and the past in our own heads and hearts does not let us off the hook of responsibility. And I assume that as feminists we would not want to be let off. We have already taken responsibility for our own lives, by defining and rejecting our

178

oppression and struggling to create new worlds and new ways of living. Our politics would have no meaning if we did not believe that there is scope for change and that we can make changes. And I believe that the creation of a feminist ethics is important on every level of our politics. In the arena of our own lives and relationships it is important because this is the most immediate sphere of action. If we cannot maintain our personal search for better ways of living, then we are failing ourselves and those we love. But I also believe we shall be failing the human community generally. Our individual actions create ripples which extend beyond our own field of vision. The clearest and most passionate arguments I have encountered for this is Barbara Ehrenreich's essay, 'Toward a Political Morality':[14]

> Let's think what it means, in the broadest sense, to be a moral person or to have a moral outlook. A moral outlook has to go beyond 'personal' matters, because the essence of morality – the reasons for judging some actions as 'good' and others as 'bad' – is the belief that there is a connection between our individual actions and the entire human community . . . . A moral position says that what we each do matters because we are each connected – through an enormous network of human interdependency – to all people and all history.

Having accepted the need for morality, or course, the questions that remain for us as feminists are those I have raised, but not solved in this chapter: What would be a specifically *feminist* morality? How would it differ from other moral systems we have rejected? How do we reach agreement on the details? And how do we put it into practice? These questions require the attention of us all.


### Postscript

I should like to express my love and gratitude to all those who have shared their lives with me and who appear (under altered names) in the journal extracts above. Needless to say, these distorted reflections tell us more about my state of mind at the times I wrote them than about the characters of my lovers, whom I admire and respect.

# 12

# I'll Climb the Stairway to Heaven: Lesbianism in the Seventies

Elizabeth Wilson

For many feminists in the early 1970s lesbianism opened like the doorway to freedom. At the same time it was like the Trojan horse that was to let loose within the very citadel of patriarchy a subversive army of female desires.

Ten years later, some of the feminists who embraced lesbianism with ideological fervour have slipped back into heterosexuality, gracefully or shamefacedly, or have acknowledged with a rueful smile that desire was unamenable to politics. Some have entrenched themselves in a greater hostility to heterosexual love; some of the 'old lesbians' of before the movement have returned to the certainties of role-playing and the outlawry of forbidden desires. The struggle continues – but what is it about?

There is something profoundly and obscurely unsatisfactory about the way in which feminists (and the Left) have talked about sexuality over the past decade or so. Feminists were talking about a Manichaean struggle between the hell of wrong desires and the heaven of a love devoid of pain. They were talking about their right to orgasm, and the thraldom of being in love. Often, to talk about sexuality was not to talk about sex at all, but about relationships, about lifestyles, about emotions. The word 'sexuality' went wider than 'sex' to incorporate ideas of identity and gender – masculine and feminine – and to refer to desire and fantasy.

Many different problems and preoccupations came to be subsumed under the word 'sexuality'. But the rush to reject personal subordination left intact many taken for granted assumptions about the nature of sexuality; many bourgeois theories remained embedded and invisible in the feminist debate; and feminism took over from established revolutionary movements a moralism about the meaning of sexual behaviour in relation to politics.

A lengthy digression into the history of ideas alone could map the multiple relationships between different strands in the contemporary feminist debate on sexuality and ideas current in society as a whole. And of course a feminist 'discourse' could not have sprung up in a vacuum. But, for example, feminists readily accepted the prevailing view that 'sexuality' holds the key to individual identity. The idea that in one's sexual life one expresses the deepest and most essential aspects of oneself is one of the established bases of modern western capitalist life. The popularisation of Freud, the privileging of the marriage relationship over wider relations with kin, the elevation of D.H. Lawrence into the writer who tells the 'truth' about sexual feeling, are some examples of how we all, the Left included, have come to accept the view that, as Raymond Williams put it (speaking of Lawrence), sexual passion represents the 'quick of life', the ultimate core of the essential self.

As a result of this assumption many feminists have come to assume that 'sexuality' holds the key to, or is the core of, the subordination of women, and also the source of female power. As one correspondent to *Spare Rib* (no.115) put it:

> I believe the erotic springs from our roots as women, and is a life-giving, powerful force at the centre of every woman. Men hate/fear this strength, have denied its existence, and have taught us to fear it ourselves. It is this fear that is the root of pornography.
>
> So I see the struggle to reclaim the erotic as a power in our lives as a fundamental attack on male sexuality and power. If we ignore or suppress it then we are once again fighting against ourselves because of the guilt and uncertainty that men have put into our heads.

This passage expresses a Reichian view of sexual energy as the most fundamental thing about us. If only we could express it properly, everything else would fall into place.

It is idealist, a denial of material reality, to believe that sexual freedom is possible so long as the vast majority of women remain economically and socially subordinate to men. The dream of shared and equal sexual pleasure within unequal marriage was the dream of the 1950s; and in the 'permissive' 1960s the dream was extended to heterosexuality outside marriage as well. Feminism came partly out of a rejection of such false dreams and we cannot return to them now. This does not mean that sexuality will fall into place 'after the revolution' but that there is a constant and complex relationship between our sexual experience and everything else, and that material provision – refuges for battered women, different divorce laws – may change sexual practice every bit as successfully as 'liberating' our sexuality or as 'understanding' and theorising.

In recent years some theorists have challenged the belief that sexuality is the core of our being, the most 'natural' part of ourselves. Work that has drawn on the writings of Michel Foucault and on Lacanian psychoanalysis has insisted that both sexual identity and gender are socially constructed. At best the sexual self is a fragile thing, wobbling on the border between the recognised and conscious 'personality' and the formless depths of the unconscious. The very notion of sexual identity becomes, according to this view, a kind of ideology – which has consequences for the notion of homosexual identity.

The feminist movement – and contemporary male gay groupings – have also not been untouched by the commoditisation in late capitalist society of sexual relations, as everything else. One aspect of this is the technologisation of the body; just as people wear headsets to go jogging, so they bring various sex aids or additions to the body to assist their sexual lives. It is not that there is anything 'wrong' with this, and it is, I suppose, a critique at the level of technology of the idea that sex is 'natural'; but technology and techniques can do relatively little to increase our understanding of ourselves and our sexuality.

The prevailing theories, whether consciously developed or part of the 'common sense' of the wider society – taken for granted ideas that we slip back into (because they're so familiar) unless we're constantly on our guard – have influenced both the experience and the theorising of heterosexuality. Further, as our culture has become more and more saturated with sexual imagery, the position and perceptions of lesbians and homosexual men have changed in relation to what is being said about sex generally. Lesbians are no longer 'Women of the Shadows' (the title of a lesbian novel written in the 1950s) in quite the way they used to be. Homosexual men are no longer perceived as effete, but have on the contrary developed a macho image.

## Lesbianism: a twentieth-century condition

For gay men it came as a revelation to realise that the 'homosexual identity' had existed in western societies for only about 200 years. Mary McIntosh's path-breaking article 'The Homosexual Role'[1] described how there were 'homosexual acts' in virtually all societies, but

182

that only in certain societies were there individuals who came to be described as 'homosexuals', a master-identity that defined all aspects of their lives and behaviour, not just what they did in bed.

Later, as Jeffrey Weeks[2] and Lillian Faderman[3] showed us, we saw that the lesbian identity was of even more recent origin and did not really come into being until the early twentieth century when the Victorian belief that women were sexless began to break down. The most famous novels from this period deal with lesbianism as an identity and as a role. The sexual practices of lesbians seemed less important than an understanding of what a lesbian *was*.

Radclyffe Hall's *The Well of Loneliness* was the most notorious of these novels. Recently, Alison Hennegan[4] has elucidated the tension that exists in this novel between nature and nurture theories of homosexuality. The author portrays the deeply masculine heroine/hero, Steven Gordon, as a member of the 'third sex', an invert: 'a person who was born with a male soul and mind trapped in a female body', one of God's mistakes. At the same time Alison Hennegan points out that there is a latent awareness of how lesbianism is the outcome of environmental experiences, and she uncovers a subtext that questions biological explanations, and points to the knowledge that Steven's dilemma exists because 'she thinks, feels and desires in ways forbidden to her as a woman', and that she has to find 'a way of living her life without constant reference to heterosexual standards and masculine values.'

Although, or perhaps because, the erotic love described in *The Well of Loneliness* is of an invert for a 'real woman', what comes across most strongly is not Steven's desire for the woman with whom she falls in love, but a romantic and highly narcissistic construction of Steven as a type of masculinity in which there nevertheless remains a haunting ambiguity. The dissonance between her woman's body, no matter how thin-flanked and boyish, and her male personality results in her being surrounded with the romantic aura of the impossible. She is one of the band of the 'haunted, tormented' and damned who transcend the degradation which is itself their glory. As Colette, who had a liaison with such a woman for six years, wrote:[5]

The seduction emanating from a person of uncertain or dissimulated sex is powerful. . . . Anxious and veiled, never exposed to the light of day, the androgynous creature wanders, wonders and implores in a whisper. . . . There especially remains for the androgynous creature the right, even the obligation, never to be happy. . . . It trails irrevocably among us its seraphic suffering, its glimmering tears. . . . She is the person who has no counterpart anywhere.

Djuna Barns in *Nightwood*, first published in 1936, also tried to analyse the attraction:[6]

> What is this love we have for the invert, boy or girl? It was they who were spoken of in every romance that we ever read. The girl lost, what is she but the Prince found? The Prince on the white horse that we have always been seeking . . . in the girl it is the prince, and in the boy it is the girl that makes a prince a prince – and not a man. They go far back in our lost distance where what we never had stands waiting. . . . They are our answer to what our grandmothers were told love was . . . the living lie of our centuries.

But that is not the worst of this romantic image. For, as Ruby Rich, feminist film critic, has said, if the androgynous boy–girl is the image of your desire, where does that place *you* as lover? The opposite of masculine is feminine, but the opposite of androgynous is – what?

After the second world war the glamour of the *femme damnée* gave place to a sensible and normalising image. We think of the 1950s as a time of repression and conservatism, yet it began to be possible then for lesbians to get away from the type of the 'invert'. In the United States, the lesbian organisation, Daughters of Bilitis, published a magazine, *The Ladder*, from 1956 to 1972, which questioned role-playing and took a reformist, civil rights stance to defend lesbians as a persecuted minority who might be deviant through no fault of their own, but who still had a right to an equal place in society. At times the magazine went further, emphasising the independence of the lesbian, and lesbianism as choice.

This was also the 'golden era' of lesbian paperback original novels, lesbian romances written not for men but for a lesbian market that was known to exist. Those by Artemis Smith, Anne Bannon and to a lesser extent Paula Christian, for example, showed lesbian sexuality and relationships as a valid way of life; Artemis Smith in particular was critical of exaggerated 'butch' and 'femme' roles, and wrote about more egalitarian relationships in which women loved and desired each other as women. Just why those novels were written at that time I am not sure, but they must have been written for the bored, thwarted housewives who were often their heroines, as well as for 'out' lesbians in 'the life' of the clubs and bars.

Maureen Duffy's *The Microcosm*,[7] published in 1965, reads like an amalgam of traditions. The novel makes a plea for lesbians not to stay in the half-world ghetto of the clubs and bars, turning their sexual orientation into a way of life. Yet although the author paints careful portraits of her characters which show the social construction of their lesbianism, the main character, Matt, is as male as they come and displays a positively chauvinist attitude towards 'women', relating to lovers as to a feminine Other, a mystery. So *The Microcosm* is ultimately unsatisfactory because of its failure to confront Matt's masculinity and to explain the significance of that subjective maleness.

Radclyffe Hall and Maureen Duffy are reticent as to the consequences of masculine and feminine role-playing for lesbian sexual practice. The bookstall novels of Artemis Smith, by no means prurient, are franker, and suggest that exaggerated roles lead to a sexual dishonesty in which the 'femme' partner is really looking for a man.

## *The seventies: Every woman can be a lesbian*

Although there undoubtedly were lesbians in the earlier Suffrage Movement, and although lesbianism was a haunting concern of the feminists and writers of the 1920s and 1930s (Virginia Woolf and Rosamund Lehmann are two obvious examples), it was only in the late 1960s and early 1970s that the second wave of feminism openly took lesbianism on board. For the first time the stigmatisation of lesbians was seen as one aspect of the subordination of women: lesbians 'had' to be punished by society because they were trying to escape male domination.

So, almost from the beginning, the women's liberation movement politicised lesbianism (as had the Gay movement). Lesbianism became one of the major themes of the contemporary women's movement, reconstructed imaginatively and theoretically to fit in with new political imperatives. One of these was to present above all a *positive* image of lesbianism: 'Gay is Good' became 'lesbianism is better'.

Although psychoanalysis has been important for some British feminists, the dominant, although often unacknowledged, theory of the feminist discourse on sexuality has been behaviourism. Lynne Segal discusses behaviourism in relation to heterosexuality elsewhere in this book. But a silent set of behaviourist assumptions has also coloured the way in which many women discussed and thought about lesbianism.

The behaviourist or conditioning model of behaviour has usually been associated with right-wing politics and oppressive 'treatments', although one of its earliest pioneers, Pavlov, was a Soviet citizen. Behaviourism has been the official psychology of the USSR, and whatever we think of the Soviet Union today, we should remember that the attraction of behaviourism to socialists at that time was that it appeared to be a completely environmentalist and therefore socially progressive theory. It suggests that the individual is initially a blank page on which anything can be written; therefore in a socialist society individuals could be conditioned to be non-violent, communally-minded, non-competitive, incorruptible, and so on, since basically we learn our responses by being rewarded or punished for them.

It is not surprising if feminists too have implicitly accepted an ideology which suggests that the conscious, willed re-education of the individual changes attitudes and desires. This is, after all, an optimistic view of human nature, if rather naïve. For feminists, it meant that not only could you learn to have orgasms, you could also learn to respond sexually to women.

Why should feminists want to 'learn' to be lesbians? Many saw erotic attraction for a man as itself a cornerstone of the subordination of women. Sexual passion sugared the pill of dependency, or even created the dependency and led to enslavement and the annihilation of self. Many women felt that a relationship with a man involved the collapse of their own identity, and it was to get away from the internalised sense of inferiority that some women turned to other women with whom alone, it seemed, they could have an equal relationship. And if sex with women turned out to be less exciting, that might be no bad thing: it made it less compulsive. Jealousy, surrender and romanticism could be abandoned, along with hard fucking.

A second reason was that in relating erotically to a woman you lived out your politics with fewer contradictions. As Lilian Mohin[8] explains:

> My political work is focused on women, on creating what it can mean to be women. Daily, I attempt to invent the theoretical ground I stand on. There are no acceptable pre-existing patterns for the women we can and must become. For me, being a political lesbian is about concentrating on women, our needs, our strengths, how to use, develop, achieve these.

Above all, there is emphasis on choice.

But the choice that feminists emphasised in the 1970s was a different choice from the choice at which lesbians gestured in the 1960s. It was more than a reaction against Radclyffe Hall's picture of the doomed invert, blighted by God with an unnatural nature which is natural to her. To see oneself in that way was close to saying one was a freak. Lesbians in the 1960s liked to see themselves as normal. Feminists in the 1970s went beyond this and experienced the adoption of lesbianism as a political rejection of women's inferior status:

> If you grow up wanting to be whole as a woman in this society, then you have to be a feminist. . . . And once you're a feminist it's almost impossible to have any kind of whole relationship with a man because there are all kinds of roles that you're taught, and even if he's really cool, you know, other people lay trips on you and it's all so ingrained. That's the only way I can see myself going really, from a strong person, to a feminist to a lesbian. It's just a very logical progression.[9]

Lesbianism no longer, therefore, involves the adoption of roles; on the contrary it comes to be seen as the escape route from the socially-constructed gender roles imposed on all women (and men) in our society. Paradoxically, the role-playing falsity of gender is now, according to this scenario, the norm of heterosexuality, while lesbianism becomes the arena for the flowering of real womanhood.

Some feminists have indeed extended the concept of lesbianism so that it comes to include all positive relationships between women. Adrienne Rich[10] has taken this view to its logical conclusion:

> I mean the term *lesbian continuum* to include a range – through each woman's life and throughout history – of woman-identified experience; not simply the fact that a woman has had or consciously desired genital experience with another woman. If we expand it to embrace many more forms of primary intensity between and among women, including the sharing of a rich inner life, the bonding against male tyranny, the giving and receiving of practical and political support . . . we begin to grasp breadths of female history and psychology which have lain out of reach as a consequence of limited, mostly clinical, definitions of 'lesbianism'.

This definition is reductionist[11] since it collapses lesbianism and feminism (and indeed femaleness) together, so that ultimately the

187

very notion of 'lesbian' disappears in a general affirmation of 'woman'.

Lillian Faderman, too, emphasises the feeling between women rather than the sex:

Lesbian describes a relationship in which two women's strongest emotions and affections are directed toward each other. Sexual contact may be a part of the relationship to a greater or lesser degree, or it may be entirely absent. By preference the two women spend most of their time together and share most aspects of their lives with each other.

Her historical account of erotic and romantic friendship between women is therefore unsatisfactory, since although the welter of material is fascinating, her theoretical vagueness simply creates further confusion as to just what the emotional and sexual significance of these relationships was.

All the definitions discussed so far positively play down the sexual aspect of lesbianism which ultimately, in the statement on political lesbianism by the Leeds Revolutionary Feminists,[12] becomes utterly redundant:

We do think that all feminists can and should be political lesbians. Our definition of a political lesbian is a woman-identified woman who does not fuck men. It does not mean compulsory sexual activity with women.

Such a definition develops logically out of a perception of sex with men as the archetypal moment of male supremacy:

Only in the system of oppression that is male supremacy does the oppressor actually invade and colonise the interior of the body of the oppressed. Attached to all forms of sexual behaviour are meanings of dominance and submission, power and powerlessness, conquest and humiliation. There is very special importance attached to sexuality under male supremacy when every sexual reference, every sexual joke, every sexual image serves to remind a woman of her invaded centre and a man of his power. Why all this fuss in our culture about sex? Because it is specifically through sexuality that the fundamental oppression, that of men over women, is maintained.

Feminists de-emphasised sex and the erotic, whether intentionally or not, partly perhaps in reaction against the 'swinging sixties' and the insistence of that period on male-defined sex with no strings attached, and the performance principle of the perfect orgasm. It might seem curious that feminists at the same time took over unchanged from the counter-culture a vehement opposition to monogamy – possessiveness, jealousy, couples and exclusiveness were just as much taboo amongst feminists as they had been in the 'pads' of the 'hip guys' and 'groovy chicks'. Yet the feminist project was a coherent one: a rejection of romantic love and its basis in intense sexual passion.

Romantic passion was not the point; it probably seemed decadent, negative and destructive. Implicitly the ideal of comradeship replaced it, and the ideal of comrades who are lovers, united in working for a higher cause and therefore above petty possessiveness, already current amongst revolutionaries early in the century if not before, is an honourable one. It is also highly rationalistic. And yet it is, in its own way, romantic too, idealising the revolutionary, the strong woman, as an exemplary type. And because it idealises it easily tips over into moralism: while not to manage to live out the ideal causes immense guilt, rage and pain.

Although many writings about lesbianism from the contemporary women's movement have talked about women's bonding rather than about sex, there have been attempts, both fictional or 'confessional' and theoretical to develop ideas about sex between women. Nevertheless, most of the women writing about psychoanalysis have been strangely silent on the subject. Neither Nancy Chodorow, Juliet Mitchell or British Lacanians have confronted it. There are books about lesbian love-making, but these come into the 'technical' category. Then there are erotic descriptions of lesbian love-making in novels, short stories and articles, such as some of those in the *Heresies* (1980) issue on sex.

Bea Campbell is one of the few women who has tried to develop a distinct theoretical and political approach. Like the Leeds Revolutionary Feminists she sees heterosexual intercourse as the moment, or virtually so, of male supremacy:[13] 'Women began to recognise conventional heterosexual practice as the glue which holds up the patriarchal order.' This is proved because 'conventional heterosexual practice – that bizarre mixture of myth and coercion – is defended more vigorously than any other precept on which our society is supposed to be founded.' Consequently, the feminist questioning of heterosexuality 'holds within it a fundamental challenge to patriarchy.' It was Anna Koedt, in her pamphlet *The Myth of the Vaginal*

*Orgasm*, who challenged heterosexuality most radically:

> Koedt suggests that 'the establishment of clitoral orgasm as fact
> would threaten the heterosexual *institution*' and that men are too
> fearful of losing their hold over women to imagine 'a future free
> relationship between individuals'. Male power relies heavily on
> the continued sexual dependency of women and this becomes
> more crucial as women seek greater social and economic
> independence.

Bea Campbell herself relies, as does Anna Koedt, on the work of
Masters and Johnson and on Shere Hite's work – all of which is
behaviourist – and this body of work *assumes* that because the clitoris
is physiologically the nerve centre for the female orgasm penetration
becomes irrational (save for reproductive purposes). Bea Campbell
therefore argues that we have to get away from a hierarchical sexuality which perceives penetration as the ultimate 'sexual act'. She
implies new and more 'democratic' explorations of a variety of sexual
pleasures, none of which can be given primacy or judged as 'better' or
'less' than any other.

She attributes a central political importance to the split in the
British women's movement between heterosexual and lesbian or
separatist feminists, which became a bitter one in the mid-1970s. A
possible solution is suggested in *Sweet Freedom*, a solution that
carries with it a number of unstated political assumptions and consequences. It is argued that heterosexual and homosexual women
should emphasise their similarities rather than their differences. The
very notion of a gay or lesbian identity is rejected. This rejection
implicitly flows from theoretical developments within the Left during
the 1970s. These developments[14] have tended to reject the idea of
gayness as an identity *because* of the understanding I mentioned
earlier: that the homosexual identity or role was a confining, restricting and stigmatised one created by the dominant and repressive
society. In order to reject the values of that society you also have to
reject the very idea that you 'are' a homosexual, and instead you
become a person who simply goes in for certain 'sexual practices':

> Lesbianism in the women's liberation movement has been as
> much about women as about homosexuality, as it is conventionally
> defined. It has been more about desire than about identity as one
> specific type or another. As such it represents a challenge to the
> very category of 'homosexuality' – and a correlating challenge to

190

the 'heterosexual' category . . . [What is advocated is ] a positive commitment to female eroticism, as something powerful and autonomous, which is shared by heterosexuals, lesbians and bisexuals – and which transcends all such definitions, robbing them of meaning except as barricades thrown up in defence of patriarchy. If the political significance of this could be seized, then femininity could be taken out of its straitjacket and celebrated rather than shunned. It could be positive and strong as well as sensual, desiring as well as desirable. It would not necessarily deny men, and it would certainly not rely on them. It would be what women wanted it to be, not what men decreed.[15]

It is right to insist that women experience desire and that desire is active. Yet the *Sweet Freedom* statement is utopian because it ignores the actual homophobia of the existing society, or at least evades the political consequence of the actual persecution of homosexuals. It is utopian because it harks back to the Marcusianism of the 1960s in which polymorph perverse sexuality was seen as the answer to a repressed world, a grand flowering of any and every sexual act which would somehow break through the death wish of our society: 'democracy' again. All this ignores the way in which sexual desire is constructed within each individual in quite specific ways. It ignores the existence of an unconscious life and, very strangely, doesn't question 'femininity'. It is therefore an empty ideal, and comes close to being simply the search for the magical orgasm in a new guise. Moreover it is the height of individualism, for the free-floating individual is pictured as engaged in a quest for erotic celebration outside the context of the social relationships that inevitably structure sex. Above all the nature of 'female eroticism' is left tantalisingly vague; and yet it is assumed that it does in some way exist. There is therefore an underlying assumption that women, or the female, or femininity is set up as essentially different from man, male, masculine. Yet how this comes about (the problematic of psychoanalysis) is ignored. Also ignored is the possibility that there could ever be similarities between what men and women might feel erotically.

## Lesbian fiction

Feminist writing is and must be a political endeavour. This creates a special problem for feminist lesbian fiction. It is possible to argue the rights or wrongs of Bea Campbell's analytical position without suggesting that her project itself is misconceived, and the whole debate

191

can remain within the parameters of an assumption that lesbianism itself is not under attack or being devalued. Fiction operates differently upon us from polemical or theoretical writing. It persuades at a different level and perhaps in a more subversive way. Is it therefore justifiable to write *anything* negative about a lesbianism that is stigmatised already in the wider society? Maureen Brady and Judith McDaniel[16] in a review of some commercially successful lesbian novels imply that it is not, for they scathingly indict the authors for marginalising lesbianism and reproducing mechanisms of self hatred:

> Several dominant theses recur in these books; the common factor is that all in some way disempower the lesbian. . . . In these novels we do not read about what we have found in our lesbian relationships – the intimacy, the support.

But what if the reality was difficult and painful? Kate Stimpson's *Class Notes*,[17] for example, one of the novels they discuss, is about discovering you are a lesbian in the 1950s, a subject likely to involve admissions of ambivalence, guilt and self-hatred.

Some novels have presented positive images of lesbian life-styles and loving. Both Rita Mae Brown's *Ruby Fruit Jungle*[18] and Marge Piercy's *Small Changes*[19] place passionate and satisfactory lesbian relationships at the centre of the action. It is good that this should happen in popular, mass-circulation novels. Yet in reading these and other lesbian novels that have come out of contemporary feminism I have been left with a sense of repetition rather than of exploration. The theme is the familiar one of self-discovery, of the searching for a lifestyle that will embody the heroine's dreams. Lesbianism as destiny, lesbianism as alternative life-style, lesbianism as enactment of sexual liberation: why are these themes unsatisfactory?

Possibly the underlying project is at fault. Perhaps fiction is not the best vehicle for positive images of love relationships. Would we after all find much to interest us in novels about heterosexual love that purveyed so wholesome a message of optimism and happy endings? As Tolstoy said: 'All happy families are alike but every unhappy family is unhappy in its own way.' And the same goes for lovers, so that fiction has sustained itself on the dramas and tragedies of thwarted or transient love, while happy couples usually seem bland and lifeless by comparison.

Many feminists who turned to lesbianism no doubt had unrealistic expectations. In the early 1970s, when large women's meetings on sexuality were first held, women used to speak out of their hopes that

192

in lesbian relationships sisterhood would transcend the difficulties of heterosexual love, or simply bypass them. When this didn't happen there was disillusionment and resentment, so no wonder that, their idealistic hopes disappointed, some women returned to men.

For some, lesbian relationships may have represented an escape from oppressive sexual desires for men – desires that were experienced as shameful and which, women felt, locked them into their subordination. Yet within relationships between women there could develop a no holds barred level of demand and need, as if women felt safer with other women to cast off all emotional restraint. Back in what Freud called the grey hinterland of the early relationship with the mother anything could happen, and it might then come as a relief to return to heterosexuality, where the rules were clearer and the boundaries more clearly marked, even if the odds were loaded against you in the game as it is played with men.

Kate Millett's novels *Sita*[20] and *Flying*[21] give blow-by-blow accounts of lesbian relationships rent with rage and agony. Tedious and compulsive, raw, self-indulgent and self-punishing, the bleeding ego of Kate Millett's heroine(s) decomposes rather than deconstructs the moment-by-moment anguish that not only dares to speak its name but dares to bare its wounds.

Was it really happier, or stronger in the 1950s? Or was it easier when the boundaries were more sharply defined? Joan Nestle,[22] writing of 'butch' and 'femme' roles, speaks of sexual courage and of outlawry, and hers is one of the few attempts to explain the different androgyny of the butch lesbian and the 'thrill of her power':

> This power is not bought at the expense of the fem's identity. Butch-fem relationships as I experienced them, were complex erotic statements, not phony heterosexual replicas. They were filled with a deeply lesbian language of stance, dress, gesture, love, courage and autonomy. None of the butch women I was with . . . ever presented themselves to me as men; they did announce themselves as tabooed women who were willing to identify their passion for other women by wearing clothes that symbolized the taking of responsibility. Part of the responsibility was sexual expertise. In the 1950s this courage to feel comfortable with arousing another woman became a political act.

## Conclusion

Many of the books I have criticised will have been important to women and given them strength or reassurance. Yet one is left with an impression of gaps, of evasions and denials. The mere fact that men have so often been cast in the role of originators of all that is dark and violent in erotic love may deprive lesbianism of a cutting edge. But then sex means so many different things to different people and how near the edge do we want it to take us?

Yet an ideology of the power of positive thinking will never help us understand the darker and more poignant elements of sexual desire, the many ambiguities of sexual attraction, the mixture of the masculine and feminine in each of us. Do we want to end up with a sort of sexual Fabianism, or else with a glittering consumerism in which erotic games become another adjunct of the lifestyle beautiful?

Perhaps Freud[23] was right, and we may need to build barriers in the way of our own satisfactions:

> An obstacle is required in order to heighten [desire]; and where natural resistances to satisfaction have not been sufficient men have at all times erected conventional ones so as to be able to enjoy love.

To deprive lesbianism of its aura of the forbidden may for some women rob it of its compulsive charm. Or we may suspect that the experience of passionate love, whether with a man or a woman, requires a psychic superstructure of what is essentially romantic imagery, and an investment of the lover with magical, remote and transforming qualities (as Lucy Goodison describes in Chapter 4), which may come close to the objectification feminism has been committed to oppose. On the other hand, perhaps Freud, who was a great romantic, simply expresses the romantic sensibility. But romanticism at least acknowledges that sexual passion is as much about imagination as biology. And it would be possible to argue that homosexuality represents the ultimate triumph of the imaginative over the biological.

Sexual identity and sexual desire are not fixed and unchanging. We create boundaries and identities for ourselves to contain what might otherwise threaten to engulf, or dissolve into formlessness. The psychic truth of desire does not always or inevitably correspond to gender, still less to biology. Women may love the feminine in men as well as the masculine, the masculine in women as well as the womanly. Passion is more than the celebration of the clitoris, nor can it be collapsed – as we have all now realised – into the politically correct.

194

In the 1960s the sexual radicals discovered the clitoris and promoted the cult of orgasm. Many of them followed in the footsteps of Wilhelm Reich and believed that the fullest orgasm was devoid of fantasy. In the 1970s the feminists discovered the construction of gender, debunked the ideology of the 'natural' and tried to construct an alternative sexual world that, paradoxically, would celebrate some essential female eroticism.

In the 1980s, perhaps we shall negotiate more humbly the dangerous and shadowed boundary between the grandiose demands of the pleasure principle and the constraints of the individual psyche. And we may learn, in a new context, that freedom is the recognition of necessity.

# 13
# Psychoanalysis and Women Loving Women

Joanna Ryan

*I*

In this chapter I want to look at some ways in which psychoanalysis can be helpful in understanding our sexuality. Clearly the scope of such a discussion is enormous, and I can only pick out some specific feminist uses of psychoanalysis and indicate the limits of these. I want to consider the central question of attraction in relation to the now widespread experience of change in sexual orientation from heterosexual to lesbian.

Our sexual relationships stand out in our lives as areas of felt irrationality, the focus of our strongest and most conflicting feelings. The phrase 'turned on', with its suggestions of switches and electricity, captures the seemingly absolute nature of attraction – how remote from conscious control our sexual feelings are, how forceful when they come, how total in their absence when they do not. There is often a tremendous difference in our feelings between people we feel sexual towards and those we don't, between lovers and friends, with little continuity between the two. This split, whilst experienced as quite natural, is itself part of the social formation of our sexuality, of the way in which it has been channelled, associated with some people and some emotions, and not with others. Sex is often written about as if it were an absolute and irreducible category of human experience, as if we knew without doubt what it is or isn't. But in fact this in itself is an assumption, a product of how our sexuality is formed and lived, that it should appear to have this discreteness from other forms of contact between people.

The notion of attraction has often been attacked as mystified and oppressive. There is a persisting tradition within libertarian and some feminist politics of trying to make sexual relationships less involuntary and exclusive, more rational. One means of doing this has been to blur the distinction between friends and lovers by substituting political sisters and comrades as sexual partners, in defiance of 'fancying'. Hence the sleeping rotas of some 1960s' communes, where the justification for sharing sex, if not the result, was the same as for other areas of domestic life: the creation of alternative structures which would allow different, less oppressive relationships to grow. Similarly now, there is a strong body of opinion that heterosexual women can decide to stop their sexual involvement with men and become, if not lesbian, at least more woman-identified. And some heterosexual feminists are insisting that men change their sexual inclinations, away from an obsessive focus on penetration and orgasm to one which accords more with what women might like or want. In all these instances sexuality is seen as subject to quite a degree of conscious control. The demand that it be so is posed not only as a challenge about who or what is attractive, but also about the nature of attraction itself. Does this have to remain a mysterious force in our lives?

Some people have been able to accommodate their sexuality in these ways, others have become confused, uncertain and often asexual, and yet others have remained stuck with familiar patterns of attraction and non-attraction, with varying degrees of guilt and compromise. Whilst we may disagree with the most voluntaristic politics as completely underestimating the strength, complexity and depth of our feelings, are we just to be stuck with old and mystified notions of attraction, or a complete collapse into the unconscious? What is the scope for understanding the sources of sexual attraction in a way that allows us some possibility of change and control in our lives and of opposition to prevailing norms, but which doesn't negate the reality of our emotions or result in untenable arrangements? One of the points at issue here is what does constitute the reality of our emotions. As they as absolute and irreducible as it is often assumed? Or is the common assumption of their fixity another way in which we construct ourselves and are constructed?

We could view the process of sexual fetishism as only an extreme example of what happens 'normally'. There, the same objects or activities are needed over and over again for sexual excitement or release, with a consequent severe restriction in the kind of relationship involved (if any), and with a rigid lack of capacity for change. Parts of the body, specific acts or scenarios, clothes, etc. are substituted for whole persons, images for actual people. It is striking that massively more men than women are involved in fetishistic or 'perverse' practices of some kind – indeed most books on the subject really are about male sexuality.[1] And from a wider point of view the whole culture of compulsory heterosexuality seems fetishistic and suited primarily to male 'needs': women have to be of a certain shape, size, age and appearance in order to be desired; certains parts of the female body are at a premium as sexual stimuli, and certain repetitive patterns of behaviour (seductiveness, passivity) are required for the stereotypically satisfying sexual act. The cultural imposition of norms and stereotypes of sexuality, and the hypervalution of specific forms of attractiveness, represent an enormous restriction of our sexual potential and diversity. It excludes vast numbers of women from being seen as sexual at all, and elevates a few to impossible or untenable standards of attractiveness. With this comes a very specific oppression of women: a deep-seated self-hatred and dislike of our own bodies, a minefield of competitiveness with other women about appearance, all of which are surprisingly hard to eradicate even with the creation of alternative values and norms. It is within this context, as well as that of the immediate family, that our specific sexualities are formed.

The supposedly absolute nature of sexual attraction extends to common ideas of sexual orientation, the assumption that we have to be one or the other – homo- or heterosexual – and that there is an identity that is our real one, whatever our actual behaviour. It is clear that the construction of a discrete homosexual identity is a relatively recent development, for both sexes,[2] and that this has necessitated the invention of a problematic third category, 'bisexual'. Although we cannot avoid using the terms involved (and often there are important reasons why, with a different valuation, we should do so), we should not adopt these categories uncritically, especially as regards the assumptions involved about sexual identity and attraction.

One of the major achievements of the women's movement has been its facilitation of sexual relationships between women. It is important that we try to understand this transformation, not only for its personal and political importance, but also because it can clarify our ideas about how sexuality is formed more generally. It certainly is not sufficient to see the process of change as only one of political choice, even though this may be a contributing factor. We have as well to look at the deeper emotional changes involved, and the basis on which our previous heterosexuality was constructed. Many psychological and psychoanalytic theories, including some feminist ones,[3] would predict that such an extensive change of sexual orientation as has occurred through the women's movement would not be possible or would only be 'superficial', and behaviourist attempts to condition adults (always of course into heterosexuality) have not been conspicuously successful.

The phrase most often used by feminists to describe this process is 'coming out'. Whilst this contains the suggestive imagery of blooming and flowering, and of needing the ground and the sun to do so, it also carries the implication, sometimes explicit sometimes not, of revealing previously hidden and unknown identities, our real or true selves. The enormous sense of self-discovery and self-realisation that can accompany a long denied acknowledgement of sexual attraction to other women is not to be ignored or underrated: nor, even now, the courage required to do so. However, to describe this as the discovery of one's real identity begs too many questions about the processes involved and what was experienced beforehand. Not only does it imply a fixed (albeit hidden) identity of one or the other kind, it also is in danger of dismissing past engagement with heterosexuality as false consciousness, an unknowing or unwilling compliance, certainly not one's real self. For women with periods of substantial heterosexuality this problem is particularly acute: however painful and unsatisfactory these relationships may have been, they cannot be disowned. To do so is to deny a part of ourselves, the needs and hopes invested, however mistakenly, in such relationships, which may well carry over into present lesbian ones.

There is, though, a problem about how to describe the change involved, without it seeming chameleon-like and mysterious on the one hand, or excessively rational on the other. We need a way of sufficiently validating the enormous leap involved without losing all sense of continuity within ourselves. Whereas there *is* a complete discontinuity in lesbian and heterosexual existence in terms of social acceptability, discrimination and the possibilities for self-disclosure, with all that this means for any one woman, it does not have to be a political cop-out to consider the substantial continuities that do exist, at least for some women, in the primary emotions involved – love, dependency, jealousy, trust, for example.

Psychoanalysis as a whole does not have much to say about lesbianism that is unpejorative or illuminating, but it does contain a form of understanding that is at least adequate to the complexity of our sexual feelings, and which can contribute to our understanding of what is involved in such a change of sexual relationships.

*II*

Psychoanalysis is far from being one unified body of theory and

199

practice, and since Freud it has developed into many distinct schools of thought. These developments have taken place in different ways: as a result of clinical and therapeutic practice in different settings, and through the introduction of new concepts and theoretical developments. The psychoanalysis that has been introduced into the women's movement represents two very different traditions and two very different sets of interest: Freudo–Lacanian theoretical writings about the construction of femininity and female identity, and the use of post-Kleinian, 'object-relations' theory in feminist therapy and writings about this. Here I shall consider some specific uses of object-relations theory, as it has been written about in the women's movement, without attempting to discuss the differences between the two approaches.

Feminist therapy has developed from quite pragmatic origins. It has had to tread a complex methodological and political path in understanding how what is social creates the individual, and what the limits of therapy are. It is no accident that feminist psychoanalytic therapy, as well as some more practical Marxist approaches[4] have turned to object-relations theory in attempting this. This branch of psychoanalysis, associated originally with Balint, Fairbairn, Guntrip and Winnicott, contains a decisive break with certain aspects of Freudian theory, with its inherent biologism, its notions of instinct and gratification, and its anatomically-based conceptions of sexuality. It contains a more inherently social view of psychological development, seeing individuals as formed in relation to, and seeking connection with, others. It replaces the notion of libidinal stages with an account of the gradual differentiation of the self, through the formation of internal 'objects' – reflections of our experience of real persons from earliest infancy which then form and structure our later relationships. I am not claiming that this school of thought is uncontentious for feminists – its perspective on mothering, for example, is very problematic – but feminist development of it has been extremely fruitful, particularly in its emphasis on the early mother–daughter relationship and the development of a sense of self within this.

Whilst disputing the Freudian notion of sexuality or libido as central to mental life, object-relations theory does not really contain a theory of sexuality as such. Instead sexuality is seen as stemming from the whole development of the personality rather than as determining it, and the goal of sexual activity is viewed as object rather than pleasure seeking. Recent feminist development of object-relations theory contains as much of a theory of sexuality and sexual identity as is to be found in previous writings.

200

## III

E.S. Person argues that sexuality expresses many aspects of personality and motivation, originating in both infantile and later experiences, and varying between individuals as to its role and importance in their lives.[5] She also argues for the critical importance of early tactile experience in mediating the relationship between infant and caretaker, and assumes that later sexuality develops out of this early sensuality: 'Because sensual pleasure is the vehicle of object relations in the real world, sexuality expresses an enormous variety of motives, predominantly dependent or hostile, and the force of sexuality exists precisely because sexuality is linked to other motives.' In particular, because of the real dependence of a helpless child on a relatively powerful adult, 'it is unlikely that sexuality will ever be completely free of submission–dominance connotations.'

Chodorow, in her far-reaching book[6], assumes that a main goal of adult sexuality is a return to a kind of 'oneness' or merging with the other. In this she is following Balint's notion of primary love and the attempts of adults to recapture it: 'This primary tendency, I shall be loved always, everywhere, in every way, my whole body, my whole being – without any criticism, without the slightest effort on my part – is the final aim of all erotic striving.'[7] Sexual intercourse, according to Annie Reich, is the 'temporary relinquishment of the separating boundaries',[8] or, according to Alice Balint, 'the situation in which the reciprocal interdependence as experienced in early childhood is re-created.'[9] Eichenbaum and Orbach express a similar idea: 'Because adult sexuality echoes aspects of mother infant pre-verbal sensuality in its very unique communication, sexuality and merger may stir up deeply resonant early physical experience before there was a definite sense of self and before language.'[10]

Merging with another is also described in non-psychoanalytic writings, though more as a peak of sexual experience than a common occurrence, and not as an echo of childhood experience. The Hite investigation included questions on why sexual intercourse was important to women, and many of the answers referred not just to closeness and intimacy, but also to various forms of merging: 'complete contact', 'breaking down barriers between self and others', 'we are one', 'becoming one in love', 'ultimate human closeness where a person can express and understand more than the mind can conceive of.'[11] (Other themes mentioned were: reassurance of being loved, becoming desirable, feeling like a woman, giving pleasure, feeling needed and special). It is as well to remember that most sexual intercourse does not approximate to these descriptions of merging: feeling disconnected from oneself or the other person, ambivalent, alienated, or only in contact sporadically, are also frequent experiences which may well be accompanied by other forms of satisfaction and pleasure apart from merging (conquest, reassurance, for example).

The idea that adult sexual activity can stir up infantile feelings in adults is basic to any psychoanalytic approach. Whilst problematic in some ways (because it is not entirely clear what is meant or why it should happen), it does point to some common predicaments in sexual relationships. That infants first of all experience themselves as totally merged with their mother (or other primary person) and then gradually differentiate separating boundaries is now a common conception. The symbiosis of early infancy is very different for infant and mother. For the infant it is a reflection of its limited consciousness and actual total dependence, without regard for the mother as a separate person with her own interests. Mother-love, on the other hand, involves an often overwhelming sense of 'reality' as regards concern for the interests of the child, to an extent that can become self-loss.

The re-experiencing of infantile states in sexual relationships is described above as though it was a relatively safe and satisfying experience, if hard to achieve. In fact, this 'merging' can only be partial and temporary (whereas the infantile state is total and timeless), since we actually are adults and retain some awareness of this and our capacity to return to our adult state should we desire to do so. And frequently it is painful and full of conflict, partly because we cannot actually become infants, and partly because of all the unmet needs, defences and fantasies stimulated by just this possibility – the craving for obliteration that Lynne Segal (Chapter 3) describes, the grief that Jill Brown (Chapter 5 (ii)) experiences, to mention only two examples. It seems it is the emotions associated with the infantile state that are stirred up so strongly rather than the state itself. The other person is felt as all-powerful, the self as needy, exposed and vulnerable (or sometimes the other way round). How acceptable such feelings are, how much trust or despair they evoke about being loved, depend on each person's history and current situation. Further, in adult–adult relationships we are also trying to be adults: both in reaction to our own child-like feelings of dependency and vulnerability, which may be too threatening, and also to care for the other person, both as adult and as child.

Despite these difficulties there are some interesting implications that have been drawn about this notion of merger. The first, described by Eichenbaum and Orbach, is that sexual connection can bring with it a fear of loss of self, and that this is particularly acute for women given the difficulties they have with developing a secure and separate sense of self as children. They describe women as either overwhelmed by sexual merger or as unable to 'let go' emotionally and physically, both consequences of an unclear sense of self and the false boundaries developed to cope with it. They maintain that in order to let go fully a defined sense of self is needed to return to, which thereby makes the experience not like an infantile state at all. Such fear of loss of self may keep women removed from sexual relations altogether or participating in them in a limited way: the result of either conscious or unconscious choices.

The implication that Chodorow draws is that heterosexual intercourse reproduces the infantile situation much more nearly for a man than for a woman, given the usual gender division of parenting: 'Men cannot provide the kind of return to oneness that women can.' Instead men come nearer to an experience of fusion with the mother in heterosexual sex than women can do, both because of the historic situation of female mothering and the fantasies and emotions associated with it, and also because of men's actual inabilities to be sensitive, caring and containing, to 'mother' in short. This creates an unequal situation in heterosexual relationships, where women can only recreate the experience of oneness at secondhand – either by identifying with the man's experience of fusion with her, or by becoming the mother to the man (child). Both are ways in which women can fail to experience either themselves as centre stage, or the great lack involved in this. The implication that Chodorow rather obviously does not draw is the absence of these particular structural inequalities from lesbian relationships, and the emotional possibilities that this opens out.

'Merging' is only one thread amongst many in sexual relationships. Loaded as it is with notions of caring and infancy, it does not convey anything very specifically erotic: for this we have to turn to discussions of sexual orientation.


*IV*

A strength of most psychoanalytic accounts is that they do not see a girl's pathway to heterosexuality as either straightforward or inevitable. Chodorow particularly, in that she is trying to break from all ideas of reproductive instinct or innate heterosexuality, emphasises the complex and highly contingent developmental processes that are involved and how heterosexuality is never established without considerable pain and ambivalence, conscious and unconscious. Her focus, like much of psychoanalytic theory, is the so-called 'change of object' that girls have to effect in order to become heterosexual, given that their first and most powerful experience of love and physical care is with a woman, that is homosexual. To become heterosexual as an adult a girl has to transfer her primary affections to someone of a different sex, a boy only to a different member of the same sex. There are many different psychoanalytic versions of this transfer, but what is widely recognised is its problematic nature, and also how incompletely, at an internal level, it ever happens.

Chodorow sees the nature of a girl's early relationship with her mother as motivating her to look elsewhere for a primary person other than the mother, and argues that the roots of eventual heterosexuality lie in the early mother–daughter relationship. She describes in some detail what she thinks happens in this early relationship, drawing on both psychoanalytic and observational literature, and contrasting it with the mother–son relationship. She argues that mothers relate to their daughters with a greater sense of symbiosis and identification than they do to their sons, to the extent that daughters may be felt as extensions of or identical to the mother. Eichenbaum and Orbach, although they have a less overridingly functionalist account than Chodorow of the effects of social roles, also emphasise the importance of gender similarity in creating identification between mother and daughter. Both appoaches concur in how this poses specific difficulties for girls in differentiating and separating themselves as individuals, and how these issues become connected to ones of loss of love and rejection.

Maternal identification does not guarantee that a daughter will feel adequately loved – quite the opposite is often the case, since, as Eichenbaum and Orbach describe, the identification is based on the culturally devalued attribute of femaleness and also mothers may perceive in their daughters, or project onto them, all the attributes of themselves that they least like (including their femaleness). Given the massive cultural preference for boys, it is hardly surprising that one common experience of women is of being inadequately loved and certainly less so than their brothers.

Chodorow adds to her account the tendency of mothers right from birth to sexualise their relationship with their sons but not with their daughters. Quite what this sexualisation of mother–son relationships consists of is not so clear, although she describes how sons become emotional substitutes for relatively absent husbands. Nor is it clear why Chodorow is so categorical about the absence of any sexualisation between mother and daughter. For one thing this differentiation assumes (which Chodorow acknowledges) the mother's exclusive heterosexuality and that this applies across the board to infants. Secondly it underplays any element of physical sensuality between mothers and daughters, which often, as Eichenbaum and Orbach point out, is an important aspect of women's memories of their mothers, but one which is largely ignored and devalued on all sides. They tend rather to emphasise the physical and erotic nature of the involvement of mothers with their daughters, but describe how this is curtailed, contained and cut off. The other aspect of sexualisation between mother and daughter that they emphasise is not with the daughter as possible object of the mother's feelings, but as similar subject, in which a mother's feelings about herself, her body and sexuality in general are transmitted to a daughter with strong undercurrents of anxiety, approval and disapproval.

Chodorow argues that a girl's 'change of object' rests on these prior developments, and is motivated by a need to get away emotionally from the mother, a form of defence against even greater primary identification and dependence. The father or other parent-figure, regardless of gender or any other attribute, becomes a symbol of independence, of separation from the mother. 'The turn to the father . . . whatever its sexual meaning, also concerns emotional issues of self and other.' This underlines how non-gender processes (dependence, separation) become related to gender through the typical parenting practices of our society where women are primary and men secondary parents. As well, the girl's very love for her mother may be a problem for her; if she feels inadequately loved and not preferred, she may look for a kind of special love from her father she cannot get from her mother. And to this we may add, as do Eichenbaum and Orbach, and many writers before them, the girl's attempts to reject the inferiority and powerlessness of women, and acquire the power that men have in the world, as personified in her father.

Chodorow also describes the father's role in encouraging his daughter to look elsewhere than her mother to fulfil some of these needs, and, crucially for her account, describes this encouragement as 'sexualised in tone', which is where the father's gender is important. This allegedly consists in the father not only encouraging the girl in role-appropriate behaviour but also making her in some way an object of his sexual interest – encouraging flirtatious and seductive behaviour but not making himself actually available sexually (though of course this does happen much more often than is generally supposed). Eichenbaum and Orbach emphasise how mothers actively push their daughters in the direction of their fathers, or men in general, as sources of emotional involvement, but at the same time convey the disappointments and frustrations of such relationships.

Along with many other writers, Chodorow emphasises that this 'turn to the father' is seldom absolute, girls remain strongly attached (internally if not externally) to their mothers, and fathers never become emotionally so dominant. The typically late and insubstantial role they actually play in a child's life may mean they are the target of much idealisation and, as Eichenbaum and Orbach recount, bitterness.

In her account of adulthood Chodorow distinguishes three components: conscious heterosexual erotic orientation to men in general; heterosexual love or emotional attachment to a man with whom there is sexual involvement; and non-sexual emotional attachments; thus propounding a split between eroticism and emotional attachment. She views women as 'getting' the first from their fathers, who are seen as 'activating' genital sexuality but not the other two components because of their unavailability as satisfying love objects in most families. We are left with a view of women as pushed and pulled out of their original homosexual intimacy into an ambivalent and very incomplete heterosexuality, where men may be the exclusive and primary erotic objects but are for the most part emotionally secondary to women: 'a girl never gives up her mother as an internal and external love object, even if she does become heterosexual.'

Chodorow makes a girl's relationship to her father crucial to her eventual heterosexuality, albeit in the context of her prior relationship to her mother. She leaves undiscussed what happens if the father is not present, or does not behave in the way described. Her notion that fathers 'activate' genital sexuality is extremely problematic: it assumes a separate category of the sexual, defined in terms of eventual orientation, that comes only via the father. A girl's pre-existing sexuality, and erotic feelings between her and her mother, are unmentioned or denied. Despite her intention to avoid any form of biological determinism, Chodorow still invokes the 'broadening of innate sex drives' as one contributing factor in the girl's interest in her father, to fill this gap in her account.

What Chodorow leaves us with in terms of heterosexuality is a deep split between eroticism and emotional attachment, explicable in terms of the fact that sexuality is developed not in relation to the person with whom the deepest attachment is formed, but with one who is relatively unavailable for a close and caring relationship. Thus eroticism and emotional unavailability are closely connected, and men (for other reasons as well) are frequently extremely unsatisfactory love objects for women. Certainly this has been one of the collective realisations of the women's movement.

## V

Chodorow provides us with a vivid account of the fertile emotional ground on which relationships between women can grow. Her account makes the attainment of heterosexuality seem at once inevitable and profoundly precarious, never achieved without major ambivalence and built upon primary feelings of attachment to women. Heterosexuality is seen to involve as much a rejection and denial of attachment to women, in the form of the mother, as a positive attachment to men. In this sense heterosexuality is a defence against homosexuality, at both a personal and a social level. The early need to separate and individuate from a primary parent figure, so often a woman, to attain some measure of independence and self-hood, interacts with the cultural disparagement of women and the hypervaluation of men as this is mediated both via the mother–daughter relationship, and in many other ways. The fear and shame that most women can experience about sexually loving other women is as much witness to the desire to do so as it is to the social stigma and personal cost involved.

What is extraordinary is that Chodorow does not herself consider the implications of her arguments for the possibility of sexual relationships between women – extraordinary because she is so insistent on the persistent importance of women in women's emotional lives, and the problematic and contradictory nature of sexual relationships with men. Her practical conclusions all concern the transforming of men to become primary parental figures and more satisfactory love objects for women, rather than the facilitation of lesbian relationships, which she virtually ignores. Her questionable account of the mother–daughter relationship as basically asexual (compared to father–daughter, or mother–son) supports this bias, given her overall framework in which sexuality is seen as 'coming from' one or other parental relationship. Though it can be very helpful to look at adult sexuality in terms of the sensual and erotic nature of particular parental relationships, and though the idea that some of these are more or differently sexualised than others has considerable meaning, we cannot let the whole understanding of where our sexuality 'comes from' rest on these ideas. To do so is to create an account that is too closed and too inevitable. Chodorow, despite her insistence on the complexity and ambivalence with which social roles are internalised via parent–child relationships, does not allow enough space for the mass of other influences that can shape sexuality (peer group pressure, the media, for example) particularly during adolescence and later. The contradictory nature of our expectations and experience which has often been the impetus for feminism; the fact that we do change from generation to generation and do not only reproduce our mothers' oppression, is as much in need of explanation as is the internalisation of patriarchal ideology. What the women's movement as shown is how powerful later experiences can be, given the rich emotional ground that Chodorow describes. It has set out to counter the cultural disparagement of women, both as this exists in the world at large and within and between ourselves, and has thereby facilitated all kinds of relationship between women that would not have been possible before, both sexual and otherwise. It has also prompted an enormous re-evaluation of our mothers, and our relationships with them.

It has always been considered pejorative to consider lesbian relationships in terms of mother-love, and not surprisingly considering the use that has been made of this: the Freudo-medical stigmatising of lesbianism as immature and hence only partially satisfactory and to be grown out of: and Wolff's[12] ambivalent interpretation of lesbian relationships as basically 'incest' with the mother – ambivalent because incest is a pathologising term, and because, despite her considerable empathy, she can only see lesbians as a stigmatised group with ultimately barren relationships. The imposition of heterosexuality is seen at its starkest: what men are allowed in terms of suitably displaced union with the mother is disallowed to women and made taboo. There has also been the argument amongst feminists that for too long women have been 'mother' to men – why should we now wish to be mothers to each other with all the connotations of powerlessness and dreaded omnipotence that this conveys? However, precisely such emotions are involved in our sexual relationships, as we have seen, and often they are even more overwhelming with women than with men, just because of where they 'come from'. Perhaps what we can do now is recognise the threads in our adult relationships that connect with our earliest homosexual affections without the necessity of defending ourselves against yet another invalidation of lesbian relationships, and without denying either the sexuality or the ambivalence involved.

*Acknowledgements*
I would like to thank Sheila Ernst, Sue Cartledge and Lynne Segal for many helpful comments.

# 14
# Sexual Theory and Practice: Another Double Standard

## Sonja Ruehl

The injunction to trust to your own experience often seems, in the area of sexuality and sexual relations, like the best piece of advice for a feminist to give or take. Relying on the authority of their own experience, feminists individually and collectively have been able to query and to some extent defuse some of the pervasive sexual mythologies of our time, whether found in the pages of the women's magazines or in the textbooks of the psychologists. Other women's subjective accounts of their sexual experience are often more immediately engaging and infinitely more authentic than accounts and theories about women's sexuality in general. And because sexuality is a peculiarly intimate part of our experience – one where we are liable to feel especially vulnerable – we may want to protect it from the intrusion of other people's ideas and views. For these reasons, the injunction to trust your own experience seems to point to another injunction: to distrust other people's theorisings on the subject of women's sexuality.

But does an acceptance of the usefulness of exploring our own experience have to imply a rejection of the usefulness of theorising our position as women and as sexual beings? I would argue that it doesn't. It is true that the very language in which theoretical discussions are carried on can be very distancing, and strangely so for a subject that encompasses emotions, sensations and the physical activities of bodies. But this doesn't mean that theories have no bearing on our everyday lives. To take just one aspect of this: any woman who has discussed her lesbianism with a psychiatrist who thinks it is a sickness, who has tried to get an abortion from a doctor who thinks that having children should be the sole purpose of sexual activity, who has brought a charge of rape before a judge who thinks men have an uncontrollable sex drive, has come across, and probably into intense conflict with, a professional in a position of power, whose

210

views of sexuality are underwritten by theories and theoretical propositions about it.[1] Indeed, one aspect of feminist engagement with theories of sexuality has been to reveal the theoretical basis of such influential views and so to criticise them and the assumptions they depend on.

In any case, the opposition between theory and experience seems less stark when we remember that it is not only theories of sexuality in the abstract which feminists have criticised and attacked – although they certainly have done that. But what has been seen as particularly insidious is the appeal to certain aspects of theories as ideological tools that have been used to justify or legitimate unequal sexual relations between women and men. The 'vaginal orgasm' controversy is just such an example where feminists have urged that a piece of theory insisting that women's orgasms are and, moreover, should be located physiologically in the vagina, is not only incorrect but pernicious because it conflates women's sexuality and reproductive role and can be used to confine women's sexual expression to 'appropriate' forms accordingly.[2] It can be used, for instance, to characterise clitoral sexuality including lesbianism as 'immature' sexual behaviour.

But feminist engagement with theories about sexuality has not been limited to criticising pre-existing theoretical positions, or their ideological use, or to tracing theoretical progenitors of popular views. Feminists have also wanted to develop theories of sexuality, and for good reason. It is, after all, we who have insisted that sexuality is an important arena – not a trivial one – for acting out women's subordination, and men's power. The slogan that 'the personal is political', taken to include sexual life, has indicated a feminist conviction that sexuality is not purely a private, individual matter. It is something about which systematic generalisations can be made concerning women, men and their relation to each other. We have put the task of explaining the relation between sexuality and masculinity/femininity on our own agenda. That is to say, we need positive theories of sexuality ourselves. Later in this chapter, I want to look at two positive developments in theorising sexuality in more detail. One is the explicitly feminist work of Lillian Faderman,[3] and the other is the writing of French philosopher Michel Foucault.[4] The latter's perspective on sexuality has influenced some feminist work on the subject (although gender is not at all one of his own primary concerns) but has also attracted much criticism and controversy. Both writers take a historical approach. But before I look at their work, I want to sketch in more general terms other feminist approaches, including reasons why feminists might be interested in looking at sexuality from a historical point of view.

One feature in common between many of the views which feminists have criticised is that differences between women's sexuality and men's are often apparently guaranteed as 'natural' differences. Differences which many feminists would regard as social (in sexual behaviour and feelings or in personality) are often treated as synonymous with biological sex differences, and hence a jump is made from treating them as 'natural' to treating them as unchangeable, inevitable, eternal. While acknowledging that there are biological differences, feminists have argued strongly that they must be distinguished from socially created ones; arguing, for instance, that biological 'sex' should be distinguished from social 'gender' (femininity/masculinity).[5] We can look to anthropology and history for evidence that sexuality is changeable and variable across cultures and over time. But in looking at our own society, what does it mean to say that sexuality is 'socially constructed'? Sexuality is in itself so hard to define or pin down, so intertwined with gender, and with so many facets of our society (with reproduction, families, commercial advertising, psychology and medicine, art and literature) that generalising about its social construction seems to require not one theoretical approach, but many.

Feminist writers about sexuality have indeed used a wide range of approaches to understand it.[6] Focusing on the way that heterosexuality and monogamous sexual relationships are privileged in our society, many have taken the family as a central feature of their explanation. They have argued that the nuclear family, the basic unit in which reproduction is organised, shapes women's sexuality to serve reproductive ends and to confine it to marriage and domesticity. Some feminists have turned to psychoanalysis in the search for a systematic account of how the 'rules' of family life come to be inscribed into an individual's psyche and to affect their inner psychic life and development, in a process in which sexuality and gender are intimately interrelated. Others have looked at the more external features of social life and have drawn attention to the range and scope of ideologies which represent sexuality to us. Sometimes they have related apparently diverse phenomena – the way that teenage magazines deal in 'romance', say, or the way that 'sex education' is presented in schools – to the development of stable heterosexual couples, marriage and hence families. Families are seen as a structure basic to society and the way that sexuality is *socially*, rather than biologically, linked to reproduction within families is of paramount importance here.

Furthermore, relating sexuality to the family as a basic social structure also enables sexuality to be connected with aspects of society further removed from the way sexuality is subjectively experienced and lived. Sexuality, via reproduction and the family, can be linked with views of the way that a capitalist economy such as ours works as a whole. Some have argued that the way the family has become separated as a 'private sphere' in the course of capitalist development, remote from the processes of production, has shaped women's sexuality through such features as wives' economic dependence on wage-earning husbands. Others have argued that there is a link between certain needs of a capitalist economy, and certain features of sexual life. For one thing, new generations of people who are reproduced are potential workers, and employers depend on having a new generation of workers, but at the same time have no direct control over their reproduction. A more indirect, ideological influence over popular views of marriage, family, children – and hence over romance and sexuality – may serve a purpose in keeping such an economic system going, over time. Feminists on the whole have avoided 'reading off' aspects of sexuality directly from features of the economy. As Maureen Mackintosh[7] notes, 'Most feminist writers do not seek to conflate production and sexuality in theoretical terms, but the close links between the organisation of production and the operation of sexual relations have been traced by feminists in the areas, for example, of prostitution, inheritance, and economic relations within marriage.' In different ways, therefore, some views of how sexuality is socially constructed refer more or less directly to a theoretical framework for understanding how the economic system forms a basis which shapes the structure of the whole society.

A different, but complementary, way in which sexuality has been analysed in relation to our type of society and its economy involves another aspect: the commercial construction of glamorous, sexy images of women which is part of modern consumerism. Feminists have seen the apparently contradictory emphasis on women as constantly available sex objects and as faithful wives as an instance of a sexual 'double standard'. While men are to some extent condoned in having active (and somewhat anarchic) sexual 'needs' as well as a role in respectable society, feminists have pointed to the ways in which this is still an either/or choice for women. A double standard applied differentially to women and men results in the division of women into the 'good' and the 'bad'; the 'nice' woman and the sex-pot whose active sexuality transcends the bounds of conjugality. Advertising is able to exploit this polarisation of women in terms of their sexuality, and constantly reconstructs images of women as sex-objects in its striving to harness the sexual pleasures of its audience to the sale of an unlikely range of consumer products. Sexuality can be seen in terms of how consumption, as well as production, is organised in a capitalist society like ours.

Of course, whether or not it is attached to particular views of the nature of capitalism, a focus on the centrality of the family and of reproductive sexuality can be extended to an analysis of lesbianism and other varieties of 'non-reproductive' sexual expression. The normative emphasis on conjugal heterosexuality creates a standard by which other sexual manifestations come to be classified as unorthodox and peripheral, if not worse. But by no means all feminist analysis has concentrated on the links between reproductive sexuality and the organisation of an economic system. On the contrary, analyses in the radical feminist tradition have emphasised reproductive sexuality as the archetypal expression of male power and aggression, which is essentially aimed at securing control over women's reproductive capacities. This kind of view has two consequences; one, that heterosexual activity is to be seen rather exclusively in terms of male dominance, so that women are seen as complicitous in it out of self-defence or submission, rather than because it is pleasurable or involving. Secondly, it puts lesbianism more centre stage because sexual relations between women become, in this view, the only haven from oppressive sexual relations. Such a view also links sexuality with wider aspects of society, but here society's basic feature is seen as a systematic and intrinsic support of male power. Sexual relations are only the most blatant playing out of this fundamental feature of society.

For this reason, radical feminist analysis is antagonistic to the derivation of questions of sexual oppression from an analysis giving primacy to the economic organisation of society. But this is not the only reason why such connections have been found unsatisfactory. Even those who accept that the economic system is the ultimate basis for social analysis also argue that the specifics of sexuality cannot just be 'reduced' to something else which fails to capture any of its subjective and interpersonal flavour.

One recent development in looking at the 'social construction' of sexuality has therefore been to distinguish different facets of sexuality from one another. Previously, 'sexuality' has often been treated in an undifferentiated fashion as something which, as a whole, can be explained with reference to other aspects of social life. The alternative is to begin by looking more closely at the separate constituents

214

of sexuality. Physical behaviour, sexual feelings and desires, sexual orientation, people's sense of their own sexual identity, the terms in which society categorises people in sexual types, these have been separated out to avoid the 'naturalistic' conflation of all these aspects with gender and biological sex (for instance, the way that having lesbian sexual desires is equated with '*being* a lesbian' or with '*being* masculine', and so on).

Of particular interest to feminists and to gay men trying to do this has been the work of various 'sexologists' who, as medical, psychological or sociological writers (and not necessarily in any context of sexual politics) have studied the field of sexuality and defined and set the terms in which we now think about the subject.[8] Since these 'professionals' of sexuality have concentrated on variations from the sexual 'norm' and not so much on the 'norm' of heterosexual monogamy itself (assumed to be unproblematic), looking at their work also puts 'unorthodox' sexuality, like lesbianism, centre stage. In a sense, an examination of the way sexology has developed tends to look first at 'unorthodoxy' as it has been studied and defined, and then to see what light this can throw on mainstream sexual norms. The two views of the social construction of sexuality I look at later, in different ways give a central place to sexology, especially nineteenth-century sexology, for the explanation of the way we now think about sexuality and how we can change it.

Before I turn to this, though, I want to say a little more about the novelty of an approach that concentrates on sexology, but which rejects the naturalistic explanations which sexologists themselves have often used. Part of this rejection is abandoning the idea that individuals have any 'true' sexual 'nature' which exists prior to social intervention and is *then* shaped by society. There is no 'essence' of a person's sexuality which could naturally belong to her or be intrinsic to an individual. Whether such an 'essence' is called a sexual 'urge' or a 'need' or a 'sex drive' or an 'instinct', such 'essentialism' is a target of attack in the views I am going on to discuss.

Although I said earlier that feminists have tended to reject 'naturalistic' explanations, this particular strand of naturalistic thinking that I call 'essentialism' has in fact been a feature of some feminist analysis and also of many ideas of 'sexual liberation' characteristic of radical ideas in the late 1960s, and which carried over into the early gay movement as well as the women's movement.[9] Influential writers such as Reich and Marcuse had a vision of an essential sexuality which, they argued, capitalism had not just shaped but 'repressed', forcing it into familistic forms necessary for the reproduction of capitalist society. If sexuality could be 'freed' from the trammels of advanced capitalism, it would provide a burst of revolutionary energy disruptive and destructive to 'the system' as a whole – as well as being good for the individual whose sexuality was thus 'liberated'. But this depended on a vision of a 'natural' sexuality underlying any social shaping, potentially anarchic, and an independent force capable of somehow overthrowing social regulation.[10,11]

Reflections of this kind of vision certainly found a place in the ways sexuality has been thought about by feminists. The emphasis on personal experience, which I mentioned at the beginning of this chapter, may I think partly be such a reflection – it suggests the idea that there is some sexual 'truth' we could discover in ourselves, by introspection almost. But, in addition, some feminists produced arguments by analogy with those of Reich and Marcuse, transposing the terms of the debate and analysing female sexuality as having been 'repressed' in the interests of men. Mary Jane Sherfey's arguments[12] that women's orgasmic capacity has been 'repressed' by the exigencies of maternity are one example.

The 'essentialism' inherent in such views was also criticised, for instance by Mary McIntosh,[13] who went on to point out some of the ambiguities in our lived experience of sexuality as feminists. A particular example she chose was that of first experiences of sexual relationships with other women. Were they to be understood as a discovery of an essential 'true self', that someone had 'really' been gay all along, and had only just discovered it? She noted that this was one very prevalent way that women accounted to themselves for their first lesbian encounter. The main alternative (and non-essentialist) way of understanding such an experience in the women's movement at the time was in terms of 'choice' – such relationships could consciously be chosen and learnt about, as 'an extension of sisterhood'. This latter way of opposing essentialism is one which is found also in the first of the historical studies I want now to turn to, which is Lillian Faderman's book *Surpassing the Love of Men*.

Faderman's book is not ostensibly a *theory* of sexuality at all, but a history of 'romantic friendships' (close emotional relationships) between women, traced from the Renaissance to the present day using a wide variety of American and European sources, both fictional and personal. Nevertheless, to understand her account of this history the reader has to grasp Faderman's theoretical position, which is a lesbian–feminist one concerned to emphasise choice in relationships and also to demonstrate the continuity of friendship, emotional closeness and romance, and to de-emphasise the singling out of sexual expression as a particularly significant way of character-ising women's relationships. Sexuality is, in this view, entirely *de*-emphasised as a separable basis for categorising either relationships or individuals and so Faderman's thesis is quite antagonistic to the distinct categorisation of lesbians on the basis of sexual preference. In fact, lesbianism as a specifically *sexual* category disappears into a wider, more diffuse notion of emotional bonding between women. As you would expect, therefore, Faderman turns an exceptionally hostile eye on the nineteenth-century sexologists who did set out to categorise humanity into distinct sexual types on the basis of an assumed essential sexuality, inbuilt into individual biology.

This means that her approach avoids the anachronism of reading back into the more distant past the categories classified and solidified only in the nineteenth century. There is no excavation of history for previously 'hidden' examples of 'lesbianism' from times when this was not a category in which women might organise their lives. Faderman does however trace links between the sexologists and certain of their predecessors – but these are seen as *literary* predecessors. Faderman sees a line of continuity between sexology and a tradition of sexually explicit male fantasy literature which she argues fed into the work of the would-be 'scientific' sexologists. Descriptions of explicitly sexual relations between women are quoted from sixteenth- and seven-teenth-century authors, who she claims used them as a titillatory device and part of a general pan-sexuality, not a sharply differen-tiated category of lesbianism at all, but simply part of a general incitement to copulation. In the eighteenth-century a pornographic literature developed in which lesbianism did become increasingly differentiated, and which developed an image of the lesbian as an exotic creature engaged in bizarre sexual practices like flagellation. This is the kind of exotic lesbian image which Faderman claims was picked up and magnified by nineteenth-century French aesthete-decadent writers as a vehicle for expressing their own ambivalent rebellion against bourgeois society. Drawing on this male literary tradition, but working within a scientific framework, the nineteenth-century sexologists then solidified the categorisation of the lesbian as a strongly differentiated sexual 'type' by arguing that same-sex attrac-tion was the expression of an inborn condition.

The possibility of defining a specifically lesbian category is thus traced through an entirely male tradition and a fictional one at that. It is seen as the culmination of a long line of products of the male imagination. It is not seen as derived from women's real sexual lives at all, not being connected with women's authentic experience and relationships. The authentic history of these, Faderman argues, is to be found in women's diaries, letters and writings and she follows through these a quite separate, parallel line of continuity in terms of the close emotional ties with other women which these documents reveal.

What Faderman sees as significant in these relationships is the intensity of emotional passion for other women, their mutual supportiveness and the degree of social recognition which such relationships have at times commanded – the only reason that 'romantic friendship' between women could not rival marriage being women's lack of economic independence. What Faderman does not see as significant in such relationships is sexuality. Rather than simply arguing that we cannot now find out whether these friendships involved specifically sexual expression (genital contact, that is) she does appear to hold a definite view that they were *not* sexual relationships. What women wanted and received from these close ties was emotional support, encouragement to intellectual activity and other sorts of independence, and shelter from the harsh world of men. Sexual desire between women is so de-emphasised in this view that it seems almost presumed not to have existed at all.

Therefore, in Faderman's history of women's friendships, there seems to be an interplay of two continuities, which on the whole do not meet because they are divided along gender lines. Concern with (genital) sexuality is seen as a specifically male concern; it is almost as if men *did* possess an essential sexuality which women are without. In this view, the alien male concern with sexuality did irrupt into women's real lives and close relationships with the nineteenth-century sexologists. They, claiming to be scientific investigators of real life and not just *literateurs*, provoked a self-consciousness in women about their same-sex friendships, which thereby became seen as sexualised. Faderman construes sexology as having unambiguously done a disservice to women generally because of this. Her own book can, I think, be read as an attempt to 'rescue' women's close relationships from this sexualisation and to displace sexual desire from the centre of definition of lesbianism too.

There are several problems with this line of approach. One is its latent essentialism in the treatment of *men's* sexuality, as I have mentioned, so that although the rigidity of defining women in terms of a sexual typology is broken down, this is at the expense of a very rigid division along gender lines. Neither does Faderman replace rigid sexual categories with a more flexible idea of women's sexual desires (which might transcend fixed and biologically construed categories), nor of a variety or choice of sexual activities. This means that there is no room, in her analysis, for women to recognise aspects of their own desires or practices in the accounts of sexologists and therefore no way of explaining why some women did come to see their own identities in terms of the categories that sexologists set up, like the 'congenital invert' of Havelock Ellis's categorisation, for example. There is no way of explaining why so many women still do experience their first lesbian encounters or desires as the discovery of a 'new self'. It leaves out of account the development of a specifically lesbian sub-culture precisely around lesbianism as a sexual category and a sexual identity women may accept to describe themselves. This, I think, points to the central weakness of the thesis: it tries to deny the extent to which sexuality actually has become an omnipresent feature in the organisation of people's lives and views of themselves – including women's. And in order to trace historical analogies for a contemporary lesbian–feminist position that emphasises political commitment over sexual expression between women, Faderman verges on denying that intense, sexual relationships can exist between women autonomously of expressions of sisterhood.

For this reason, it seems to me that a theoretical approach which criticises the contemporary valorisation of sexuality, and can query the rigid categories and biologism of nineteenth-century sexology but still leave us with a way of thinking about specifically sexual expression, is more useful. Something of this possibility is given by the work of Foucault and developments in the history of sexuality which have built on his approach.

There are in fact points of similarity between Faderman's work and Foucault's. In a different way his *History of Sexuality* also advocates a de-emphasising of sexuality and expresses a hostility to nineteenth-century sexology which he sees as having invented a rigidifying taxonomy of sexual types. This rigidity is underpinned by the essentialist ideas of the sexologists, whose categories he sees as partly having shaped the possibilities of sexual expression, not just described them. Categories of sexuality were seen by the sexologists of the nineteenth century as inscribed into individual biology in an intrinsic kind of way; and later *experienced* as such by individuals who recognised something of themselves in the categories. They thus created new possibilities for regulating people's conduct and persuading them to regulate themselves. In short, the categories of sexuality have become imprisoning for individuals whose lives are to an extent administered around them.

Given these similarities, it is not surprising that Foucault is complimentary about Faderman's work and the novelty of her approach.[14] But what is also interesting is that his interviewers have taken him up precisely on the question of Faderman's refusal to consider sexual expression explicitly; querying this on the grounds that her attitude confines women to an asexual realm of sentiment in a way that actually colludes with traditional attitudes to women. Foucault's reply is made not in terms of any analysis of the position of women (in his own work, gender relations are notably absent in fact), but on the general grounds that any analysis not conducted in terms of laws, repressions and prohibitions on sexuality is a refreshing change, productive of new ways of analysing sexuality outside the terms he considers were wrongly utilised in the 1960s.

In his own work, he mounts a strong attack on the idea that sexuality has been monolithically 'repressed' and can equally as monolithically be 'liberated'. He casts doubt on the idea that the history of sexuality has been one where the dispassionate light of science has been gradually shed on the murky mysteries of sex. Rather, nineteenth-century scientific endeavour invented new possibilities of control because it socially constructed sexuality as a realm of knowledge, susceptible of rational discussion and therefore of regulation. Far from sexuality having been 'silenced' in the Victorian era, he argues that there was in fact a positive explosion of different ways of talking about it, of different 'discourses' on sexuality.

In fact, in this view 'sexuality', in so far as we are able to think of it as a coherent or unified whole, is a unity produced by the discourses about it – sets of ideas and defining concepts – and not a pre-existent 'thing' which can simply be referred to. This raises the problem of what the relation between these discourses and the 'realities' of sexual life is supposed to be, and the place of experience in the account. Feminists influenced to some extent by Foucault's perspective have had to confront this question. Rosalind Brunt, for example,[15] argues:

> What is generally called 'sex' is a highly-mediated cultural pheno-
> menon, directly experienced only by immediate participants,
> consigned to secrecy and privacy and not (usually, regularly)
> directly available to witness-by-others. Curiosity, desire for
> knowledge about the norms of sexual conduct, is thus primarily
> catered to not by immediate access but through the mediation of
> 'discourse'. 'Sex' enters the public domain as a topic to be talked
> about or visually and verbally represented – whether as 'por-
> nography' in magazines, film and video, various forms of 'erotica',
> the sexual 'confessions' of famous or fictitious people in news-

papers and paperbacks, the sex 'quiz' in the popular press with 'self and partner ratings' and the various documentary texts drawing on popular psychology, medicine and common sense with information on what to 'do' and how: the sex 'manuals'.

She and other feminist writers have treated these discourses and representations as important in providing in themselves definitions and ways of thinking about sex.

But at least, in Foucault's view, the process of social categorisation which he deprecates is built onto a multifarious set of possible physical sexual activities and desires. He does not deny that bodies are capable of a range of sexual pleasures, only claiming that a grid of categories and rigid definitions has been superimposed onto these. Objecting to the idea of 'a lesbian', say, having an inbuilt and permanent sexual identity, as an invention of essentialist psychology, does not mean that it is necessary to deny that same-sex sexual activities or desires between women pre-existed such categorisation. This is why it seems to me that this is a more useful view than Faderman's – and it also explains why the question Foucault's interviewers asked him was a pertinent one.

Because Foucault's analysis focuses on the social process of sexual categorisation, some of those wanting to use his ideas have argued that his approach leaves a space for other explanations – of how sexual desire is formed in the first place, for one thing, including psychoanalytic explanations.[16] Others have seen his approach as possibly complementary to explanations with the rather different focus of the development of a stable sense of sexual identity for particular individuals, forged between their personal experiences and society-wide, publicly-known categories. His work can be seen in conjunction with that of the so-called 'symbolic interactionists', the most influential of whom probably being Gagnon and Simon[17,18] who emphasise the plasticity and relativity of personal sexual histories but are not concerned with the more general process of categorisation. 'Symbolic interactionism' emphasises the socially learnt nature of sexuality for individuals, which Gagnon and Simon express through the idea that people have to learn a 'sexual script' as they grow up, before they can function sexually. This metaphor has also been used in feminist writing in the interactionist framework, such as that of Stevi Jackson.[19] She has used it in analysing rape, and the way rape is accounted for, and has also looked at the way children acquire sexual knowledge.

But Foucault's views are not compatible with other ways in which feminists have analysed sexuality as socially constructed. His view is that sexuality is regulated in a variety of ways and that these also actually constitute or construct what we understand as sexuality. This conflicts with analyses which see sexuality as socially constructed in a more unified strategy, around the family, with the help of a unitary state, in the interests of a capitalist system. Feminists influenced by Foucault's approach have explicitly criticised the emphasis on the family as 'the' unit 'in charge' of the organisation of sexuality, evident in much feminist writing.[20]

Another objection to Foucault's analysis voiced by some feminists and others, including Marxist commentators, is that his is an 'idealist' view. He seems to regard the assumption that people have a coherent 'sexuality' almost as an idea invented by the sexologists. Also, the history of sexuality in this sense, is the history of discourses about sexuality – a history which seems to be only traceable through internal links between discourses. So, critics ask, what is the relation of such discourses to 'real life' supposed to be? Some would prefer an approach that anchored an analysis of sexual life historically in the changing material circumstances of work, family and reproduction. Foucault himself eschews theorising such connections, but this remains a problem for those who would like to integrate some of Foucault's insights with an approach to history that rejects the view that ideas have an independent force in shaping historical change.

Rosalind Coward points out that Foucault's analysis concentrates on unorthodox sexualities, because these have been exhaustively and minutely defined in legal and medical discourses. The conjugal, heterosexual 'norm' is explained in terms of its difference from the *un*orthodox, rather than the other way round, which a focus on the family would do. There is thus disagreement between Foucault's view and feminist analyses which give centrality to the family as a basic structure around which sexuality is shaped and which invoke a unitary notion of state power to support this. His approach is antagonistic to other views of history based on a more unified, holistic view of society such as a Marxist one and this makes it unsatisfactory to those trying to link in a view of sexuality strongly with a general conception of society giving primacy to production. Singling out 'sexuality' as a historical object of analysis makes it difficult to integrate Foucault's perceptions with a more conventional – or indeed, with other radical – approaches to history.[21]

Debates over the place of the family and reproduction in the analysis of sexuality, and the importance of the ways that sexuality is represented to us through different cultural forms, continue.

Although I started with the proposition that the 'social construction' of sexuality was an idea common to feminist writers, there are clearly divergences of opinion as to what that might mean. Given the importance of the cultural divide between heterosexuality and lesbianism, attempts to theorise this will also remain on the agenda. What I have tried to do in this chapter is to single out some of the different strands of thought that might contribute to these feminist projects.

*Acknowledgements*
I would like to thank the editors of this book, and also Marsaili Cameron, John Clarke and Simon Watney for ideas and helpful comments on an earlier draft.

# Notes

## Chapter 1: pages 1–7

1. A. Rich, 'Husband-right and father-right', in *Lies, Secrets and Silences*, Virago, London, 1980, p. 216.

## Chapter 2: pages 8–29

1. Stella Browne, 'The sexual variety and variability among women', *British Society for Study of Sex Psychology*, no. 3, 1916.
2. Charles Darwin, *The Descent of Man*, 1871.
3. See Dr Mercier, in Allbut (ed.), *A System of Medicine*, vol. 7, 8 vols, 1896–9.
4. See Anna Davin, 'Imperialism and motherhood', *History Workshop Journal*, no. 5, 1978; and Jane Lewis, *The Politics of Motherhood*, Croom Helm, London, 1980.
5. August Forel, *The Sexual Question*, 1906.
6. E. Sloan Chesser, *Women and Womanhood*, 1912.
7. Forel, *op. cit.*
8. Josephine Butler was a prominent feminist in the campaign against the Contagious Diseases Acts 1860s–1880s, which provided for the compulsory medical inspection and detention of prostitutes in certain garrison towns and ports.
9. See Sheila Rowbotham and Jeffrey Weeks, *Socialism and the New Life*, Pluto Press, London, 1977.
10. There has been relatively little published research on the social purity feminists of this period, but see Sheila Jeffreys, 'The spinster and her enemies', *Scarlet Women*, **13**, part 2 (Women Only), 1981.
11. Cicely Hamilton, *Marriage as a Trade*, 1st edn 1909, reprinted by The Women's Press, London, 1981.
12. Mrs P. Sherwen, *Freewoman*, 25 January 1912.
13. Isabel Leatham, *Freewoman*, 7 December 1911.
14. Christabel Pankhurst, *The Great Scourge and How to End It*, E. Pankhurst, London, 1913.
15. See E. Noel Morgan, *Freewoman*, 8 August 1912, who argued that for women to have time to emancipate their sex they needed celibacy.
16. See Beatrice Webb, *My Apprenticeship*, 1920, p. 222.
17. See Kathleen Oliver, *Freewoman*, 15 February 1912.
18. Kathleen Oliver, *Freewoman*, 29 February 1912.

19. See Frances Swiney, *The Bar of Isis*, 1907.

20. Juliette Heale, *The Woman Pays*, 1916.

21. Swiney, *op. cit.*

22. Pankhurst, *op. cit.*

23. See Hamilton, *op. cit.*, and 'The Crux', in *The Charlotte Perkins Gilman Reader*, ed. Ann J. Lane, The Women's Press, London, 1980.

24. Heale, op. cit.

25. An essay on Mrs Pankhurst in the 'Post-Victorians: A Reed of Steel', 1933, reprinted in Jane Marcus, *The Young Rebecca*, Virago, London, 1983.

26. Swiney, *op. cit.*

27. See 'The New Moralists', *Freewoman*, 4 January 1912.

28. Browne, *op. cit.*

29. See 'A.B.', *Freewoman*, 1 February 1912.

30. *The Clarion*, 20 December 1912.

31. Grace Smith Carter, *Freewoman*, 15 February, 1912.

32. Heale, *op. cit.*

33. Oliver, *Freewoman*, 15 February 1912.

34. *Freewoman*, 13 June 1912.

35. Mary Allen, *The Pioneer Policewoman*, 1925.

36. *The Shield*, February 1915.

37. Allen, *op. cit.*

38. *ibid.*, p. 137.

39. See for example, 'Rosalind', in Frank Mond (ed.), *The Burden of Women*, 1908; and Jeffreys, *op. cit.*

40. *Freewoman*, 23 November 1911.

41. 'Some problems of sex', *International Journal of Ethics*, July 1917.

42. *Freewoman*, 22 February 1912.

43. See Beatrix Campbell, 'A feminist sexual politics: Now you see it now you don't', *Feminist Review*, **5**, 1980.

44. Ruth Hall, *Marie Stopes*, Virago, London, 1978.

45. Preface to 7th edn, *Married Love*, 1919.

46. Campbell, *op. cit.*, p. 4.

47. *Dear Dr. Stopes, Sex in the 1920s*, Ruth Hall (ed), André Deutsch, London, 1978, p. 86.

48. Marie Stopes, *Married Love*, Putnam, London, 1918, p. 48.

49. Helena Wright, *The Sex Factor in Marriage*, Williams & Norgate, London, 1930, p. 58.

50. *ibid.*, p. 83.

51. Havelock Ellis, *Sex in Relation to Society*, 1910; English edition Heinemann, London, 1937.

52. Gray's introduction to Wright, *op. cit.*, p. 16.

53. See Campbell, *op cit.*, for a fuller discussion.

54. *Enduring Passion*, Putman, London, 1928, p. 117.

55. *ibid.*, p. 42–3.

56. Sonja Ruehl, 'Inverts and experts', in *Feminism, Culture and Politics*, R. Brunt and C. Rowan, (eds), Lawrence & Wishart, London, 1982.

57. Maude Royden, *The Moral Standards of the New Age*, League of Church Militant, 1925.

58. Wright, *op. cit.*, p. 29.

59. Campbell, *op. cit.*, p. 5.

60. See, for example, Ruth Hall (ed), *Dear Dr. Stopes, op. cit.*

61. See OWAAD, 'Black women and health', in *No Turning Back*, The Women's Press, London, 1981.

62. E. Sloan Chesser, *Love without Fear*, 1941 (reprinted throughout the 1940s, 1950s and 1960s).

63. Maxine Davis, *The Sexual Responsibility of Women*, Heinemann, 1957.

64. Chesser, 1941, *op. cit.*

65. *Women*, 28 February 1952.

66. Chesser, 1941, *op. cit.*

67. See CCCS, 'Resistance Through Rituals', *Cultural Studies*, **7/8**, 1975.

68. Jeffrey Weeks, *Coming Out*, Quartet Books, 1977.

69. Victor Chamberlain, *From Adolescence to Maturity*, The Bodley Head, 1952.

70. See 'Feminism as feminity in the 1950s?' *Feminist Review* no. 3, 1979; and E. Wilson, *Only Halfway to Paradise*, Tavistock, London, 1980.

71. Cambell, *op. cit.*

72. Helena Wright, *More about the Sex Factor in Marriage*, 1947.

73. Alfred Kinsey *et al.*, *Sexual Behaviour in the Human Female*, Saunders, USA, 1953.

74. Geoffrey Gorer, *Sex and Marriage in England Today*, Nelson, London, 1971.

75. Walker, Kenneth and Fletcher, Peter, *Sex and Society*, Penguin, 1955.

76. Audrey Leathard, *The Fight for Family Planning*, Macmillan, 1980.

77. D. Hart-Davis 'Permissive Britain', *Sunday Telegraph*, 30 November 1969, quoted in Leathard, *op. cit.*

78. See Janice Winship, 'Woman becomes an "individual" – femininity and consumption in women's magazines, 1954–69', CCCS, 1980; and see Rosalind Coward, 'Sexual liberation and the family', *m/f*, no. 1, 1978.

79. Campbell, *op. cit.*

80. William Masters and Virginia Johnson, *The Human Sexual Response*, Little, Brown & Co, USA, 1966.

81. See Lucy Bland, 'It's only human nature? Sociobiology and sex differences', *Schooling and Culture*, no. 10, 1981.

82. Stopes, *Married Love, op. cit.*

## Chapter 3: pages 30–47

1. Letter to *The Leveller*, 19 March–1 April 1982.

2. P. Whiting, 'Female sexuality: its political implications', in M. Wandor (ed), *The Body Politic*, Stage One, London, 1972, p. 189.

3. *ibid.*, p. 209.

4. *ibid.*, p. 212.

5. A. Hamblin, 'The suppressed power of female sexuality', in S. Allen *et al.*, *Conditions of Illusion*, Feminist Books, 1974, p. 87.

6. *ibid.*, p. 95.

7. See, for example, M. Foucault and R. Sennett, 'Sexuality and solitude', in *London Review of Books*, vol. 3, no. 9, 21 May–9 June 1981.

8. W. Masters and V. Johnson, *Human Sexual Inadequacy*, Boston, 1970, p. 62.

9. E. Stephens, 'The moon within your reach: a feminist approach to female orgasm', *Spare Rib*, no. 42, December 1975, p. 15.

10. L. G. Barbach, *For Yourself: The Fulfilment of Female Sexuality*, Signet, 1975, p. 19.

11. *ibid.*, p. 53.

12. *ibid.*, p. 27.

13. *ibid.*, p. 29.

14. *ibid.*, p. 77.

15. *ibid.*, p. 82.

16. *ibid.*, p. 84.

17. *ibid.*, p. 29.

18. *ibid.*, p. 173.

19. *ibid.*, p. 19.

20. S. Hite, *The Hite Report*, Dell, 1976, p. 434.

21. *ibid.*, p. 386.

22. *ibid.*, p. 528.

23. A. Meulenbelt, *For Ourselves*, Sheba, London, 1981, p. 15.

24. *ibid.*, p. 8.

25. *ibid.*, p. 95.

26. *ibid.*, p. 107.

27. *ibid.*, p. 207.

28. Stephens, *op. cit.*

29. A. B. Snitow, 'Mass market romance: pornography for women is different', in *Radical History Review*, no. 20, 1979, p. 143.

30. Janus, Bess and Salters, *A Sexual Profile of Men in Power*, Prentice-Hall, 1976.

31. M. F., 'Two women write about their experiences with men', in *Spare Rib*, no. 91, 1980, p. 49.

32. M. Marcus, *A Taste for Pain*, Souvenir Press, London, 1981, p. 61.

33. *ibid.*, p. 123.

34. Meulenbelt, *op. cit.*, p. 106.

35. Kate Millett, *Sita*, Ballantine Books, London, 1976.

36. A. B. Snitow, 'The front line: notes on sex in novels by women, 1969–79', in *Signs*, vol. 5, no. 4, Summer 1980.

37. *ibid.*, p. 710.

38. Anna Coote and Beatrix Campbell, *Sweet Freedom*, Picador, London, 1982, pp. 227–8.

39. *ibid.*, p. 231.

## Chapter 4: pages 48–66

1. The leaflet, headed 'Everything tends to reduce lovers to objects', is marked BIB 2, bubble CPP – bm.

2. This lack of discussion of the subject is pointed out by Daphne Davis, 'Falling in love again', *Red Rag, A Magazine of Women's Liberation*, no. 13, p. 12. Elizabeth Wilson also notes with regret the way that socialism and feminism have neglected romance, in 'Fruits of Passion', *City Limits*, No. 74,

March, 1983.

3. This point is expressed more fully by Davis, *op. cit.*, pp. 12, 13.

4. From Alison Buckley 'For Tasha', in *Art and Feminism*, Laurieston Hall, 1977.

5. Rosie Boycott, 'Falling in love again', *Honey*, IPC Magazines, 1982. The article is a detailed personal account of the start of an intense love affair.

6. Marge Piercy, *Small Changes*, Fawcett Publications, Greenwich, Conn. 1974, p. 193.

7. *ibid.*, pp. 194, 195.

8. *Ink in Love: Exploding the Romantic Myth*, Ink No. 29, 21 February 1972, p. 12.

9. This is one of a number of personal accounts by women which for reasons of privacy I am leaving anonymous. I am indebted to a number of other women who have discussed their experiences with me, have read this piece and expressed encouragement and valuable disagreements, as well as giving helpful contributions and suggestions about changes. In particular I would like to thank Sue Cartledge, Inga Czudnochowski, Marie Maguire, Jo Ryan and Stef Pixner.

10. Again, this point is made by Davis, *op. cit.*, p. 13.

11. Buckley, *op. cit.*

12. Piercy, *op. cit.*, p. 195.

13. Erica Jong, *How to Save Your Own Life*, Panther Books, London, 1977, pp. 203, 204, 207, 208.

14. See note 9, above.

15. Piercy, *op. cit.*, p. 197.

16. Piercy, 'Burying blues for Janis', in Lucille Iverson and Kathryn Ruby (eds), *We Become New: Poems by Contemporary American Women*, Bantam Books, 1975, pp. 4–5.

17. *ibid.*

18. Slim, 'If I loved me half as much as I love you', in *Country Women*, issue 24, pp. 18–20.

19. Jong, *op. cit.*, p. 207.

20. *Ink in Love, op. cit.*, p. 8.

21. Frederick S. Perls, *Gestalt Therapy Verbatim*, Bantam Books, London, 1971, p. 10.

22. This point is made in Ralph Metzner, *Maps of Consciousness*, Collier Macmillan, London, 1971, p. 152. Showing that projection is not unique to this century, Stendhal discusses the same process under the term 'crystallisation'. See Stendhal, *Love*, trans. by Gilbert and Suzanne Sale, Penguin, Harmondsworth, 1975.

23. See Liz Greene, *Relating: An Astrological Guide to Living with others on a small Planet*, Coventure, London, 1976, pp. 149–150.

24. Raymond Durgnat, *Eros in the Cinema*, Marion Boyars, 1966.

25. Perls, *op. cit.*, p. 40.

26. Metzner, *op. cit.*, p. 152.

27. Jane Roberts, *The Nature of Personal Reality: A Seth Book*, Prentice-Hall, New Jersey, 1974, p. 382.

28. See Roberto Assagioli, *Psychosynthesis*, Turnstone Books, 1975, pp. 25–6.

29. Melanie Klein, *Envy and Gratitude and Other Works 1946–63*, Hogarth Press, 1963, p. 100.

30. Jane Rule, 'Homophobia and romantic love', in *Outlander: Stories and Essays*, The Naiad Press, Florida, 1981, p. 184.

31. Piercy, *Small Changes*, p. 211.

32. Jenny James, *Room to Breathe*, Coventure, London, 1975, p. 151.

33. See, for example, Dion Fortune, *The Esoteric Philosophy of Love and Marriage*, The Aquarian Press, Wellingborough, 1974, pp. 60–2.

34. Davis in *Red Rag, op. cit.*, p. 13, makes this point and suggests that we may imagine we are in love when all we are feeling are sexual desires or hunger pangs.

35. See note 9, above.

36. For a fuller account of this theory, see David V. Tansley, *Radionics and the Subtle Anatomy of Man*, Health Science Press, Devon, 1972.

37. For a brief account of this method, see Brian and Marita Snellgrove, *The Unseen Self*, Kirlian Aura Diagnosis, Carshalton, Surrey, 1979.

38. Bela Grunburger, 'Narcissism in female sexuality', in Janine Chasseguet-Smirgel, (ed), *Female Sexuality: New Psychoanalytic Views*, Virago, London, 1981, p. 71.

39. Alexander Lowen, *Bioenergetics*, Coventure, London, 1976, p. 67.

40. This term comes from the books of Carlos Castaneda. See, for example, the incident where Castaneda 'sees' the 'lines', in *Journey to Ixtlan*, Penguin, Harmondsworth, 1974, p. 267.

41. This idea is suggested by the Arica spiritual teachings.

42. Perls, for example, distinguishes 'confluence' from real contact which consists of the appreciation of differences. See *Gestalt Therapy Verbatim*, pp. 271–2.

43. As Davis points out in *Red Rag, op. cit.*, p. 12.

44. For many of the ideas in this passage, and particularly here, I am indebted to the therapeutic work of Jenner Roth in her sexuality workshops and in her individual therapy practice in London.

45. See note 44.

46. See note 44.

47. Rule, *op. cit.*, p. 185.

48. Slim, *op. cit.*, p. 20.

49. Gestalt therapy offers some simple and useful techniques for owning fantasies and projections by role-playing. See Sheila Ernst and Lucy Goodison, *In Our Own Hands*, The Women's Press, London, 1981, chs. 3, 6.

50. *Ink in Love, op. cit.*, p. 9.

51. See note 9, above.

52. *Ink in Love, op. cit.*, p. 12.

## Chapter 6: pages 89–104

1. I have not offered any practical ways of resolving difficulties with sex – it should be clear why. *Cosmopolitan* magazine published an article in June 1982, 'Baby *interruptus*', by Jane Filstrup, containing advice which women may find helpful. Its political perspective, however, is pretty much what you'd expect.

2. The medicalisation of ante-natal 'care' is not necessarily conducive to healthier women and babies. See works by Ann Oakley and Barbara Katz Rothman, n. 3, 4, below.

3. See Ann Oakley, 'Wise Woman, Medicine Men', in the *Rights and Wrongs of Women* ed. Ann Oakley and Juliet Mitchell, Pelican, Harmondsworth, 1976. Barbara Katz Rothman, *In Labor: Women and Power in the Birthplace*, Junction Books, 1982. Doris Haire, *The Cultural Warping of Childbirth* ICEA, 1974 (International Childbirth Education Association) (NCT). Adrienne Rich, *Of Woman Born*, Virago, 1977. Ann Oakley, *Becoming a Mother*, Martin Robertson, 1979. Ann Oakley, *Women Confined*, Martin Robertson, London, 1980. Barbara Ehrenreich and Deirdre English, *For Her Own Good*, Pluto Press, London, 1979.

4. See Ann Oakley, *Housewife*, Pelican, 1976.

5. Transition to Parenthood Project, Thomas Coram Research Unit, 1982.

6. Channi Kamur, Prospective Study of Sexual Activity during Pregnancy and After Childbirth, University College Hospital, reported in AIMS paper on Pregnancy, Parenthood and Sexuality Conference, London, January 1982.

7. Brian Jackson, 'Now the baby's here, how's your sex life?' *Living* Magazine, June 1980.

8. See *Episiotomy: Physical and Emotional Aspects*, ed. Sheila Kitzinger, NCT (undated). Sheila Kitzinger and Rhiannon Walters, *Some Women's Experiences of Episiotomy*, NCT, 1981. Lesley Saunders, critical review of the above books, *AIMS* newsletter, Winter 1981/2.

9. I do not dispute that for some women hormonal or anti-depressant drug treatment has markedly alleviated their immediate distress. It is important that the research should be recognised and adequately funded as a step towards the de-psychologising of women's illnesses.

10. See Ann Oakley's books on motherhood (quoted above). Vivienne Welburn, *Post Natal Depression*, Fontana, London, 1980.

11. See *The Politics of Sexuality in Capitalism*, Red Collective, 1973. Sheila Ernst and Lucy Goodison, *In Our Own Hands: a book of self-help therapy*, The Women's Press, 1981.

### Chapter 7: pages 105–123

1. Anna Coote and Beatrix Campbell, *Sweet Freedom*, Picador, 1982.

2. *Spare Rib* is a London-based, monthly feminist magazine.

3. Redstockings, 'Feminist revolution', *Redstockings*, 1975.

4. Robin Morgan, *Going Too Far*, Vintage Books, 1978.

5. Redstockings, *op. cit.*

### Chapter 8: pages 124–140

1. Much more has been said about women's sexuality in relationships. My focus here is on men's. This means that there is a danger of implying that only men are subject to those feelings in relationships, and the resistances that result. I know that's not true. What is true is that their needs and desires in relationships have been camouflaged by 'knowledge' about men's sexuality and what is underneath their sexual relationships has not been scrutinised.

2.  All the quotations come from my research. (Wendy Hollway, *Identity and Gender Difference in Adult Social Relations*, unpublished PhD thesis, University of London, 1982). Italics indicates emphasis used by the speaker. In this article I have altered the transcript slightly where it has made the meaning more clear or shortened the quote. This has meant editing out pauses and repetitions but not changing the meaning.

3.  Lucy Bland and Wendy Hollway, 'What's natural about sexuality? The problem for feminism of biological accounts of sexuality and sexual desire', *Feminist Review*, 13 (forthcoming).

4.  By the term 'discourse', I mean a system of statements which cohere around common meanings and values. The meaning of the term is similar to a 'set of assumptions' but the way 'discourse' has been theorised (most importantly by Michel Foucault, *The Order of Things: An Archaeology of the Human Sciences*, Tavistock, London, 1970 and *The History of Sexuality, vol. 1, An Introduction*, Allen Lane, London, 1979) emphasises how these meanings and values are a product of social factors, of powers and practices, rather than an individual's set of ideas. My use of the term here also enables me to make the link with language and grammar where people are positioned (and position others) by the use of personal pronouns in sentences. For an extended discussion of these theoretical issues see J. Henriques, W. Hollway, C. Urwin, C. Venn and V. Walkerdine, *Changing the Subject of Psychology*, Methuen, London, 1983, forthcoming.

5.  This tendency in psychoanalytic theory is exacerbated by the way it reduces content to process. For example, Freud emphasised that the object to which desires attach themselves or around which fantasies develop was displaced from the real object and therefore of little significance. This view fails to see the systematicity in what is projected onto whom. I believe that it is here that gender (or race or class) as a *social* system of differences is necessary for the analysis.

6.  This would suggest that a heterosexual man's desire for the Other is even stronger, and therefore even more threatening, than a heterosexual woman's (displaced) desire. Men's greater repression, and more driven resistance to women's powerfulness (as they experience it through their vulnerability) would make sense in this light.

7.  Several men have described to me the same phenomenon when they were young, particularly when they fell in love with older women. But there's also a danger of overgeneralising. I think many men get into relationships with women who are less experienced and less confident (apparently) than they are and, by retaining this power inequality, never experience the vulnerability. Yet they don't feel entirely satisfied and will be the ones who pull away from the relationship.

8.  Women do too, though the opportunity has not been equally available.

## Chapter 11: pages 167–179

1.  Louise Eichenbaum and Susie Orbach, *Outside In . . . Inside Out*, Penguin, Harmondsworth, 1982.

2.  G. Wickes, *The Amazon of Letters*, Putman, New York, 1977. Natalie Barney was a famous lesbian and the centre of an artistic and literary circle in

Paris for the first half of this century.

3. Angela Carter, *The Sadeian Woman*, Virago, London, 1979.

4. Carl Jung, *Memories, Dreams, Reflections*, Collins, London, 1973.

5. Alexandra Kollontai, *Sexual Relations and the Class Struggle*, trans. Alix Holt, Falling Wall Press, Bristol, 1972.

6. The Red Collective, *The politics of sexuality in capitalism*, London, 1973.

7. Pat Califia, 'Feminism and sadomasochism', in *Heresies*, no. 12, Heresies Collective, New York, 1981.

8. *The South Bank Show*, London Weekend Television, January 1983.

9. Jaqui Duckworth and Joy Chamberlain, *Home Made Melodrama*, London, 1982.

10. Adrienne Rich, *Dream of a Common Language, Poems 1974–1977*, W.W. Norton, New York, 1978.

11. G. Rubin and others, in 'Talking sex', in *Feminist Review*, no. 11, London, Summer 1982.

12. *Sex Issue, Heresies* no. 12, New York, 1981.

13. Red Collective, *op. cit.*

14. B. Ehrenreich, 'Toward a political morality', *Liberation*, July/August 1977.

## Chapter 12: pages 180–195

1. Mary McIntosh, 'The homosexual role', *Social Problems*, vol. 16, no. 2, Autumn 1968, reprinted in K. Plummer (ed), see note 14 below.

2. Jeffrey Weeks, *Coming Out*, Quartet, London, 1977.

3. Lillian Faderman, *Surpassing the Love of Men*, Junction Books, London, 1981.

4. Alison Hennegan, Introduction to Radclyffe Hall, *The Well of Loneliness*, Virago, London, 1982, p. ix.

5. Colette , *The Pure and the Impure*, Penguin, Harmondsworth, 1980, p. 68.

6. Djuna Barnes, *Nightwood*, Faber & Faber, London, 1963, p. 194.

7. Maureen Duffy, *The Microcosm*, Hutchinson, London, 1965.

8. Lilian Mohin, *Love Your Enemy? The Debate Between Heterosexual Feminism and Political Lesbianism*, Only Women Press, London, 1981, p. 60.

9. Angela Stewart-Park and Jules Cassidy, *We're Here: Conversations with Lesbian Women*, Quartet, London, 1977, p. 140.

10. Adrienne Rich, *Compulsory Heterosexuality and Lesbian Existence*, Only Women Press, London, 1981, pp. 20 ff.

11. See Bonnie Zimmerman, 'What has never been: An overview of lesbian literary criticism', in *Feminist Studies* vol. 7, no. 3, Autumn 1981.

12. Leeds Revolutionary Feminist Group, 'Political lesbianism: The case against heterosexuality', in *Love Your Enemy*, 1981, p. 5.

13. Anna Coote and Beatrix Campbell, *Sweet Freedom*, Picador, London, 1982, p. 219. I refer to this chapter of *Sweet Freedom* on the assumption that it was largely the work of Bea Campbell, since it follows closely from and develops out of her article 'A Feminist Sexual Politics?', *Feminist Review* no. 5, Summer 1980.

14. Kenneth Plummer, (ed), *The Making of the Modern Homosexual*, Hutchinson, London, 1981.

15. Coote and Campbell, *op. cit.*, p. 228.

16. Maureen Brady and Judith McDaniel, 'Lesbians in the mainstream: Images of lesbians in recent commercial fiction', in *Conditions* vol. II, no. 3, Summer 1980, pp. 82, 103.

17. Kate Stimpson, *Classnotes*, Avon, New York, 1979.

18. Rita Mae Brown, *Ruby Fruit Jungle*, Daughters Inc., Plainfield, Vermont, 1973.

19. Marge Piercy, *Small Changes*, Fawcett Publications, 1974.

20. Kate Millett, *Sita*, Virago, London, 1978.

21. Kate Millett, *Flying*, Hart-Davis McGibbon, London, 1974.

22. Joan Nestle, 'Butch-Fem Relationships', *Sex Issue, Heresies*, 1981, p. 22.

23. Sigmund Freud, 'On the universal tendency to debasement in the sphere of love', *Standard Edition*, vol. 11, The Hogarth Press and the Institute of Psychoanalysis, London, 1910.

### Chapter 13: pages 196–209

1. Robert Stoller, *Perversion: The Erotic Form of Hatred*, Delta, New York, 1975.

2. Mary McIntosh, 'The Homosexual Role', in K. Plummer (ed), *The Making of the Modern Homosexual*, Hutchinson, London, 1981.

3. Ethel Person, 'Sexuality as the mainstay of identity: Psychoanalytic perspectives', in C. R. Stimpson and E. S. Person (eds), *Women: Sex and Sexuality*, University of Chicago Press, 1980.

4. Paul Hoggett and Sue Holland, People's Aid and Action Centre, *Humpty Dumpty*, no. 8, 1978.

5. Person, *op. cit*

6. Nancy Chodorow, *The Reproduction of Mothering*, University of California Press, Berkeley, 1978.

7. Michael Balint, 'Critical notes on the theory of pregenital organisation of the libido' (1935), in M. Balint (ed), *Primary Love and Psychoanalytic Technique*, Tavistock, London, 1952.

8. Quoted in M. Balint, *The Basic Fault*, Tavistock, London, 1968.

9. A. Balint, 'Love for the mother and mother love' (1939), in Balint, *op. cit*.

10. Eichenbaum and Orbach, *Outside In . . . Inside Out, op. cit.* 1982.

11. S. Hite, *The Hite Report*, MacMillan, New York, 1976.

12. Charlotte Wolff, *Love Between Women*, Duckworth, London, 1971.

### Chapter 14: pages 210–223

1. Susan Edwards, *Female Sexuality and the Law*, Martin Robertson, London, 1981.

2. Beatrix Campbell, 'Feminist sexual politics', *Feminist Review*, no. 5, 1980.

3. Lillian Faderman, *Surpassing the Love of Men*, Junction Books, 1981.

See also my own review of this book in *History Workshop Journal*, Autumn 1982, for a more extended discussion.

4. Michel Foucault, *The History of Sexuality*, Allen Lane, London, 1979.

5. See Janet Sayers, *Biological Politics*, Tavistock, London, 1982 for an extended account both of the ideological use of biological arguments and also the place of biology in different feminist analyses.

6. Michèle Barrett, *Women's Oppression Today*, Verso, London, 1980. Ch. 2 gives an overview of approaches.

7. Maureen Mackintosh, 'Gender and economics', in *Of Marriage and the Market*, ed. Young, Wolkowitz and McCullagh, CSE Books, London, 1981.

8. See Mike Brake, *Human Sexual Relations*, Penguin, 1982, for extracts from the work of major sexologists and also for current comment on sexual theory and politics.

9. Simon Watney, 'The ideology of GLF', in *Gay Left*, 1980.

10. See Jeffrey Weeks, 'The development of sexual theory and sexual politics', in Brake, *op. cit.*

11. See also Stephen Heath, *The Sexual Fix*, MacMillan, London, 1982.

12. Mary Jane Sherfey, *The Nature and Evolution of Female Sexuality*, Vintage Books, 1973.

13. Mary McIntosh, 'Sexuality', in *Papers on Patriarchy*, 1976.

14. In an interview, *Entretien avec M. Foucault*, by J. P. Joecker, M. Ouerd and A. Sanzio, in *Masques: revue des homosexualités*, no. 13.

15. Rosalind Brunt, 'An immense verbosity; Permissive sexual advice in the 1970's', in *Feminism, Culture and Politics*, ed. Brunt and Rowan, Lawrence & Wishart, London, 1982.

16. See Weeks, in Brake, *op. cit.*

17. J. H. Gagnon and W. Simon, *Sexual Conduct*, Aldine Publishing, 1974.

18. See also Ken Plummer, *The Making of the Modern Homosexual*, Hutchinson, London, 1981.

19. Stevi Jackson, *Children and Sexuality*, 1982, and 'The social context of rape; sexual scripts and motivation', in *Women's Studies International Quarterly*, Pergamon, Oxford, 1978.

20. Rosalind Coward, 'Sexual Liberation and the Family', *m/f* no. 1, 1978.

21. This is something I think Jeffrey Weeks tries to do in *Sex, Politics and Society*, Longman, London, 1981. See also 'Foucault for historians', *History Workshop Journal*, Autumn 1982.

# Biographical Notes on Contributors

*Tricia Bickerton* is thirty-five and has one son. She originally trained as an actress, worked in political and fringe theatre, and taught drama and English. She now teaches therapeutic skills to self-help therapy groups, runs workshops at the Women's Therapy Centre, London, and works as a therapist.

*Lucy Bland* at present lives in Birmingham where she is a member of W.O.N.T. (Women Oppose the Nuclear Threat) and Birmingham Feminist History Group. She teaches Women's Studies for the Open University and for the extra-mural department. Despite a training in Sociology and Anthropology she is trying to do historical research into women's sexuality and has published several articles on the subject.

*Jill Brown*: 'I was born in 1950 and grew up in a small village outside Cambridge. I have done various things, including visiting lesbian feminists in Canada and America; working for local government; going to Warwick University; being active in the women's liberation movement and the Communist Party; living in Italy. I now live in Bristol and spend my time working for Women's Aid, working out new forms of feminist childcare and money sharing, enjoying and learning from my daughter, deepening my relationships with women, and keeping hold of a vision of the world without oppression, loneliness and separation.'

*Jo Chambers* was born in 1948: 'What I would like you to know about me is that my essence, though often hidden, is one of joy. I love the trees and the stars and the wind, and I am proud to be a native of the flat fens of East Anglia. I am now settled in the West, where I am actively engaged in the women's movement, endeavouring to bind together political action, creativity and personal relationships.'

*Lucy Goodison* is an active socialist feminist who is also involved in massage, dance and Greek history. She lives in East London and has one child. Her other publications include *In Our Own Hands: a book of self-help therapy* (co-authored with Sheila Ernst), (1981); *Divide and Rule – Never!* (1979), an anti-racist booklet for schools; a pamphlet, *Women and Migraine* (1979); and she contributed a chapter to *Why Children?* (1980).

*Deborah Gregory*: 'I was born in 1943 and spent the 1950s and 1960s focused on the oppression of just about everybody except me. Gave birth to a child in Paris, 1968; accidentally stumbled into the women's liberation movement in England in 1970 and become a born-again radical feminist. In 1981 I left for the peace and quiet of Vancouver Island, Canada, where I am on the collective of *Everywoman's Books*, and am about to become a fitness instructor.'

*Angela Hamblin* was born in London in 1940 of Irish parents. She joined the women's liberation movement in 1971 and since then her work has appeared in *Conditions of Illusion* (1974), *Spare Rib, Isis, Hard Feelings* (1979), and *One Foot on the Mountain* (1979). She also edited and published *The Other Side of Adoption* (1977). She is a former member of the London Rape Crisis Centre Collective and is currently a member of a women writers group. She is divorced and has two sons and a grand-daughter.

*Wendy Hollway* teaches applied psychology at Birkbeck College, London. She is a member of the *Feminist Review* collective and has been involved in research on women's identity and on gender difference.

*Sonja Ruehl* lectures in economics at the Open University, where she has also worked on an inter-disciplinary women's studies course. Involved in the women's movement since 1970, she has written about economics, social policy and sexuality, reviewed books and films for *Gay News*, and is a member of the *Feminist Review* collective.

*Lesley Saunders* has two young children and lives apart from their father. She writes poetry, book reviews and articles on many aspects of women's lives. She is involved in feminist self-help therapy and art.

*Lynne Segal* teaches social psychology at Middlesex Polytechnic. She is an Australian and came to live in England in 1970, and has been politically active as a socialist feminist since then. She co-authored *Beyond the Fragments* (1979), helped edit *No Turning Back* (1981), and edited *What is to be done about the Family?* (1983). She lives with her teenage son in a collective household.

*Elizabeth Wilson* teaches applied social studies at the Polytechnic of North London. She has written four books: *Women and the Welfare State* (1977); *Only Halfway to Paradise: Women in Postwar Britain 1945–1968* (1980); *Mirror Writing* (1982); and *What is to be Done about Violence Towards Women?* (1983), as well as articles in many journals and newspapers. She has been active in the women's liberation movement since 1971.

## About The Women's Press

The Women's Press is a feminist publishing house. We aim to produce lively, intelligent books by women chiefly in the areas of fiction, literary and art history, physical and mental health and politics.

Since we began in 1978 we have published a wide range of non-fiction in a variety of areas. We have commissioned major new books and our list also includes important works by American feminists, as well as reprints of classic non-fiction.

In the area of politics we have recently published two major works on pornography, *Pornography: Men Possessing Women* and *Pornography and Silence*; an anthology of writings from the Women's Liberation Movement, *No Turning Back*, and a collection of conference papers *On the Problem of Men*. We are the publishers of the essential radical feminist texts *Gyn/Ecology* by Mary Daly and *The Dialectic of Sex* by Shulamith Firestone.

Also among our books are *In Our Own Hands: A Book of Self-Help Therapy* by Sheila Ernst and Lucy Goodison; *Why Children?* in which women talk about their decision to have or not to have, children; *Our Mothers' Daughters* by Judith Arcana and *Female Cycles* by Paula Weideger, now reprinted. Recent titles include *The Handbook of Non-Sexist Writing* and *Feminist Theorists*.

We have published the first major illustrated monograph on *Paula Modersohn-Becker* by Gillian Perry, as well as *Women Artists*, a full appraisal with over 300 black and white illustrations by Karen Petersen and JJ Wilson, and the first collection of cartoons by Paula Youens, *Lone Thoughts from a Broad*.

Among our recent titles are a new anthology of writings by Susan Griffin, *Made from this Earth*; *Through the Flower*, an autobiography by Judy Chicago; *Women, Race and Class* by Angela Davis.

Please help us to continue publishing by buying our books, by bringing them to the attention of bookshops, educational institutes and libraries and by sharing with us your comments and suggestions.

To receive our complete list of titles please send a large stamped addressed envelope. We can supply books direct to readers. Orders must be pre-paid with 45p added per title for postage and packing. We do however, prefer you to support our efforts to have our books available in all bookshops.

The Women's Press,
124 Shoreditch High Street, London E1 6JE.

Stephanie Dowrick &
Sibyl Grundberg, editors
**Why Children?**

Eighteen women – mothers in 'nuclear' families, single
mothers, women bringing up children to whom they did
not give birth, lesbian women, heterosexual and bisexual
women, women who have decided not to have children –
talk about the most important decision they may ever
face: to have or not to have children.

Social Questions/Politics   198 × 126   272pp   3855 6   £2.75


Sheila Ernst and Lucy Goodison
**In Our Own Hands:**
A Book of Self-Help Therapy

Now in its second reprint, this book has established itself
among self-help groups, in therapy training courses and
among countless individuals – women and men – as a unique
instrument of the power each of us has 'to change
ourselves and to help each other'. Offers a political critique
of psychotherapies; advice on how to choose a therapy,
and how to set up self-help groups; and exercises for use
alone or with others.

Psychology/Politics   210 × 135   336pp   3841 6   £4.50

## Nor Hall
## **The Moon and the Virgin**

An exploration of myth, symbol, poetry, fairy tales and dreams to uncover and reclaim the female archetypes: 'life energies and forms that structure psychic growth'. Nor Hall invites us to 'delight in being all things', through a matriarchal vision, opposing the patriarchy's 'allegiance to the letter of the law'.

*Illustrated*

Psychology   210 × 135   304pp   3862 9   £3.95


## Judith Arcana
## **Our Mothers' Daughters**

Probably the most honest and searching book to date about that first and most important relationship, the resonances of which last through our lives. Through interviews with 120 women, the author points to ways in which we can 'confront the reality of our mothers, as the women they are, and as they live in us'.

Psychology/Women's Studies   198 × 126   256pp   3864 5   £2.95

Scarlet Friedman and
Elizabeth Sarah, editors
## On the Problem of Men
Two Feminist Conferences

Feminists analyse political and personal problems for
women inhabiting a world dominated by male power.
Subjects include the family and parenthood,
heterosexuality, monogamy, the role of 'non-sexist' men,
transsexualism and male violence.

Women's Studies   198 × 126   272pp   3887 4   £4.95


Paula Weideger
## Female Cycles

Greeted on its first publication as 'the best book on
menarche, menstruation and menopause to have appeared
so far' *(New Society)*, this remains unsurpassed in its genre.
A practical, scholarly and political book.

Health/Women's Studies   198 × 126   paperback 276pp   3829 7
£3.95
Hardcover 2822 4   £5.95

# Andrea Dworkin
# **Right-Wing Women**
## The Politics of Domesticated Females

*Right-Wing Women* is a work of appalling and prophetic vision, by one of the most outstanding and passionate thinkers in the contemporary women's movement.

The author sees the waves of rape and woman battering, the backlash campaigns in America and elsewhere against Jews and homosexuals, abortion, and family welfare benefits, not as ultra-right aberrations but as various and consistent manifestations of the coming crisis of the patriarchy — one with patriarchal society's historic economic and reproductive exploitation of women. The crisis, she believes, is upon us.

In the sense in which Andrea Dworkin uses the phrases, right-wing women, 'domesticated females', anti-feminists, are neither foolish nor malicious. They are women who have faced the true nature of male power, and chosen collaboration as their strategy for survival. Feminists too, she argues, must face up to the nature of that power.

Andrea Dworkin is the author of *Pornography: Men Possessing Women* (The Women's Press 1981), acclaimed as one of the most courageous and powerful analyses of the role of pornography yet written; and *Our Blood: Prophecies and Discourses on Sexual Politics* (The Women's Press, 1982).

Women's Studies   198 x 126   256pp   3907 2   £4.95

Andrea Dworkin
**Pornography: Men Possessing Women**

Recognised as one of the most important books on
pornography yet published, *Pornography: Men Possesing
Women* analyses the books, films, advertisements of the
multi-million dollar pornography industry, and shows us
that pornography is at the heart of male supremacy.

Women's Studies   210 × 135   304pp   bibliography   index   3876 9
£4.75

Mary Daly
**Gyn/Ecology**
The Metaethics of Radical Feminism

A truly revolutionary feminist text, that examines the
forces that have bound the minds and bodies of women in
this and every other culture through the centuries, and
liberates language itself with the exhilaration of its thought.
'Outrage, hilarity, grief, profanity, lyricism and moral
daring join in bursting the accustomed bounds even of
feminist discourse' Adrienne Rich

Social Ethics/Politics/Women's Studies   197 × 130   512pp
Paperback 3850 5   £4.95
Hardcover 2829 1   £8.95

# Kim Chernin
## **Womansize**
The Tyranny of Slenderness

In this challenging book, Kim Chernin argues that
our society's increasing demand that women be
*thin* is no accident of history but has a political
meaning. It is, she insists, an unrecognised aspect
of male violence against women; it has to do with
the male-imposed image of the child-woman, and
the threat to male culture that a mature woman,
and a mature woman's body, represent.

Dieting, Kim Chernin argues, may be dangerous
to our health, and when we starve ourselves or
stuff ourselves we are giving up the attempt to
change the patriarchy which denies us the right to
grow.

'Kim Chernin quietly and thoroughly undermines
— one hopes forever — the popular, widely
endured tyranny of "thinness" over women's
bodies and souls. To read her is to experience an
immediate and distinct feeling of liberation'
Alice Walker.

Health/Women's Studies   198 × 126   208pp   3914 5   £3.95